SOFTWARE QUALITY

ASSURANCE

AND MANAGEMENT

SOFTWARE QUALITY

ASSURANCE

AND MANAGEMENT

MICHAEL W. EVANS

JOHN J. MARCINIAK

A Wiley-Interscience Publication

JOHN WILEY & SONS

New York · Chichester · Brisbane · Toronto · Singapore

Library of Congress Cataloging in Publication Data:

Evans, Michael W.
    Software Quality Assurance and Management.

    "A Wiley-Interscience publication."
    Bibliography; p.
    Includes index.
    1. Computer software—Quality control.   I. Marciniak,
John J.   II. Title.

QA76.76.Q35E93   1986   005.1'4   86-1713
ISBN 0-471-80930-6

Printed in the United States of America

10 9 8 7 6 5 4 3

To Charlotte and Diana,

The Inspiration

PREFACE

Software development is a complex process requiring the careful integration of diverse disciplines, technical activities, and administrative project controls. Quality is built into software products through the management and technical procedures which are defined and implemented to assure schedule and budget compliance and correspondence to user requirements.

The role of software quality assurance is to act as an early warning to management, customer, and project personnel. The disciplines should accurately identify not only when software quality problems exist, but also when project conditions are such that the development of a quality product is impossible.

Quality personnel are faced with a broad charter, to evaluate the technical and development health and status of a software development project. Satisfaction of this charter requires an in-depth understanding of the technologies and methodologies associated with software development, the flow of work and responsibility within a project as the development proceeds, and the tasks that must be supported if the project is to succeed.

The development of complex software systems is arguably one of the most challenging enterprises encountered by mankind. First, computing is pervasive; its effects are felt in every field of modern endeavor, from the fight against cancer to the space program which would have been impossible without computers. Second, the sheer speed with which computing technology has advanced and been introduced across all elements of society has caused a vast technology explosion. Technology has advanced more rapidly than our ability to develop complex systems within expectations of cost and schedule. In short, software has been the long pole in the tent with respect to the fruitful use of computers in society.

In almost every major system developed or acquired by commercial or government organizations, software or firmware plays a major part and has become an increasing management concern. It takes too long to develop, causing the entire system to slip its schedule, and commensurately raises development costs. In addition, when delivered it does not perform as expected. In fact, requirements that were to be implemented in software have had to be scaled down in order to make a reasonable delivery schedule.

This problem has focused major management attention on the productivity of software development, the cost associated with the development, and the quality of the delivered product. Software productivity, or the rate at which software can be delivered, is limited by current development practice. Software scientists generally believe that software productivity will not dramatically improve without major technology breakthroughs creating more automated programming techniques. Many scientists believe, however (and the authors agree), that the rigorous employment of modern disciplined software engineering practice can achieve significant software quality improvement over current practice without a corresponding increase in cost. By concentrating on engineering practices to achieve software quality, concomitant improvements in software productivity will also be attained.

This book deals with the software development process and managing that process in such a way as to attain quality software while improving the productivity of software development. It treats the software development process as a whole and is not oriented toward specific personnel in the software development organization. It deals with quality techniques that are employed in the software development process as well as management controls needed to monitor and direct that process. A large part of the book deals with the software project infrastructure—that combination of management technique and development process that forms the basis for the sound development of the software system.

This book describes an integrated approach which will provide effective software quality assurance in a project environment. The approach recognizes the need for software quality assurance personnel to understand the software development process and the intricacies of managing and controlling the evaluations in the context of the project situation. The approach is disciplined and tailored to the software environment. If followed, software quality will be engineered into the software life cycle.

MICHAEL W. EVANS
JOHN J. MARCINIAK

Morgan Hill, California
Arlington, Virginia
June 1986

ACKNOWLEDGMENTS

This book is based on the experience of the authors through a variety of project and management situations. The experience gained and the knowledge garnered have proved invaluable and we hope the chapters that follow will prove valuable to the reader.

This book would have not been possible without the support of our wives, Charlotte Evans and Diana Marciniak. A special thanks and note of appreciation are due Charlotte, who entered volumes of information, redid countless pages of text, and was a constant source of support.

There were a number of people who were generous with their time who provided reviews of the manuscript and information and material. Joe Dormady of the Burroughs Corporation provided several reviews of changing information. We would like to thank Lisa Reinbold of Teknowledge and Marilyn Stewart of Logicon for their reviews of the early manuscript and their many constructive recommendations. To Stan Brown and Lieutenant Colonel Howard Wendt of the U.S. Air Force, Dr. Larry Yelowitz of the Ford Aerospace Corporation, Larry Fry and John Penasack of Sanders Associates, our thanks and appreciation for their reviews of the final manuscript. Based on these reviews substantive changes were made. We would like to acknowledge Lewis Picinich, Paul Houk, and Karl Pearson of Expertware, Inc., who provided valuable input on reviews and walk-throughs; Joseph Cavano of the U.S. Air Force's Rome Air Development Center for his review of the chapters on process and product metrics and material provided from recent RADC studies in this area; and Robert Kent of the U.S. Air Force's Electronic Systems Division for his material on management level software metrics.

We would be remiss if we did not thank Patty Boss Reitman, who spent endless hours editing and reorganizing the manuscript. Few technical writers could have accomplished what she did in so short a period.

We also must acknowledge Don Arnoldy, who produced the art in this book. Besides making sense of the rough art we provided, Don designed the cover for this book as well as the cover for *Productive Software Test Management*, an earlier book by Michael Evans.

Finally, we would like to again thank Jim Gaughan, our editor, for the encouragement and support that made this book possible.

M.W.E.
J.J.M.

CONTENTS

PART II. SOFTWARE QUALITY

SOFTWARE QUALITY

ASSURANCE

AND MANAGEMENT

PART

I

LIFE CYCLE SOFTWARE ENGINEERING ACTIVITIES

1

INTRODUCTION

Quality must be built into the products of software development from the beginning through the definition of an effective development environment and the controlled application of monitoring procedures.

The conference room hushed as the program manager walked in. Under his arm he carried a folder containing the charts describing the program status. As he pulled the charts out, the software manager watched nervously, realizing that what was being presented did not accurately reflect the true state of the program. Compromises had been made in quality to save the schedule, short cuts had been taken to meet budgets and, most importantly, the development environment which had been planned from the beginning of the project had never been implemented because of conflicting priorities. Week after week he had reported good news while suppressing the bad. The overriding hope was that things would get better if they could only get to the next milestone.

PROBLEM: CAPTURING THE TRUE STATE OF THE PROGRAM

This scenario is all too common, illustrating the first step in a series of events which ultimately impact the success of the program and the acceptability of the system. The causes are rooted in the very fabric of the project. From the early stages of development program monitoring emphasis was on measuring current budget and schedule performance rather than assessing the long-term system impacts of program decisions. There was no ongoing review or evaluation of the effects of development problems. There was no assessment of the impact of software development decisions (or lack of decisions) on the quality of the system and the health and well being of all segments of the program. The software manager missed subtle early indicators of poor quality: poor productivity; the inability to define or implement a consistent set of tools, techniques, and project methodologies; and data products quickly done to meet a schedule milestone. He had relied on information from internal functional organizations rather than employing a qualified external organization to provide accurate, objective information concerning the project status and its resultant impact on software quality.

If this situation is allowed to continue the problems will become more acute. They will finally become visible when the customer interface has been damaged, when budgets and schedules have been exceeded, and when the technical quality and integrity of the system have been jeopardized.

What can managers do to insulate themselves from these problems? How can they ensure that the data used as the basis for critical decisions accurately portrays the true state of the program? How can the manager ensure that software quality is not being overlooked until the final test phase?

The astute software manager will recognize that the problems associated with software quality must be addressed early. Solutions must be built into the development process. From the beginning valid requirements, implementation of a program environment characterized by a smooth, controlled data flow, complete and effective quality checks at all stages of the software development, and application of external controls and monitoring procedures to continuously assess the adequacy of the development process and the quality of the products being produced must be implemented and continually enforced by all management levels. There cannot be early compromises with software project discipline, technical quality, or development rigor to achieve short-term budget, schedule, or minor customer success. The manager must constantly be aware that, although short-term problems are difficult to deal with, they pale in comparison with the problems associated with an unacceptable system or a missed software delivery date.

What can the manager expect in an environment like that described in the opening scenario? During the early stages of the development there is unbridled optimism on the part of all managers associated with the program. The common theme is, "This time the system will be developed right." During this period the program is a whirlwind of activity, and unless the software project manager is careful, essential planning, including quality management planning, gets deferred.

Later a period of disillusion sets in. System components which appeared straightforward in the beginning become complex. Difficult decisions, dismissed earlier by a wave of the hand, now must be dealt with. The development process so clearly understood during the early stages is beginning to crack under the weight of changing requirements, design constraints, and unspecified interfaces. Issues of quality, development rigor, and long-term planning take a back seat to more visible activities focused on the crushing need for signs of immediate progress.

Eventually the problems of poor quality, ineffective controls, and project disillusionment lead to a state of desperation. The theme of the project becomes, "If I can just make it to the next milestone, things will get better." The inadequate development controls; inaccurate interface specifications; the laissez-faire program and software development environment; and a lack of accurate status information have combined to inhibit the success of the software development and impact the long-term prognosis for software acceptability.

Unless these situations are dealt with quickly and effectively they ultimately cause the development to grind to a halt. Meaningful progress ceases. Even simple activities prove overwhelming, and instances of quality are accidental rather than an integral part of the system. A catastrophe has occurred.

Early application of software quality discipline could have avoided this disaster. By integrating software quality disciplines into the project structure early, visibility into the development process and products would have been achieved. This early emphasis would yield a planned structure of recurring project reviews and audits fully supported by management and technical personnel. Software quality tools, techniques, methodologies, ⌐⌐d personnel should be selected and applied based on the specific software ⌐⌐ɑ project characteristics. Finally, the budgets for the project should be structured from the beginning of the project to ensure adequate resources are available, when needed, to develop a quality product.

SOFTWARE QUALITY CHALLENGES AND EXPECTATIONS

Quality must be built into the software system from the very beginning— by instituting an effective development environment.

Quality has been a pursuit of humanity for a long time. In the past quality was typically a singular accomplishment associated with the work of one individual or a small team. The early artisans were known for the quality of their work. It was only the introduction of mass production techniques during the industrial revolution that required attention to quality as a means to control the consistent manufacture of quality products. The automobile and garment industries are early examples of mass production industries dependent on the ability to consistently produce large quantities of goods. While yesterday's products exemplified the personal quality of an artisan's reputation, the quality of today's products have enormous economic implication. The ability to produce a quality product could make the difference between having a long term and profitable market or an early Chapter 11 (bankruptcy). The economic implications are clear—in runs of thousands, the difference of 1 percent in acceptable parts can mean millions of dollars, especially in a highly competitive marketplace.

In order to deal with this quality issue special management mechanisms were created to verify manufacturing practice and a number of techniques employed to focus on quality. Many remember the Zero Defects and Quality Circles programs. While these programs met with some success, the predominant belief today is that quality must be built into the product in the process of development and manufacture. One large manufacturer advertises that "the quality goes in before the name goes on." That is certainly the thesis of this book.

The issue of quality in hardware is certainly different than for software. Hardware quality programs are largely intended to audit and inspect manufacturing practices as countless different pieces are manufactured. Software, however, is not mass produced so that development and manufacture of the software system are synonymous. This fact has caused difficulty within industrial organizations as quality assurance personnel came into conflict with the personnel developing or manufacturing the product. In truth the quality of software is the concern of all: those who have the major responsibility for development, those who have the responsibility to monitor the process to assure the quality of the system, and above all, those who have management responsibility.

The measurement of software quality is not yet a science and will not be until effective means are developed, accepted, and implemented to qualify the software. Should quality be measured in terms of the number of errors found and fixed during some period of time relative to the size of software? Perhaps it should be associated with the ability of software to perform a task over a period of time with a quantifiable degree of reliable performance. It is not presently practical to address quality as a formal absolute.

Simply stated, quality assurance is the total effort by all concerned with the software development to ensure that a quality product is developed, regardless of the specific definition of how quality is measured.

For those familiar with the subject, there are several activities or management methodologies that have been employed to directly or indirectly deal with software quality. To put this book in the correct context, we will briefly examine three of them. They are a quality program, software quality assurance, and independent verification and validation.

A quality program is a management and organizational approach to ensure that proper procedures are used to develop software and the inspection of that process to ensure compliance with those procedures. This typically turns out to be an audit-type approach, conducted largely by personnel who are not software development practitioners. This process of building a quality assurance organization was conceived to try to create quality in software using an approach similar to the approach used to assure quality in hardware systems. The big difference, of course, is that hardware quality assurance involves watching the production process after the equipment has been designed, developed, and validated. When carried over into software development and production, this approach found the development process synonymous with the production process; therefore, software quality assurance personnel found themselves involved in the software development process. This process of observation is markedly different from building quality in the development process. If software development is pursued on the basis of a sound software engineering process, the quality of the product will be assured.

Another methodology being practiced with varying but generally good success is independent verification and validation (IV&V). This methodology was conceived in the early days of major software systems development, principally in strategic missile systems. Because of the enormous impact these systems have on international political events and the requirement for safety the product had to prove operational integrity without any opportunity to actually use the system. IV&V was developed to provide that integrity through the use of a contractor other than the developing contractor (independence), to assure the integrity of the development process (verification), and to assure that the developed and delivered product met operational requirements (validation). IV&V is an active technical role conducted by technical personnel who independently check the development team, and participate in and/or conduct their own analyses and tests of the product.

It must be remembered that IV&V was conceived when software engineering was in its infancy; therefore, the direct check by qualified technical personnel added confidence and integrity to the development process. As software engineering matured, IV&V has also evolved in terms of methodology and application. In addition to the confidence-building example discussed previously, IV&V is used to supplement the engineering management team, which typically is short on software engineering expertise and spot check development, especially when things are not going well. This latter approach is sort of like adding fertilizer to the lawn—it creates a short-term benefit which subsides after a period of time. The most common dispute with IV&V is that if the engineering team were composed of well qualified personnel and were following sound engineering practice, IV&V would be unnecessary, except perhaps to provide an unbiased check on the development team, who may hide the facts when things go awry or, worse yet, fail to recognize their predicament.

Which brings us to software quality assurance and the subject of this book. The approach that this book takes is that quality is a result of the application of sound engineering practice. This book will treat the process of development and not the "bandaids" that have been applied to software development in the past. This does not obviate quality assurance programs or IV&V, these management techniques still have a place. However, over time they should evolve to a point where they properly supplement the development process.

One caveat is worth mentioning. Eventually software "quality" is something that must be measured. In the current state of development, this is not totally possible. Metrics, which are the measures of software, are currently being developed and have been used on a few programs on an exploratory basis. They are a long way from being validated as accepted practice, or implemented across a wide range of developments. At this time, quality assurance relies heavily on subjective analysis. Thus, all the more reason for concentrating on the adequacy of the software development process itself.

This book treats software quality from two complementary engineering perspectives, the "process" and the "products" associated with software development. The development process is based on the integration of engineering and management tasks across the software development life cycle. For example, requirements that are specified in the early phases of the development process are related to the design in an orderly and structured manner. In like manner, the requirements set forth in program specifications are translated into test requirements and ultimately appear in test documents. The concentration on instituting an orderly process assures that all requirements are allocated into the system design and are tested in the test program. It is this concept of process that conveys one dimension of quality assurance.

The other dimension is the quality check of individual components of the system development. The system comprises numerous products: design specifications, test plans, top level and detailed designs, requirements specifications, and so forth. The product orientation examines each of these products as a snapshot in time. For example, has the test plan been developed in accordance with accepted documentation standards? Does it address all of the key topics and areas of concern to the development? Does it contain all of the requirements of the system that should be included in the plan? It is this concentration on a specific product that is the other dimension of quality assurance.

There are many good reasons for dealing with software quality assurance along these two dimensions. The foremost of these are the different skills and organizations that are employed in the development process. In any development project there will be certain people who are dedicated to the program for its entire development period, and others who will be used at specific points in time. From an engineering perspective, a senior analyst may be needed during requirements analysis and top level design, but not for detailed coding and testing. From a management viewpoint, quality assurance or test personnel are only needed for those periods where their skills can contribute to the development. Thus, concentrating on the "products" of development allows management to bring to bear the correct resources for the task at hand, assigning dedicated project personnel to maintain quality throughout the "process" of development.

To complement this "process" and "product" dimensional view, the book will treat the individual techniques used to ensure quality. Techniques, in this sense, are individual procedures that are employed—the tools of software quality assurance. Throughout the book techniques will be described that are used in the process of orderly engineered development and to check individual development products. One example is the technical review procedure: how to prepare for the review, who participates in the review, what happens at a review, and follow up actions after the review is concluded.

This book, then, deals with software quality assurance as a practiced discipline of the total software development process, including all of the personnel resources that are involved in that process.

THE QUALITY DILEMMA

The goal of software quality is elusive in an actual project environment. The measures differ between projects, and criteria vary as a function of the specific characteristics of the project, the needs of the user, and the application requirements of the system and software. Quality measures used for small systems are not always appropriate for large ones. Criteria for quality applied to real-time applications are not always relevant when dealing with non real-time systems. Complex software requires different monitoring procedures than trivial applications. Quality criteria vary dramatically depending on the phase of the project at which the evaluation takes place. As described in subsequent chapters, the measures of quality must be specific to the project being evaluated and must assess the effectiveness of the entire development process, not just individual segments.

Software quality must be planned into the project, engineered into the products of development, and be monitored by assessing not only individual segments of the project or single data products but also by evaluating the interactions and interrelationships between them. Quality goals must be clearly defined, effectively monitored, and rigorously enforced. The project must focus on the quality issues of the project from the outset, ensuring that quality criteria are consistent with defined requirements. Throughout software development, the management of software quality must be an overriding concern of all project personnel. Quality must be planned into the project structure, constantly evaluated, and corrections applied when deficiencies are identified.

The remaining chapters deal specifically with problems of software quality assurance. The book has been written for personnel responsible for software quality at all levels of customer, program, and software project organizations. It also describes how development, support, and project control personnel interact with software quality assurance and why this is an essential component of project success.

2

SOFTWARE QUALITY: INTRODUCTION TO LIFE CYCLE ACTIVITIES

The quality and effectiveness of a software product is determined by the process used to develop it and the attributes of the products which comprise it.

The rapidly changing nature of systems and software development makes the evaluation of quality difficult. New application types, improvements in technology, innovations in development techniques and tools to support them are generating new and more rigorous demands for improved software quality assurance techniques. As these changes accelerate, the software quality assurance disciplines must keep pace or the effect will be felt throughout the industry.

More than any other discipline, software engineering has felt the effects of change. The application of new methods, the use of unproven methodologies and the reliance on untried software development environments have made the implementation of software the "problem child" of the engineering world. The industry is in the midst of a technological explosion fueled by change within government, industry, and academia.

The positive effects of this explosion have resulted in the development of systems which only five years ago were considered well beyond the state of the art. Consider electronic banking, space technology, computer enhancement of visual imagery, military applications, expert systems and other applications of artificial intelligence technologies. Project the changes these and other equally dramatic applications of computer systems have had and will continue to have on our lives. The effects are enormous, and will continue to be.

On the negative side, however, the risks associated with this revolution are as significant as the benefits. As computers pervade more areas of our lives and control more of our environment, the potential effects of unacceptable software quality become increasingly disturbing. In many cases our ability to specify requirements; to design, develop, and test systems; and to maintain the software systems once deployed has been outstripped by the complexity and characteristics of the systems themselves. When assessing the effects of this shortfall, consider the potential effects of a banking system of questionable accuracy, of an unreliable software system supporting a manned space mission, or a military system which reports incorrect data or data in the wrong format. The need for absolute, predictable software quality becomes evident.

The challenges facing software quality assurance are significant. The disciplines must provide an accurate assessment of the effectiveness of the software development process, reliable projections of software reliability and user acceptability, and anticipate operational effectiveness and the quality of the products of software development. To be useful, software quality assurance must consider not only individual components of the development process or single data products but how these individual parts interact in the context of the system and software development process.

This, and the following chapter, describe the process of software development, the practices and procedures which are applied to the development, and the project infrastructure which determines the software development environment.

Software development is a complex process requiring the careful integration of diverse disciplines to be successful. These include the tailored application of technology, effective management practices, and administrative project controls. The software project must prove equally competent in all areas.

SOFTWARE ENGINEERING—THE LINK TO QUALITY

Why does one project succeed while another, using identical tools, techniques, and methodologies, and having similar software attributes, fail? The answer lies in the degree of success that the project has in defining an effective environment for developing, managing, testing, and controlling the products of software development. Projects which are characterized by high motivation, a clearly understood set of project goals, and a smooth flow of work, data, and responsibility within the project normally result in higher quality products. These parameters constitute an effective software engineering environment.

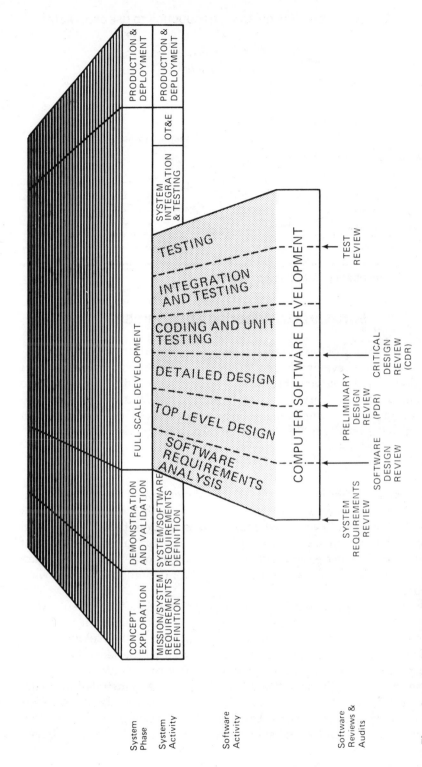

Figure 2-1. System development life cycle.

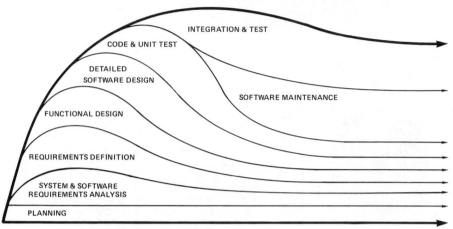

INTEGRATION & TEST

CODE & UNIT TEST

DETAILED
SOFTWARE DESIGN

SOFTWARE MAINTENANCE

FUNCTIONAL DESIGN

REQUIREMENTS DEFINITION

SYSTEM & SOFTWARE
REQUIREMENTS ANALYSIS

PLANNING

Figure 2-2.   Engineering development lifecycle.

Software Engineering Environment

From the beginning of the system development, the effectiveness of the system and software development environment; experience with development methodologies, development controls, and engineering disciplines; and the requirements for software quality go hand in hand. This relationship continues throughout the implementation and becomes the major factor which determines the quality of the end products of software development.

Life Cycle Phases

As illustrated in Figure 2-1, the software development life cycle is composed of several phases, each of which ends with the occurrence of a milestone event, and each of which produces an identifiable combination of documents or software items and results in a formal review or set of reviews. This life cycle serves as the foundation on which all software project planning is based and is the first level of definition of the software infrastructure.

The following lifecycle description describes the milestone events, data products, development phases, and review requirements. It is by no means the only development standard, does not fill all development requirements, and should not be embraced by all as the ideal solution to the problems of software development. It is representative of the actual activities occurring during software development. As illustrated in Figure 2-2, the life cycle consists of several discrete yet overlapping phases. During the development several baselines (or groupings of completed, approved data products) are established at the completion of each development phase.

System Definition

The system definition phase is usually the most complex and important phase of software development. It is here that initial requirements are set down, defining the system that is to be built, and the system and software project is structured and defined. The conduct of this phase is crucial to the software development. During this phase user requirements are detailed into the formal definition of a system—a process that is dependent on the understanding that the developers have of the user's problem and his or her environment—and the software environment is planned. The nature of software systems is such that a great amount of the system is procedural in nature; that is, the software captures the process of management and/or engineering procedure, military operational procedure, and so forth. In other words, it is a process that is extremely dependent on the specific personnel performing the task at any given time and will change as new personnel are brought into the environment. The product of this phase is a statement of requirements; however, the process of collecting those requirements is the essence of the phase's activity. It is this process that provides for a healthy communications process and rapport between the user and developer, a condition that is requisite for sound development. The culmination of that process is the requirements specification, and it is this document that will be used to design, cost, and schedule the subsequent development.

While the requirements definition is of paramount importance, there are a number of other activities that occur, at a lower level of importance, that have great effect on the project. For example, a user may decide that he or she needs 10 display formats with certain information contained in those formats. An innovative system analyst can implement these display formats in any number of ways, each of which will have different impacts on the cost and schedule of the project while not appreciably changing basic requirements. A number of trade-off studies need to be conducted to determine exactly what the system will look like and how it will be implemented in hardware and software. These activities constitute an important part of this phase of development.

System Engineering Studies.   System requirements must be subjected to trade-off and optimization studies to ensure that the system meets total system requirements in the most cost effective manner. Usually the user will concentrate on operational requirements, however, and ignore issues such as supportability. These other requirements must be considered early and will have an effect on the cost and schedule of the project. The following are examples of the categories of studies that may be conducted during this phase of development:

1.   *Feasibility Studies.*   These studies may be conducted to ensure that the use of computer resources is appropriate to the task under de-

velopment, that the requirements can effectively be met with the proposed equipment, that development risk has been bounded, and that the preliminary cost estimate is within reason.

2. *Trade-off Studies.*   These studies are generally conducted to develop alternative means to satisfy system requirements, essentially to reduce the cost and risk of development or to explore alternate system configurations that may infer enhanced system performance at the same or almost the same cost of development. Logistics, technology, schedule, cost, and resources are some of the items that are considered in the trade-off studies or are the subject of trade-off. The following are illustrative of trade-off issues:

    a.   Programming language and computer architecture

    b.   Security requirements

    c.   Support concepts

    d.   Technical approaches

    e.   Operational alternatives

3. *Risk Analysis.*   These studies identify high risk development areas and alternate means of development to reduce risk. Risk may be associated with some high technology performance factor such as the speed of performance or the use of a particular development environment that may not be as mature or as complete as required for the development. Risk assessment is an ongoing process throughout the development process and effects considerations of cost of development, schedule, and performance.

Two reviews, the system requirements and the software design reviews, culminate in the definition of the software system.

Software Design

There are two levels of design, top level and detailed. The top level design is the first step in the transition of requirements to a physical system. It is here that the organization of the system starts to take shape. Requirements are allocated to individual parts of the system: to the individual hardware subsystems and software subsystems. This partitioning of requirements is called the functional allocation of requirements. It is "top down" because the design starts from the top, the set of requirements. For example, in a simple system software may be allocated to the executive subsystem and to only one software subsystem or computer system configuration item. Depending on the complexity and size of the overall system, the top level design may proceed through a number of subordinate levels. The conclusion of the top level design is somewhat arbitrary; it depends, again, on the complexity of the system, the judgment of the software designers, and other factors. It generally concludes when all of the requirements have been allocated such that a reasonable picture of the design of the system is in hand. This process ends with a preliminary design review, at which the design team, the key managers of the development team, and the end users review the design with the purpose of ascertaining that the project is proceeding satisfactorily and that all requirements have been accounted for within the design. The manager is concerned that the milestone achieves this purpose for he or she wants a check that he or she is on track with respect to schedule and cost. The key document of this phase is the top level design document. The components of top level design include:

1. *Requirements Allocation.* The logic used to assign requirements to individual components is described. Requirements for interfaces (external and internal), as well as processing time and memory size requirements are detailed.

2. *Functional Flow.* The general system flow of processing and data are detailed. The purpose and mode of operation of each component (at least the key ones) should be described.

3. *Interrupts.* Interrupts are detailed, including external and internal interrupts.

4. *Data.* Both global and local data requirements are detailed. Some of the attributes of global data are: description, type, representation, size, units, limits, accuracy, and location.

5. *Components.* Each top level component should be thoroughly described in terms of its inputs, local data, interrupts, timing and sequencing, processing, and outputs.

During this phase there are other activities that may take place. A good bit of the software development planning must be detailed. A software test plan should be developed. Standards and conventions, if not already in place, should be completely specified. A database design (document) should be detailed and the software configuration management plan and software quality assurance plan should be completed if they have not been already completed in the requirements analysis phase. In any event the major function of this phase is to allocate the total set of requirements to the major components of the system.

The detailed design phase is exactly what it implies—the completion of the total design of the system in preparation for implementation or production. The major product of this phase is the detailed design (document), and the phase culminates in a critical design review. The purpose of the phase is to complete all tasks necessary to begin implementation or production. The purpose of the review is to assure that the design is complete and satisfactory and that the system is indeed ready for production.

The detailed design describes, in detail, the structure and organization of each computer software unit such that coding of the components can take place after design review. The design builds on the top level design with additional detail until the design is totally specified. Detailed design ends when each component has been satisfactorily defined—usually each component will be assigned a certain number of minimum coding statements (one to two hundred). A key part of this phase is to assign all requirements to components such that there is complete traceability from the top level requirements document to the detailed design. Each component description should contain a description of global data, external interface implementations, component inputs, local data, component outputs, interrupt requirements, processing requirements (control, algorithms, special control features), error handling, data conversion, outputs, and so forth.

While the detailed design (document) is the most important product of this phase, there are a number of other activities that take place. The database design should be completed. If the system is complex, an interface design may be required. This design should be completed during this phase as well. Informal test procedures, a software development folder, software test descriptions, and a software programmer's manual should be completed or at the very least started during this phase.

The culmination of this phase is the critical design review. At this review all of the documents that are produced during the phase are subject to review; however, the principal review is with respect to the detailed design.

Coding and Unit Testing

The coding process can take place any number of ways, but is usually undertaken in a deliberate, planned manner whether a top down coding process, using stubs and drivers to test the interim results before the next layer/layers are completed, or in a bottom up manner integrating and testing units (modules) as they are coded. The program manager (or program management team) will decide beforehand what particular approach will be used and that will be described in the software development plan. In a bottom up approach the individual units are built and tested informally by the coder. They are reviewed (e.g., in a walk through) prior to committing them to a baseline in the software development library and then are integrated with other units during the build process to form higher level units or computer software components (CSCs). In a top down approach the individual units are tested using simulated sources referred to as stubs and drivers (to simulate lower level units that have not been coded) and then integrated as the development process proceeds down through the build process. In like manner a review is conducted as each unit is completed and tested by the individual developer.

No matter what the development or build strategy, after each unit is reviewed it is placed under configuration control in the software development library. This is probably the most important step in the development process. The retention of the identification of source and object code, along with its documentation and test results, is critical to the development process.

Test and Integration of Computer System Configuration Items

While there is a certain amount of integration and test in the coding process, this phase does not begin in earnest until enough units have been integrated to form a major set of CSCs such that it is reasonable to begin computer system configuration item (CSCI) integration testing. A manager may decide that all of the code (and units) should be built before beginning CSCI integration testing; however, that is not a practical strategy since the CSCs will normally be on different schedules. In order to maintain an orderly development process with reasonable resource leveling this process can begin earlier.

Since testing depends on having interfaces with the other parts of the system, integration starts naturally as the need develops to test units together. In essence the tests are now conducted in a more formal way in that there are prescribed test plans and procedures and the tests are witnessed by independent test personnel along with quality assurance personnel. The CSCI test and integration process culminates when the complete CSCI has been assembled, has been tested in accordance with the software test plan and individual CSCI test procedures, and has been reviewed by an independent team. Again the CSCI is placed in the software development library along with test results documentation and the source and object code. The primary product during this phase is a completed CSCI that has been tested and baselined according to the prescribed functional and performance requirements of the software requirements specification, the design specification, and the detailed design.

Integration and Test

The last phase of the development process is the integration and test of the system into a deliverable product. This, naturally, is more than a software task, involving integrating the software CSCIs with the hardware that the software must run on and interface with. The product of this phase is the completed system. The developer should be able to demonstrate that the system has been developed and tested in accordance with the system specification and software requirements specification and that the product is accurately described by its documentation.

Development Baselines

Three customer-approved baselines are established during the software development life cycle. The three baselines are:

1. *Functional Baseline.* This baseline denotes the end of requirements definition activities. All requirements of the system are defined in the functional baseline.

2. *Allocated Baseline.* This baseline denotes the end of high level design activities. The allocated baseline is established with the approval of the functional design.

3. *Product Baseline.* This baseline describes the as-built software system or subsystem in terms of its functional, performance, and operational characteristics. It is first established with the approval of the draft of the detailed design. It continues in effect through software build, integration, and test. The final product baseline is established after successful acceptance of the software.

Other baselines that are normally controlled are specific to a project. These are system or subsystem requirements, interim functional and detailed design, test data, and the other information approved by the program or customer through a life cycle phase.

The life cycle is specific to the characteristics of the project being developed. Each life cycle will vary according to the size and complexity of the system under development. In each of the phases there may be parallel paths of development for a complex system where there is corresponding hardware development and many software subsystems while a straightforward software development with minimal hardware development and a single software system may only have one sequential development path.

While this material discussed may be more or less an idealistic view of the development process, these events must take place in any orderly, well-managed development process. What will vary are the individual techniques employed such as top down design and the phasing of the overall events. In a simple system it may be possible to have an orderly serial development and progression of events. In a more complex system, a number of CSCIs may be involved with commensurate hardware development, and a number of parallel development processes may result. Within each process the procedure and practices are basically the same and the management challenge is to integrate these parallel developments into an integrated process for the system under development.

It is worthwhile to mention at this point the function of configuration management. While there are a number of parallel activities that are occurring throughout the development (quality assurance, independent testing, reviews, and so forth) configuration management is an extremely important part of the process itself. As products develop they are baselined at appropriate points in the development process and it is the configuration management function that is responsible for this process. Without a credible configuration management system, the development process can easily fall apart. Imagine testing code that was not properly described by its documentation or integrating units while the development activity was still in the process of making changes to the code such that the testing baseline was shifting. This becomes even more critical when code from two different development groups is being tested and integrated. If these configurations are not controlled the integration process cannot proceed and the product will not get developed.

3

THE SOFTWARE PROJECT INFRASTRUCTURE

The software project infrastructure is the discriminator which separates a successful project from one which is unsuccessful. It is the means by which a set of specified user requirements are translated into an operational system capability.

In his book, *Controlling Software Projects,* Tom DeMarco made an interesting and disturbing observation.

> *So many (software) projects fail in some major way that we have had to redefine "success" to keep everyone from becoming despondent. Software projects are sometimes considered successful when the overruns are held to thirty percent or when the user only junks a quarter of the result. Software people are often willing to call such efforts successes, but members of our user community are less forgiving. They know failure when they see it.*

This observation, based on a study of over 200 commercial software projects, is backed up by many like examples in the government, in the commercial sector, and in the academic communities. Many causes for this dilemma are voiced throughout the industry. Our tools are poor. Our training is inadequate. We use antiquated methodologies. The programming languages we use are archaic.

The cause of problems of software development are rooted in all of these. However, a major reason for poor software quality is the inability to understand and effectively apply a sound software project infrastructure.

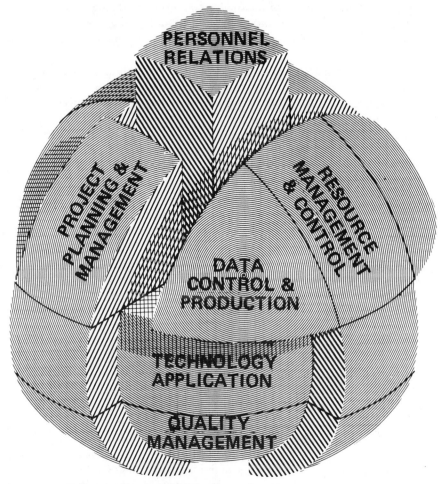

Figure 3-1. Software development puzzle.

As depicted in Figure 3-1, the software development process consists of many components which must fit together to create a total and integrated project environment. These individual project pieces must interface and interact effectively within other segments of the project if the project is to function efficiently. It is not as essential that any individual project tool, technique, methodology, or segment of the infrastructure be a model of effectiveness as it is that the individual pieces fit effectively in the overall context of the project environment. As with the puzzle, what is most important to software quality and project productivity is not the individual pieces but the interfaces between related project segments. Unless the interfaces are clearly defined and supported, individual tools, techniques, project methodologies, and project control techniques will not have the hoped-for effect on quality and project productivity. For a project to achieve the promised productivity and quality gains attributed to new and innovative software engineering practices, the emphasis must be on the total, integrated project environment. All components of the development process—management, project planning, project control, manual and automated tools, techniques and project methodologies, technology, and the data products which are required and developed as part of the implementation—must fit together.

The project infrastructure is the discriminator between successful software projects which produce quality software products and less successful projects. All elements of the infrastructure—technical, administrative, project management, customer and program interactions, and data management and control—must mesh smoothly. The project must be characterized by a controlled flow of data and clear transition of responsibility as software development moves from phase to phase. There must be clear project focus, reflected in objectives and development goals which flow from the top of the organization down through the technical staff and a clear coordinated application of technology to the requirements of the project and the technical characteristics of the application. There must be commitment on the part of all segments of the organization to meet schedules, budgets, and technical requirements of the program.

SOFTWARE DEVELOPMENT LIFE CYCLE—ITS RELATIONSHIP TO THE PROJECT INFRASTRUCTURE

The software development life cycle model, as described in Chapter 2, is an essential basis for a successful software project. It represents the process by which the software will be developed. It identifies discrete events which may be scheduled and measured during the life cycle. It describes the logical relationships between data products, reviews and project milestones, as a means for evaluating the productivity and quality of a software project. It is important to have a basic understanding of this serialized process, however, this simplistic model is inadequate to deal with real world environments—particularly those where parallel development of hardware and software is common.

SERIALIZED LIFE CYCLE MODEL—THE WATERFALL SYNDROME

As illustrated in Figure 3-2, the common software development model is patterned after this serialized software development life cycle. This model treats the process of development as a serial process: each phase flowing into the next—with each phase, from a time perspective, considered to be independent. This "waterfall" perspective is illustrative of the types of activities which occur in developing software; however, is more theoretical than practical. While it is important to study this life cycle from the stand-

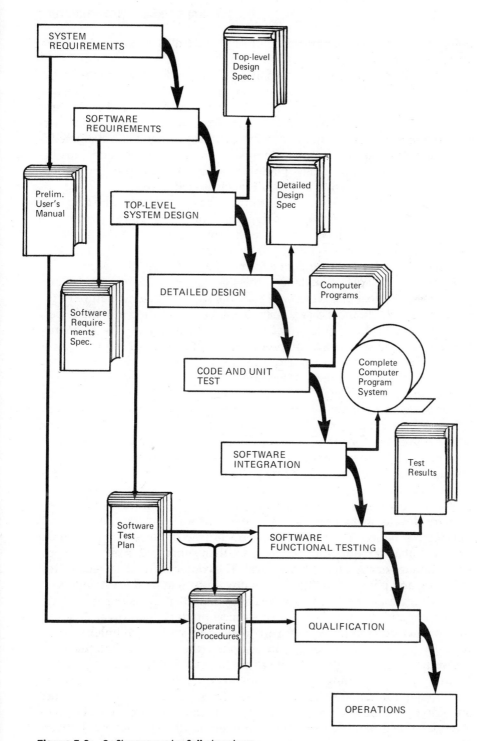

Figure 3-2. Software waterfall structure.

point of basic software engineering precepts, it is also important to understand its deficiencies.

A major problem with using this life cycle model for development is the incompatibility between the requirement to adequately review software project documentation prior to a formal review and the need to proceed with other project tasks in order to maintain the overall integrity of project development. Before a major review, the documentation to be evaluated is often complex and voluminous. Because of the complex relationships between technical data products, planning documentation, and test requirements, this documentation is difficult to adequately assess.

The data is submitted for review and the project proceeds. The data contained in the document changes as the project proceeds, that is, as technical requirements are modified and additional information becomes available. Often, because of internal changes to a submitted document after or during the review process, the results of a formal review are invalidated.

Even in the best of circumstances, this formal review and approval of proposed changes does not work well considering the dynamic nature of the software project. In most cases, changes cannot be factored into the review process because of schedule pressures or project limitations. The frequency of essential changes to software products and the impact of changes on the technical integrity of the software project forces decisiveness. There is a continuing need for timely project decisions. Technical progress on a software project cannot be impeded or delayed by an inability of a program or customer board to evaluate a proposed internal change, a modified software interface, or a test parameter. Schedules will be missed. Quality will suffer. This requirement for prompt action is incompatible with the need of customer and program personnel to ensure that data which has been reviewed and approved is not invalidated by project decisions in which they do not participate, or at least review, before implementation.

When the serialized life cycle model is followed, it is difficult to accurately monitor development progress and assess software quality. The software developer produces a series of data products in accordance with predefined or prenegotiated requirements. These are then submitted to either the program monitor or customer for approval. The contents are reviewed at a formal "dog and pony" show held at a software system or subsystem level.

These reviews should provide visibility into the process of software development and the integrity of the technical products. However, in an actual project situation, the software review process is complex. Unless ridiculously long review periods are provided, the reviewer find that there is insufficient time to fully evaluate all documentation. Instead they "do the best they can," sampling some documentation, fully reviewing some, and performing a minimal review on others. Documents are approved which shouldn't be, technical problems are missed, critical relationships between the operational requirements of the system and the system and software system design are not uncovered, the integrity of the proposed test program

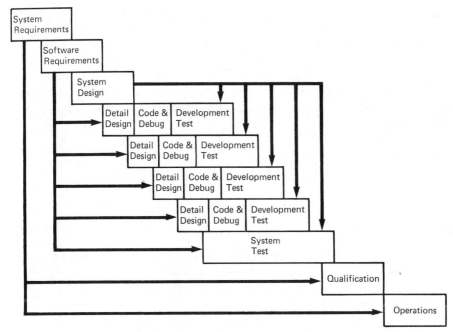

Figure 3-3. Software development overlap.

is not adequately assessed and technical and development risks are ignored. The document review is conducted to stay on schedule, rather than provide an essential analysis of the technical integrity of the project.

With the strict use of this development model, when nontrivial problems are uncovered, they require a major effort to correct. Budgets must be found, schedules must be adjusted, and the effects and impacts on related data products must be assessed and, if necessary, updates to these products must be made. There is a ripple effect throughout the project at a time when most software projects have limited fiscal or schedule options to adjust with the perturbation.

REAL LIFE CYCLE MODEL

In practice, software development is closer to the life cycle model illustrated in Figure 3-3. In this model, software development is a series of parallel miniprojects, each building on an incomplete data set, providing a specific piece or category of data to other miniprojects and requiring data from prior or concurrent parallel phases. The occurrence of a formal project review does not signify the completion of a development phase. It only authorizes the start of the next phase of development. Traceability and data control are the threads that link phases and tie individual project activities together.

This point, although subtle, has enormous impact on the project infrastructure. What it means is that the project is in reality many parallel activities ordered by development priority and technical risk. All data developed must be traced to a changing set of requirements; the data products are not really complete until the end of the project and even then they change. Control over this process and consistency between the data products that pass from phase to phase are the critical components of the software project infrastructure.

PROJECT INFRASTRUCTURE

Simply stated a project infrastructure is the integration of all assets, both human and machine, combined with engineering discipline and management procedures that are dedicated to building a sound software product. The emphasis is on the "integration" of all the activities of development which have to work together in a cohesive manner. Engineering does not, and cannot, act on its own independent of, for example, the quality assurance organization. A team effort is required. While this may seem altruistic, it should be viewed as a worthwhile goal in project environments. The project infrastructure provides the basis to help achieve this goal.

The technical aspects of the software project infrastructure are the integration of many individual tools, techniques, and methodologies used to satisfy the development needs of the project. As previously described, there is a technical flow to the development which places distinct, and often widely divergent technical requirements on the development process. Each of these technical requirements requires its own distinct set of technical solutions to ensure that it is adequately supported in the context of the project environment. These solutions or methodologies fall into many separate project areas. It is important to distinguish between a tool and methodology. A methodology is a prescribed way of doing something, akin to disciplined engineering practice or procedure. A tool is a mechanization of a procedure or methodology. Methodology categories are:

1. Management methodologies which are the means by which the software project is planned, organized, and controlled; that resource requirements are projected, scheduled, applied, and monitored; and the project direction, focus, and development progress is determined, channeled, and kept on course.

2. System requirements methodologies which facilitate the identification, definition, and specification of a valid set of user and system requirements. These methodologies may provide consistency checks on the requirements as they are developed, assist in the allocation of requirements to system architectural components, and

monitor the data products as they are produced to ensure system traceability and testability.

3. System design methodologies which support the definition, decomposition, and allocation of requirements into successively lower levels of functional definition and identify data requirements as the decomposition is conducted.

4. Prototyping methodologies which facilitate the rapid development of a prototype system which reflects the projected operational capabilities of the system long before any production software has been developed.

5. Software design methodologies which translate the functional requirements resulting from the execution of the system design methodologies into a complete, documented software structure ready for coding.

6. Software coding methodologies which facilitate the production, review, and support of software code which is compatible with the design, supports the requirements and needs of the application, and is consistent with software development within the standards and conventions.

7. Software development testing methodologies which support the process used to qualify the software modules and units prior to release for integration into a load module configuration.

8. Software testing methodologies which facilitate the integration of software first into load machines then into executable subsystem configurations and then qualify the software against the functional requirements allocated to it.

9. System test methodologies which integrate software subsystems into an executable software system configuration and then integrate the software and hardware into system configuration. The second stage of system testing qualifies the system against the system requirements.

10. Data production methodologies which define the relationships between engineering data products, or determine the hierarchal relationships between these data products and the documentation end items which include them and support the production and quality control of them.

11. Baseline configuration management and control methodologies which facilitate the management, control, and updates of customer approved end items.

12. Engineering data management methodologies which control the flow of engineering data within the project, ensure the validity of all project approved data items, and control the integrity of the data when used by more than one area of the project simultaneously.

13. Quality control methodologies which evaluate the integrity and acceptability of data products as they are produced and assess the integrity of the software development process.

14. Project monitoring and control methodologies which assess the progress of the software project against plans, monitor resource expenditures, and control the flow of data, the transition of responsibility, and the allocation of work.

There are myriad methodologies developed or supported by companies, acquired or adapted from the outside or developed by the project and modified for project use to support each of the individual areas of the project infrastructure. Each of these has been developed with a different model of software development than that required by the project, each has a different set of data input requirements, results in a unique set of outputs, and requires varying degrees of expertise and project support to implement effectively. The challenge facing the software project is to select from these methodologies those that most adequately support the particular needs of the project, tie them together into a consistent technical environment, and apply them to the project such that their use and problems associated with their application may be predicted rather than unknown.

The quality implications associated with this definition of the technical environment are significant. If methodologies do not link correctly, if they can't be supported or properly employed by the staff, then software quality and project productivity will be diminished.

Despite this, consider for a moment how the technical environment of the project is defined. Often the organization developing the software does not have an understanding of the environment which will be used to produce the software. The methodologies are selected based on customer, company or staff pressure in an *ad hoc* fashion. They are selected based on "flash" rather than actual project need. They are not tailored to the needs of the project, nor do they link with related methodologies to form an integrated technical environment. As shortfalls are found in the environment, compromises are made in the integrity of the development process or in the quality of the engineering data just to make the project work. The scenarios often result in the production of software which is not consistent with design, nontestable, nontraceable to requirements, and cannot be controlled. This, from a quality perspective, is "Armageddon."

Why don't methodologies always work across a broad spectrum of applications? Consider how the concepts are often defined.

Software which is being developed in a research environment, where the primary emphasis is to test a concept or build a prototype system to evaluate a particular architecture, can tolerate a significant amount of technical inefficiency. There is time to step back and redefine technical data when problems are uncovered.

Directed research has similar features to the pure research environment described previously, however, the research is conducted against a rigorous set of requirements, and perhaps a limited or fixed schedule and budget. In this environment there is some latitude for technical inefficiencies; however, not to the extent of a pure research environment. The product of this activity is still proof of concept rather than product delivery.

A third category, scheduled development, is by far the most common focus of software activity. These project environments are schedule and cost driven and must result in a product compliant with requirements, and the software, once deployed, must perform up to the expectations of an end user. This software environment, whether applied to the development of large or small software, nonrealtime or realtime, or complex or trivial applications has a common denominator; software quality and project productivity must be predictable and meet some level of expectation.

It is extremely important in this third environment that methodologies are selected that are consistent with project goals and resources, have proven off-the-shelf capabilities and provide an integral set of life cycle capabilities. By selecting methodologies after definition and as part of the project technical environment, there is increased probability that the research methodologies will result in predictable, useful, and relevant results. The following criteria are useful for selecting project methodologies:

1. They have been proven in an actual software development environment with similar characteristics to ensure valid comparison.

2. The engineering data products which result from implementation of the technique can be integrated with related data elements, fit into the technical and documentation environment of the project, are verifiable, and can be controlled by the project control practices.

3. The staff has sufficient direct experience with the technique to effectively apply it to the project, utilize it to solve specific project problems, and support it in the context of the software project environment.

4. The technique and supporting components fill a specific, discrete project need and can be brought into the project environment without a major upheaval in the project structure. The cost of the technique must be outweighed by the benefits derived by its application.

The specific methodologies must be acquired, evaluated, and translated into practical applications within the context of the specific engineering environment of the project.

These techniques, if judiciously applied to the project and completely integrated into the project structure, will be of enormous benefit to the project. These benefits will only be realized if the particular technique is considered in the context of the complete technical environment, not as an entity by itself. This puts a different perspective on the selection or application of a particular technique to the software project environment.

QUALITY GATES

At key points in the development process a set of quality gates must be integrated to monitor and ensure the quality and integrity of data products before they are used by the next levels of development. This gating of the development process ties the quality assurance and configuration management and control disciplines into the development activities.

These gates include formal reviews in the case of completed data products, requiring external customer, program, or system development concurrence. The quality gates also include internal reviews conducted to evaluate data items used internally by the software project. These informal reviews include walk-throughs, inspections, and a structure of peer reviews to check the quality of the software and software-related products as they are being developed.

The quality gates provide a means of evaluating the process being used to develop the software, conformance of the software project to the needs of the program, and the technical requirements, goals, and objectives of the system. These parameters are evaluated through preplanned, regularly scheduled and structured project audits. These audits gate the development process, providing an objective assessment of the degree to which the development process or project deliverables meets the criteria specified in the project plans, agreed to program and customer form, and development standards and technical standards of quality.

Formal Reviews

These reviews serve as the quality gates through which all customer approved data products must pass before the data is used by other segments of the project concurrently. The formal reviews are those which evaluate completed end items. The successful completion of these either establish or augment a project baseline.

The formal reviews establish, with customer and program participation, a means for evaluating and approving each of the baselines as they are developed. Formal reviews should be defined to evaluate the technical integrity of the project.

System Requirements Review

This review evaluates interpretation that the engineering staff has made of the specified user requirements. It also analyzes the trade-offs and system analyses conducted to evaluate the requirements and define an architecture and support configuration.

Software Design Review

This review presents and evaluates the overall software architecture and the preliminary definition and allocation of functional requirements. It is the first purely software technical review and should consider:

1. Quality and technical integrity of documentation presented and reviewed
2. Stability and integrity of requirements presented
3. Completeness and adequacy of software interface definitions and specifications
4. Program languages used and the rationale leading to the selection
5. Software standards and conventions and technical methodology selection
6. Project complexity evaluation
7. Operating system and support software selection
8. Data management selection
9. Personnel selection, application, and qualifications
10. Development facility selection and planned application
11. Project management plans and procedures

Preliminary Design Review

This review provides a means for evaluation and approval of the progress, consistency, and technical adequacy of the selected design approach to satisfy the allocated performance requirements contained in the functional specifications. A preliminary design review (PDR) will be held for each major component of software. At the PDR, the following actions should be performed:

1. Review all detailed functional interfaces between the software subsystem and other subsystems, and between the software and related equipment. Action should be taken to ensure that interface design requirements are adequately identified and solutions documented.
2. Ensure that the software processes or tasks and their functions have been identified, and review the functional interfaces between the processes.
3. Review word lengths, message formats, available storage, memory maps, and other considerations included in the functional specification.
4. Review critical timing requirements and estimated run times.

5. Ensure that the design meets the functional, performance, interface, and design requirements in the requirements specifications, interface specifications, database specifications, and the software/software interface specifications.

6. Review the human interaction aspects of the software, and ensure that the requirements of the user's manual are supported by the design.

7. Review the qualification test plan and all available test requirements, documentation, and tools. Ensure that the incremental builds provide for adequate testing of requirements.

8. Review the project standards and conventions.

9. Review the software development facility, including configuration and availability.

10. Review the software development plan and the software project management plan including detailed schedules, personnel requirements, manning, internal management milestones (e.g., unit test and releases), and resource allocation. Review status monitoring and reporting.

11. Review any critical technical and contractual issues.

The PDR should be approved by the customer, with approval being the point at which design is baselined under configuration management. The PDR establishes that it is prudent to proceed with the detail designs.

Critical Design Review

This review establishes that it is prudent to proceed with the coding and software integration. During the critical design review (CDR), the integrity of computer program logical design is established. Also during this review, the design language representation of the design, the unit development folders, and the "build-to" design specifications are scrutinized. These documents are made available to the review group and technical management prior to the review. At the CDR, the following actions are performed:

1. Review the compatibility and traceability of design with the functional specification.

2. Review the detailed design and other descriptive documentation to establish compatibility with the system design.

3. Ensure that the interface requirements are satisfied and are specified in detail. Review the detailed user interface.

4. Review interaction of the software with the database.

5. Review the test and analytical data such as logic diagrams, algorithms, and storage allocation charts.

6. Review the design specification, with the exception of the program listings (which will be produced only after coding), and ensure that the software is specified at a level of detail that permits the writing of code without further design.

7. Review the computer loading, interaction rates, processing rates, processing time, and memory estimates.

8. Ensure that the design meets the functional, performance, interface, and design requirements in the segment requirements specifications, interface specifications, database specifications, and the software/software interface specifications.

9. Review the current detailed development and test plans. Ensure that the incremental builds plan for requirements to be tested, the modules to be included, and the test procedures to be used.

10. Review the development facility capability to support fullscale code and integration.

11. Review critical technical and contractual issues.

The CDR is conducted on the software after the detail design is essentially complete. Its purpose is to establish the integrity of computer program design at the level of functional flow diagrams of computer programs, logical design prior to coding and testing. The "build-to" design specification is to be reviewed at CDR; it is subject to change and will not be baselined and controlled until after the development effort is complete. The CDR will be approved by the customer.

Test Review

The test review is conducted in two parts. The first assesses the readiness of the software to support the required test activities while the second assesses the adequacy of the testing and the reported results.

Engineering Reviews

Engineering reviews are internal to the software project and are the quality checkpoints that ensure the integrity of engineering data before it is used by other project segments.

These quality gates are the essential project "checks and balances" which build integrity into the software products. They are the checkpoints that ensure that the many individual pieces of data which comprise a software system are consistent with software project standards and requirements. These gates ensure that the engineering data is of sufficient quality to attain the quality requirements of the application. The reviews also ensure that development shortcuts are not being taken which would invalidate the integrity of the software project or the products which result. Each individual data product or step in the development process should be subject to approval at a quality gate before it is accepted by the software project or controlled at a project level.

Walk-Throughs

Walk-throughs are interactive, informal evaluations conducted by the project personnel to review specific data products. The walk-throughs are chaired by a walk-through leader who schedules the walk-through, chairs the meeting, and evaluates the results. Walk-throughs should be focused towards a small, narrow objective. They should be nonthreatening, designed to uncover problems, conduct a "what if" analysis of the data product and ensure product acceptability. The walk-through is not designed to identify poor performance or personal shortfalls. Walk-throughs should always evaluate the products against project standards and design, not against undocumented opinions or assumptions. If the walk-through is not structured and if the data products are not controlled after approval, the walk-through is a waste of time.

Inspections

Inspections are static, reviewing data products against project standards and requirements in a noninteractive manner. Unlike walkthroughs, inspections do not necessarily involve the individual who developed the data product. Inspections involve a qualified individual sitting down with a single data product and evaluating it against a documented set of standards. These requirements may be described in checklists. The data products which are approved through an inspection may not be baselined after completion since the inspection may be required just to authorize the start of a new activity, not to authorize use of the data by different organizations.

Internal Reviews

The internal reviews are more formal than walk-throughs, evaluating more than a single data product. These reviews are localized to the software project. Reviews are closer to the "dog and pony" show than walk-throughs. They are structured, requiring stand up presentations of development, technical, and risk characteristics of the object of the review. As with walk-throughs, the data products approved through a review should be baselined.

Quality Gate Categories

These review categories serve as schedule milestones and provide assurance that all data products are of sufficient quality to satisfy project needs and standards and that the requirements are translated into design, development, test, and integration project activities.

The formal project reviews are the points at which the quality, adequacy, and technical integrity of customer approved baselines is established. These reviews provide a first tier of baseline qualification and, when integrated with other review evaluation procedures, are an essential factor in the quality equation. All data approved by the customer through a formal project review should be baselined through formal configuration management procedures.

The project walk-throughs, internal reviews, and inspections provide the means by which internally developed data products are evaluated and approved prior to project control. There are many types of walk-throughs and inspections which may be applied to evaluate software data quality. These include:

1. *Requirements Evaluation.* Evaluates the requirements received from the customer for completeness, consistency with related software systems, and for testability, traceability, and technical integrity.

2. *Operation Concept Evaluation.* The system and software operational concept should be reviewed.

3. *Software Requirements Evaluation.* Evaluates the basic proposed architecture of the software system and the initial allocation of requirements of the various components of the software configuration.

4. *Functional Design Evaluation.* At each level of the functional decomposition, a walk-through should be conducted to ensure technical integrity and validity.

5. *Design Analysis Evaluation.* An evaluation should be held for each software unit preceding the functional allocation and overall design concept.

6. *Unit Design Evaluations.* This evaluation should occur on completion of the unit design and the unit test definition, when the design is completed on paper and not coded beyond that level. The evaluation should concentrate on adherence to requirements, design, interfaces, and on the relationship of the module(s) to the software subsystem. An evaluation should be held for every unit to review the intended design.

7. *Code Evaluation.* This evaluation occurs on completion of coding. The code evaluation should ensure that acceptable coding techniques and adherence to standards have been rigorously followed during the coding. The code is verified against the design to identify any coding errors and against standards to ensure compliance.

8. *Unit Test Evaluation.* This evaluation occurs on successful completion of unit testing. The evaluation should validate the final module source code, should review the unit test scope, and test materials for completeness and accuracy.

9. *Build Evaluation.* A build review is conducted prior to the demonstration of a build to the software manager. It is in two parts: (1) evaluating the plans and procedures for the build, and (2) evaluating the results of the testing.

10. *Acquisition/Reusability Evaluation.* A review should be conducted to evaluate software prior to acquisition by the project for use in the software system or subsystem configuration. When successfully completed, this evaluation should authorize procurement or application of the component. The review should be the specific functional support to be provided by the software, the technical compatibility of the software architecture, the documentation quality, and compatibility with project standards.

All data which is approved through a project walk-through or internal review should be placed under software project configuration management and control.

Technical Environment

The technical environment provides the structure used to define, design, develop, and test all software. The technical environment is characterized by the concurrent conduct of many diverse engineering tasks, each having its own technical requirements and resulting in a discrete set of engineering data. The development phases are linked through the data products produced by each development phase, and through the tools, techniques, development methodologies, and project support and control facilities which structure the project environment. The technical environment is an integration of manual and automated procedures and practices controlled through project management and control procedures. As illustrated in Figure 3-4, the functions which are associated with data management and control are what drive the production of software.

Derivation of the system requirements is a precursor to all development and test planning, as well as providing the basic criteria by which the customer will accept the system from the contractor. For this reason the buyer of the system should provide a major input to the definition of requirements as well as approving the requirements before system and software design is initiated. After approval, configuration management and control of requirements is essential if the integrity of the project is to be assured.

System and Software Requirements

Specification of software requirements is the first technical task of the software development activity. The requirements are the basic specification of what the integrated software system must do to satisfy the allocated requirements of the system. As with the methodologies used to specify system requirements, those used to specify software requirements should

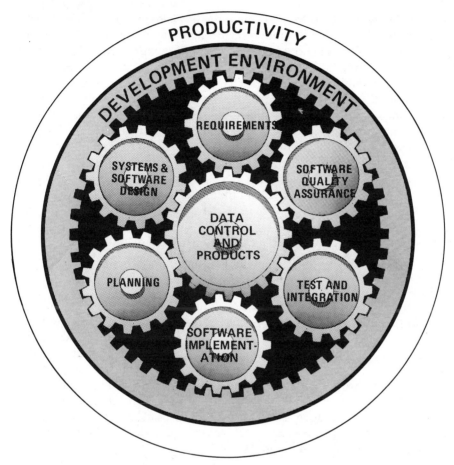

Figure 3-4. Software data relationship.

provide clearly testable and traceable requirements, controlled at an individual software subsystem level. These requirements are the common link between software test planning and the technical development.

The methodologies used to define and document software requirements must interface with those used to specify system level requirements. These methodologies result in an allocated set of software requirements on which the functional design process may be initiated. These requirements form the basic functional criteria for software acceptance testing. When allocated to software subsystems, they are reviewed at the project level through internal project reviews and, if required, at a customer review. After review, they are placed under the baseline and data management segments of software configuration management.

The definition of specific requirements, both system and software, is iterative. At the lowest level these requirements should be individually specified. Each requirement should be traceable downward through the design, to the code and finally through each of the levels of testing and be capable of verification through a discrete test, through inspection or through analysis. Each requirement should be nonambiguous, expressed in such a way as to minimize misinterpretation. Finally, the specification of requirements should be tailored to the individual characteristics of user requirements.

There are different types and categories of requirements. For example, performance requirements specify how a system responds, while operational requirements specify what a system does—how it satisfies the user with respect to what he or she wants the system to do for him or her. Each individual requirement category has different specification requirements, as well as different attributes which measure the adequacy, quality, and integrity of individual requirements in the project context.

This requirements taxonomy is important. The techniques used to specify each set of requirements; the form of the specification for each area; the reviews, audits, and evaluation techniques to assess the integrity of the requirements, and the project control techniques which ensure the testability, traceability, measurability, and integrity of the requirements are all important components.

Requirements track through the development process and are managed according to their separate needs. Operational and functional requirements describe from a system perspective what the system must look like to be compliant to the needs of the user. These requirements are built into the design through successively lower levels of functional and detailed design and evaluated through all levels of integration and functional testing.

Quantitative requirements, performance, and resource utilization are initially defined in budgets, allocated to individual design components through the design process, and evaluated through demonstration and inspection of individual and integrated code products.

The final category of requirements are those delivery requirements which are essential to acceptance of the system. These fall into two primary subcategories.

1. Those attributes which, from an application and operational perspective, must be implicit in the software when integrated into the system configuration. These attributes should be explicitly demonstrated during system integration testing.

2. Those attributes concerned with the form, structure, maintainability, and support of the end products of the development; the documentation, the code, the support environment, and the tools and testing products and results.

In order to ensure the quality and acceptability of the software when it is used in the system environment, all requirements must be integrated into the software system and the data products which support it. A system which supports operational and functional support requirements but does a poor job supporting delivery requirements will not result in a quality system. Likewise, systems which may efficiently support all performance or resource constraints of the application but are operationally or functionally deficient will not be acceptable for supporting the needs of the user. The software infrastructure provides the means by which these requirements are built into the products of development. The specifics of the infrastructure, the tools, techniques, project methodologies, and development practices differ based on the type of requirement being addressed.

Functional Design

Functional design decomposes the functional requirements of the system into successively lower levels until the software systems design process can proceed. The lowest level of abstraction represents the basic division of the subsystem. These may then be described in a detailed design representation for implementation.

Detailed Software Design

Software functional requirements provide the basis for derivation of the detailed design for each of the subsystems and units. The detailed design process starts when functional requirements are decomposed and documented in functional specifications. When the functional design is complete, subsystem functionality is described in a manner consistent with the needs of the next design step and test phases of the project.

Coding and Unit Testing

The code represents the tangible commodity of the development process. The actual process and methodologies used for coding should be rigorous, frequently monitored through walk-throughs and inspections. The process integrity of the coding process should be the responsibility of the individual responsible for implementation; however, adherence to standards, use of good practice and procedure, and the integrity and currency of documentation versus code must be ensured by the manager or supervisor responsible for the development. The project should provide the tools, support, and controls necessary to ensure productivity and code quality.

The frequent use of independent inspections to assess progress and monitor quality and standards compliance is essential. Poor code or loose standards in this phase will be hard to correct later. Evolving code should not be baselined until completion of informal testing.

Test and Integration

The focus of all project activities and the measure of the effectiveness of the development process is the project experience during the period of test and integration. These tasks represent the bottom line of the software devel-

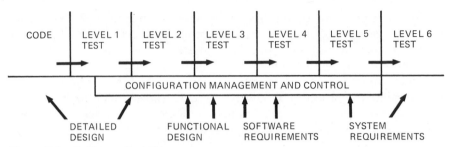

Figure 3-5. Software test flow.

opment process. The activities during this project period are the means by which design integrity is verified, traceability to requirements validated, and operational integrity established.

Test and integration is not the period of the project when quality can be built into the products of development. It's too late. Poor documentation cannot easily be fixed during test. Nonexistent requirements cannot be defined here. Poor design cannot be easily corrected as a by-product of test and integration. Quality must be built in throughout the development process, it can't be added later.

There are separate and distinct methodologies for each test level which must be defined and linked to the design methodologies and to each other through the plans and data developed during the software development process. The system test levels significantly affect the software planning process. Software subsystems must be tested in accordance with requirements allocated through the system design methodologies; interface integrity must be demonstrated before the subsystems are integrated into an operational configuration; and the software test levels and system test levels must be tightly coupled to permit the concurrent qualification of integrated system and software subsystem releases.

The methodologies applied to the software test category should be consistent with the design and implementation methodologies used to define, design, and develop the software. There should be clear correspondence and traceability between the test specifications and the design specifications which result from the design process. If hierarchical design methodologies are used, and the development proceeds in a hierarchical fashion, hierarchical testing methodologies which integrate the system from the top down are most appropriate. If, on the other hand, the development does not rigorously follow a hierarchical pattern due to functional, schedule, or resource requirements, a blending of testing methodologies for software integration is most effective. As illustrated in Figure 3-5, during test and integration the project should be characterized by a structured flow of data.

At the first level, *the module level,* the implementation of the smallest element of development, normally the module, is evaluated. This testing level is usually conducted by the development staff and verifies that the module compiles without error. This test level is the first check that the module has been developed in accordance with project standards and conventions.

At the second level of software testing, *unit level testing*, individually qualified modules are integrated into a unit configuration. A unit is a logical grouping of modules, normally one to 10, which support an identifiable, traceable software function or group of related functions. At one unit level, modules are integrated in a hierarchical fashion tracking the execution sequence of the software within the unit. Units are qualified in two aspects. The first verifies that the implementation of the unit is in accordance with the design and that all execution paths through the software execute reliably. The second component of unit testing validates that the unit, as implemented, satisfies its allocated functional, interface, and performance requirements. Unit tests are conducted by the development staff. At the completion of unit testing and approval at a walk-through, the unit is released for software integration.

It is at this point that software is placed under project level configuration management control. The unit design, code, and test information is baselined after successful completion of the various levels of software walkthroughs.

At the third level of testing, *software integration testing*, qualified units are integrated into software builds for functional and interface testing. Builds are logical subsets of the overall software capability. They are selected because of schedule and functional compatibility. Identification of components for individual builds must be consistent with schedule projections and compatible with the functional design of the software. As a prerequisite to this level of testing, early planning of build structure and content is essential. As with unit testing, builds are integrated in a hierarchical fashion, tracking the execution sequence of the software. During this testing, qualified units are integrated into an operational configuration data relationships and internal execution characteristics, including performance benchmarks, are verified against the software design; and internal execution sequences and support characteristics are verified.

At the fourth level of software testing, *software subsystem testing*, the integrated builds are qualified against functional requirements allocated to software subsystems. A subsystem is a major component of the software system defined by functional completeness, hardware support, testability considerations, and interface characteristics. Where the previous test levels were concerned with evaluating internal aspects of the software subsystem execution, this test level looks at the software from an external perspective. This test level is planned, executed, and evaluated by an independent test team that has not participated in the software design or implementation. The test team should develop all test plans and specifications exclusively from system functional, performance, and interface specifications.

The fifth level of software testing *integrates qualified software subsystems* into an operational system configuration. These tests are in two parts. The first is to qualify the internal software system characteristics against design specifications and data requirements, control interactions between the executing subsystems, and assure the internal integrity of the integrated software system. The tests are planned, executed, and evaluated by system engineering personnel familiar with system design and the role of software in the system configuration. Completion of these tests qualifies the software for the second part of system integration. This initial stage of system testing is an extremely critical stage of integration. Most often the problems uncovered through this testing occur due to interface errors: misunderstandings, inaccurate specifications, incomplete design, and inaccurate implementation of specifications. At the previous test levels the interfaces between internal software components are exercised and qualified. If the previous test levels are properly conducted these level 5 tests focus on the intersubsystem software interfaces.

The second part of system integration testing takes an integrated software configuration and integrates it with the system hardware. These tests should exercise each of the major hardware and software interfaces using a predefined test set. If properly planned, the system integration tests should be incremental, phased to the build test schedules. This allows for incremental addition of system capability over a long period of time rather than a single, turn-key integration of a full system configuration.

At system testing (level 6) the software is operationally qualified with the actual system hardware. The tests are executed using qualified, controlled, and documented software and hardware configurations and live, reproducible, and controlled data sources. All problems are formally documented and tracked. Corrections are made by the software organization and regression is tested and qualified prior to integration into the test configuration. The amount and type of regression testing are determined by project level review of the problem. The test requirements are documented in the system level test plan.

PART II

SOFTWARE QUALITY

4

PLANNING FOR SOFTWARE QUALITY

The planning of software quality assurance must be an integral part of the project infrastructure. The plans must provide technical and quality gates through which all project data must pass and management tasks to monitor project effectiveness, development risk, productivity, and project performance.

The successful development of a software system requires the presence of five factors:

1. A preplanned project environment tailored to the needs, characteristics, and development requirements of the application.
2. A smooth blending of technology, project discipline, and development control based on firm requirements and an integrated set of project plans tailored to the characteristics of the project.
3. Application of tools, techniques, and project methodologies covering each phase of development linked together through project controls and data products. They are tailored to project technical characteristics, personnel experience, and technical, administrative, and management constraints of the project.
4. A smooth, controlled transition of data consistent with technical and development standards of the project; a predefined, effective flow of responsibility as the implementation proceeds from phase to phase and as responsibility shifts from organization to organization; and a

set of quality gates which monitor and evaluate the quality of the data before the impacts associated with poor quality affect the quality of the end products of the development.

5. A staff that is technically competent to produce the software, motivated to meet schedule and cost commitments, coordinated to ensure that the activities of one organizational element mesh properly with other segments of the project and that the activities of all segments of the project are focused and directed towards a common set of goals and objectives, and that the staff is committed to produce a quality product consistent with project standards, operational and performance requirements, and the development requirements of the project.

The extent that each of these factors is important to the quality of the software depends on the perception of the observer. V.'hat drives the end user, and as a result determines his or her view of the software development, differs substantially from the view of the system or software organizations. Likewise, these organizations have different quality definitions and criteria which determine the quality assurance approach. A uniform quality management or quality assurance plan is not achievable. A plan must be written and implemented by each organization concerned with software quality to reflect their individual requirements. These plans describe the particular quality requirements and software attributes essential to the organization: criteria of acceptability, the scoring technique to be used, the product, and process and product relationship and techniques to be used to measure quality.

QUALITY REQUIREMENTS FOR PLANNING

Before developing a plan to evaluate software quality needs and requirements, the essential system goals, objectives, and requirements to be met must be defined. As has been described these are process and product related. They are based on the perceptions of the various organizations concerned with the quality of the software. These perceptions are described in the following section.

As illustrated in Figure 4-1, software product quality can be depicted as through a series of concentric rings. As one goes deeper into the development hierarchy individual measurements will change and the attributes used to measure them will vary.

Customer Quality Needs

The customer's quality perspective differs dramatically from that of the program and software development staffs. The customer is interested in two primary factors:

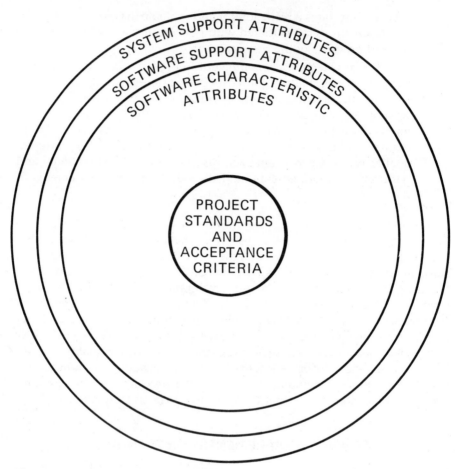

Figure 4-1. Product quality relationships.

1. *Responsiveness.* When the system is delivered, will it meet the unique and environmental constraints and meet the promised benefits when put in the support configuration?

2. *Risk Reduction.* What are the cost, schedule, and technical risks that will impact the quality or application of the system?

The process and product development factors which are important to the customer are those which address these concerns.

As illustrated in Figure 4-2, the quality concerns of a customer are hierarchal. At the top level is confidence in the developer's ability to deliver a product consistent with the customer's perceived needs. The quality concerns and the specific process and product factors which are monitored, and how low in the quality scoring tree they go during the development, are a

Figure 4-2. Customer quality concerns.

function of customer confidence. The less confidence the customer has, the lower in the hierarchy these factors will be monitored.

If there is limited customer confidence in software development integrity, there is a second level of quality concerns which move to the top of the hierarchy. These are the technical management and implementation performance on the project relative to the initial criteria and constraints established for the project. This level relates to the life cycle data products and activities.

The third level of the quality hierarchy is the technical quality of each individual data product and the process used to develop these products. If problems are perceived with life cycle products or development performance, the customer concerns are with the next level technical data products and process. This level of concern is with the project infrastructure: the products, tools, techniques, methodologies, and project management and control. When customer quality concerns reach this level, the customer quality assurance takes on a different perspective. Rather than being a check on process and product effectiveness and compliance to project requirements, it becomes a day by day analysis of the project. At this level the customer is concerned with the implicit quality of the implementation levels rather than the products which result. From the developer's standpoint, this is a difficult environment.

The next level of customer concern, and in many instances the final consideration leading to project termination, is the software development cost and schedule performance. Although these parameters are always tracked, from a customer standpoint, the quality implications do not become predominant unless the customer confidence, life cycle, and project infrastructure levels are violated. If, however, these levels are not consistent with customer expectations, these parameters take precedence.

The lowest level of the customer quality hierarchy is the ability to deal with the risks and realities of the software development problem. At this quality level the customer is concerned with recovery rather than development. The integrity of the development process and products, and the project cost and schedule performances takes a secondary role for a short time. Once customer quality concerns reach this level, serious project problems are not far behind.

As illustrated in Figure 4-3, the product attributes which most concern the customer are those which most affect the operational integrity of the software when integrated into an operational configuration. These attributes are typically not visible until the system has been integrated into its operational environment. Rather than fall prey to the "big bang" form of system acceptance, customer quality concerns extend into the end products which result from each phase of development.

These lower level development and product attributes provide the project technical, administrative, and control environment. The process used to develop and control these products is also of concern to the customer since the process provides the assurance that the system will satisfy the requirements of the application. These process concerns are first with the system development and test practices used to develop a system from its component parts and the software development practices employed at each phase of software implementation.

Program Quality Concerns

The program manager is interested in two primary factors.

1. Ability of the software project to meet program cost and schedule commitments

2. Ability to develop a contractually acceptable quality product technically consistent with other program areas

The process and product software quality attributes which are most critical to the program and which have the most effect on the perception of quality relate to these factors secondarily.

As illustrated in Figure 4-4, the program quality requirements are different than those which drive the customer. The primary quality considerations center around development cost and schedule performance. At this level, process is of more concern than product factors.

The measures used are both after the fact and predictive. Cost and schedule performance on completed tasks is an essential program consideration since these identify project efficiency and development effectiveness. Predictive measures are also essential in that they provide an early warning to the program management of impending project shortfalls which will result in quality impacts. A program quality concern is to ensure that poor cost and schedule performance will not result in an unacceptable system and

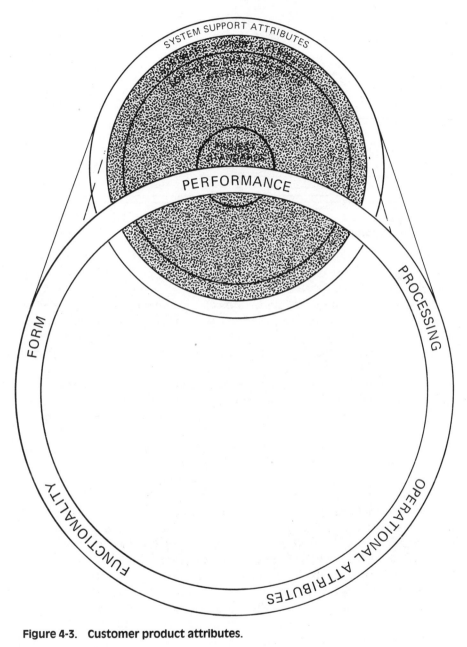

Figure 4-3.   Customer product attributes.

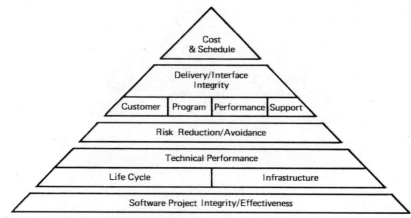

Figure 4-4. Program quality concerns.

that additional resources will not have to be applied to solve a critical quality shortfall.

If cost and schedule performance indicate a problem, the second level of concern is with the quality implications of those shortfalls or the acceptability or interface integrity of the software in a system configuration. These concerns are with the ability of the software project to develop acceptable quality and still meet the revised project constraints. They are with the technical characteristics of the life cycle products being produced and the integrity and productivity of the process being used for production. The program quality concern at this level is, "Can we do it and not have it cost more money or time?"

The third level of program quality concern is whether the software project sufficiently addressed the quality implications of program and software development risks, and whether those risks acceptable. Can the project develop quality data (acceptable to the user) considering the risks implicit in the implementation? This level of program concern provides a "warm fuzzy" feeling that, in spite of cost and schedule and product quality problems, the problems are well in hand. This level of analysis may also result in a "wringing of hands, grinding of teeth" when it is clear that the risks are incompatible with the development or quality constraints or criteria of the project. If the development risks have not been adequately addressed, or if they seem unacceptable to the program, the next level of concern becomes the technical attributes and process characteristics of the software project infrastructure.

At this point, the quality concerns have extended far down into the development. The program quality concern now is to "micro evaluate" the product and process being used for development. Program managers do not necessarily understand what is being assessed, nor, in many cases, do they understand the quality implications or infrastructure impacts. Recommendations often have short-term return rather than long-term support payoffs. Actions often have a negative, often catastrophic, effect on the quality of the software development end products.

If this level of program quality concern is reached, it is very difficult for the software project to recover. The lowest level program concern is whether the software project can ever develop a quality product within the constraints imposed by the development environment. This quality decision is essentially binary and results in a project go/no-go decision.

From the perspective of the program, the product attributes which most affect the quality of the software product are those which ensure that the software will perform as advertised when integrated into the system configuration. These attributes, illustrated in Figure 4-5, describe certain characteristics of an integrated software system. The program can and does collect data which are indicators of software quality throughout the software development. By applying reviews and audits of the software project, inspections of data products, independent evaluations of technical quality, and program level control over all customer or program approved data, the process and product quality as it relates to the program is determined.

The program level concerns about software quality extend through the process used to develop and control the end items of each phase of the software project and to the attributes of end items when they are delivered to the program for integration or delivery to the customer.

Development Perspectives

The development organization has two primary quality concerns:

1. That the process used to develop the software will be complete, will be achievable, and will result in acceptable software
2. That the products developed will be adequate to meet the requirements of the software application and will be acceptable

As illustrated in Figure 4-6, the quality concerns of the development organization differ substantially from those of either the customer or program management.

At the top level, the concern is that the development process will be adequate and result in an acceptable product. The primary software quality concern is that there are, because of the process being used to develop the software, potential surprises which will impact the quality of the product or the productivity of the project. At this level the concern is that the technology to produce the software will not adequately support the development requirements, that each individual component of the planned software technology has been properly integrated into the project environment, and that the staff has sufficient expertise to use the technology to implement the software.

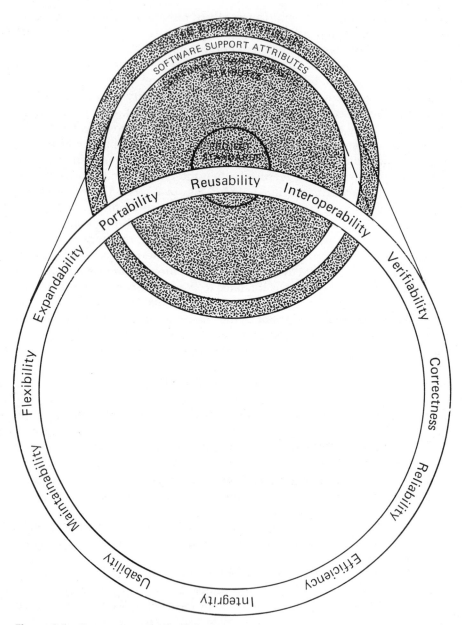

Figure 4-5. Program product attributes.

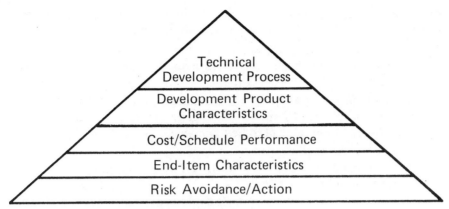

Figure 4-6. Development quality concerns.

The second quality level is the ability of the software organization to produce an acceptable software product compliant with the requirements and needs of the application. The concern usually takes several forms:

1. The software infrastructure must be sufficient to satisfy the technical requirements of the application.
2. The essential software product attributes must be achievable within the resources or in accordance with the constraints of the project.

If the development organization is confident that the process being used is adequate, the products should fall into line. If, however, there is a problem with the process, the product worries will quickly become predominant.

The third quality level, cost and schedule performance, is always a concern of the software organization because of the customer and program emphasis. These concerns become predominant, however, when the development process breaks down and there is a corresponding impact on the quality of the products of development. These cost and schedule concerns center around whether sufficient resources can be applied to the project to result in an acceptable product. Cost and schedule concerns are perhaps the most frustrating from the standpoint of the development organization. When the cost and schedule concerns become the highest quality concern there is very little that the development organization can do to rectify the situation. The money and development time has either been used or didn't exist in the first place. The development organization can only increase the budget or schedule, reduce the scope of work, or increase productivity.

The fourth quality level, the ability to develop the individual end products required by the project, becomes predominant when it becomes evident that the cost and schedule constraints are unrealistic. When this quality level is reached the project management becomes obsessed with restructuring the end items and delivery schedules to try to minimize budget and schedule exposure. The concern has two dimensions:

1. Is there a more efficient way to structure the end items and not impact the quality of the software?
2. Can the project get by with reducing the technical content of the end items to buy short-term schedule gains, making up the shortfalls later when more time becomes available?

The end item concerns are a "last ditch" effort to meet the development requirements of the application.

The lowest level of the development quality pyramid is whether there is any way to restructure the project to avoid or minimize development risks if the process, product, cost and schedule, and end items are blown. At this point, the software development is being driven by the problems being experienced during development rather than the technical, implementation, or development demands of the project.

As illustrated in Figure 4-7, The product attributes of most development concern are those which most affect the technical integrity of the software as it is being implemented. These attributes are visible as the software is implemented and as it is being integrated into executable configurations. The quality concerns of the development organizations include concerns about the adequacy and consistency of each individual software data product and that it meets the project standards, fulfills the intended role in the project, and is usable in the specific areas of the project where it is applied.

The development organization is concerned not only with the integrity of individual data elements but how these elements fit into the end products which result from each phase of development. These small, low level development product attributes are the basic documentation and definition of the software project technical, administrative, and control environment. The process used to develop these software development products is of primary concern to the development organization. The software project tools, techniques, and methodologies which comprise the software development process provide the assurance that the software be traceable, testable, and, when integrated into the system, will satisfy the requirements of the application. These process concerns involve the software development and test practices used to develop a software system from its component parts and the specific software development practices employed to develop each individual software subsystem.

ELEMENTS OF QUALITY PLANNING

The general areas that form the foundation of quality plans are:

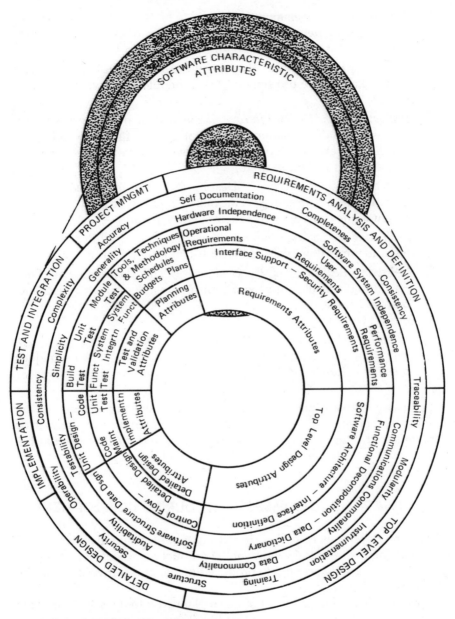

Figure 4-7. Development product concerns.

1. *Quality Assurance Practices.* The specific tools, techniques, and requirements for project quality monitoring require an understanding of the software development process, as well as an in-depth understanding of the application requirements.

2. *Software Project Planning Evaluation.* The evaluation of software planning parameters is the most essential project review and perhaps the most difficult to accomplish.

3. *Evaluating Requirements.* Poor requirements will ultimately impact every phase of the project: budgets, schedules, and technical integrity.

4. *Evaluation of the Design Process.* If the system and software design processes follow a planned methodology, are firmly rooted in requirements, and are rigorously managed and controlled, the quality of the design will be assured.

5. *Evaluating Coding Practices.* Despite the rigor associated with requirements and design specifications, poor coding practices may preclude the development of acceptable software.

6. *Evaluating the Software Integration and Test Process.* Integrity of the test and integration phase is the surest indication of software quality.

7. *In-Process Evaluation of the Management and Project Control Process.* Project management and controls are essential for project success and must be monitored and evaluated in the context of the project environment.

8. *Tailoring of Quality Assurance Procedures.* Although the quality assurance discipline follows a consistent structure, the techniques must be tailored to each project individually.

The plans for software quality assurance and management must identify the relationship between process and product factors, identify how the specific attributes that describe each may be evaluated, and identify criteria that may be used to assess and measure the quality of the factors.

SOFTWARE QUALITY ASSESSMENT DURING DEVELOPMENT

During the development period, the evaluation of quality has two forms: (1) evaluating the technical validity of the product as it is developed and (2) the ability of the software staff to produce the required software within the constraints of the project.

Software quality management must be planned into the structure of the project and be in place throughout its life. There are three separate organizational structures that support the function:

1. A structure of management and project controls that monitors the expenditures of resources, progress against plan and against resource expenditures, and quality of products against contract commitments. These are customer, management, and project activities.

2. Independent quality assurance activities which assess project integrity and product quality using independently derived criteria and using totally independent evaluations and reporting techniques. These may take the form of independent quality audits or reviews or be active analyses of product integrity conducted as an independent verification and validation of product characteristics.

3. Internal program and project monitoring techniques which are implemented as an integrated set of quality gates to assess the quality of developing data products and authorize their use by other areas of the project.

The planning of the quality management areas of the project must be complete. It must address the different quality perceptions and also describe, from the perspective of each of the organizations charged with evaluating software quality, how they will conduct the evaluations. This cannot be done through a single software quality plan.

PROGRAM PLANNING RELATIONSHIPS

The early structuring of a program should have three primary parallel parts: program planning, allocation of work, and definition of system level requirements.

Program Planning

The initial planning of program development requirements provides the basis on which the structure of the project may be based and meaningful projections of cost, schedule, and resource requirements may be developed. These requirements identify parameters which the technical segments must address if system level requirements are to be adequately supported and if the resultant system is to adequately satisfy the requirements of the end user.

The program plan is the essential starting point for development of any system in that it lays out the structure for the program and the requirements for development. The plan defines essential program relationships and controls and communicates organizational structure, requirements, and responsibilities, as well as external reporting and support requirements. The program plan describes what each individual segment of the program organization must do to ensure a smooth flow of work, data, and responsibility. The plan describes how various program segments are to be coordinated and planned and how program activities are to be focused towards a narrow set of defined goals and objectives. This program plan is the critical first planning step.

In order to develop these initial program plans, the program characteristics, contract requirements, and user expectations should be analyzed and
a structure defined which represents the worst case or most stringent application of the requirement or project discipline. This should provide the
basis for the specification of the project environment and be documented in
the program plan; the hardware, software, and system configuration development plans; and second level project planning documentation. This
phasing of resources, project disciplines, organizational elements, and technical and management controls serves as the basis for the allocation of resources and projecting costs and schedule requirements for the program.

The phasing of program plans to a common set of predefined requirements should be a precursor to all software planning. This planning is done
early in the development, laying the groundwork for all development of
software subsystems; it is modified on a regular basis to reflect changing
program conditions and development realities.

This period of the project is the most critical from a manager's standpoint
since it is during this period that the structure of the project is defined; the
technical requirements and characteristics of the project are developed; the
cost, schedule, and resource constraints which limit the prerogatives of
the software manager are identified; and development, management, and
project control procedures and techniques are defined and implemented.

Despite the importance of this early planning to the ultimate success of
the program, it is often difficult for a manager to find time or resourses early
in the development to perform these functions. As previously described,
the typical program is normally front-loaded with a myriad of essential
short-term tasks which require the direct participation of the program manager and his or her staff to complete. Early customer reviews, program planning meetings, project staffing, budget negotiations, and organization
development all compete for the program manager's time and dilute the
limited resources available to the program organization early in the implementation. Long-term problems such as program planning, meaningful
cost and schedule projections, critical early test planning activities, and
planning and development of a productive program environment are often
deferred in lieu of these short-term requirements in the hopes that after
these crises are over time will be available to address the pressing long term
issues of the program. Unfortunately, the reality is that there is never time
available in a program situation.

Once the program manager falls into the trap of trading short-term requirements for long-term planning requirements, he or she has sown the
seeds of poor productivity and unacceptable quality. The commitments on
the manager and staff increase, requiring more time rather than less to complete. As the project proceeds through the design and development stages,
the time that the manager hoped would be available for planning evapo-
rates. Early program planning, which would have brought order to these
later project phases (requirements definition, design, coding and test), has

not been done resulting in a project environment which, at best, is unproductive and, at worst, results in development chaos. Quality does not become a factor in this type of development.

The program manager must recognize the importance of this early planning to the long-term health of the project. This planning, and the specific requirements for it, should be integrated into the program environment, sharing equally in importance with the early technical activities and milestones. These program activities should be under the direct supervision of the program manager. In the case of the Program Plan, the program manager should have primary responsibility for defining the plan's content and in determining the requirements for the tools, techniques, methodologies, and program management procedures and controls.

This initial program planning establishes the environment and constraints which determine the software development prerogatives, control the software project's ability to produce quality products and develop software responsive to the needs of the end user and system environment. If the program environment is loosely defined; if the management, technical, and program controls are ineffective or not implemented; or if resources allocated by the program to the software project are not adequate; the quality of the software product will suffer.

Additional Project Planning Relationships

Several program planning documents other than those that describe software establish the system development environment and impact the ability of the software project to produce a quality software system responsive to the system requirements. The first of these, the System Engineering Management Plan (SEMP) is critical to software project integrity. The plan normally has several parts which, in aggregate, establish the program's overall engineering environment. The plan defines what engineering resources, controls, technical approaches, and methodologies are to be applied to system development to ensure the quality and integrity of the system when developed. From an engineering standpoint, SEMP describes what will be required to specify an adequate set of requirements and convert these into a system architecture consistent with the constraints identified in the program plan.

The SEMP documents the process to be followed in specifying the system, deriving the design, developing and testing the products, and, finally applying the controls to ensure the integrity of the process. A poorly thought out plan, or a plan which does not reflect the technical, administrative, or management environment will have a devastating effect on development productivity or the quality of all system components, not only those relating to software.

The other plan which establishes the program engineering environment is the Hardware Development Plan. This plan performs the same program function as the Software Development Plan, only for the hardware components of the system. The Hardware Development Plan does not impact the software segments directly during the early stages of development. In a typical program environment, the hardware and software segments of the project are developed independently, interacting only through configuration management and control, systems engineering, and program management and control. Although the effects of the hardware development shortfall begin to impact software quality and development productivity during the first stages of software testing, the critical impacts become evident during the latter stages of system integration. During this stage of the program, all poorly engineered hardware components must be corrected. All interfaces which were not properly implemented must be fixed. All system requirements or hardware performance which were not satisfied must be addressed.

Integrated Program Plan

All these documents—the Program Plan, the Software Development Plan, SEMP, and the Hardware Development Plan—define the integrated program engineering management and development environment. The plans are hierarchal; requirements tree downward from a common set of program development and control requirements. From these requirements, a system engineering structure is defined which satisfies the program goals and objectives and is consistent with documented program constraints, limitations, and essential program relationships.

At the lowest level of the engineering planning process the requirements for hardware and software development are documented, as well as specific procedures for managing and controlling the process.

This relationship is critical to the success of the software project and the quality of the products which are produced. If software is produced in a program environment which is unclear, inconsistent, or ineffective, the quality of the software will be questionable despite the rigor of the software development and the effectiveness of the software engineering process.

SOFTWARE QUALITY ORGANIZATION REQUIREMENTS

Software quality management is a tool to monitor the process used to develop, integrate, and demonstrate the software components of the system; and to monitor the technical quality of the software data products, and the responsiveness, technical quality, and operational integrity of the software when integrated into a system configuration. Software quality management acts as the technical gatekeeper, evaluating data products as they traverse from program segment to segment. Software quality management acts as the eyes of the customer, the program manager, and the software project to evaluate technical and operational compliance of the data products during development, the productivity of the software development personnel, and the effectiveness of the controls and processes being used to implement, integrate, and demonstrate the software.

The organizational and procedural segments that are used to monitor and assure software quality should be distributed throughout the program organization and monitor all categories of data: system engineering, hardware, software test and integration, program development constraints, and technical and development risk assessments. The structure for software quality assurance combines formal and informal reviews, walk-throughs, audits, independent tests, and tools, techniques, and methodologies into an integrated, cohesive, and comprehensive structure.

Quality Organizational Requirements

Quality is the responsibility and goal of the entire project organization. Previous chapters have concentrated on the project infrastructure and the process of, and products of, development in order to describe how quality is built into a modern software development project. This chapter describes the organizational aspects of the project with special emphasis on quality. The project will generally be either a small team of people for small projects or a large team of matrixed personnel for a sizable project. Since the matrix organization is the norm for most large companies, this will be used as the baseline for describing how quality is built into the organization. The subject of smaller projects and organizations will be treated as a special topic, as will the topic of Independent Verification and Validation (IV&V). The primary emphasis will be on concepts rather than on specific organization; that is, organizations will not be developed, but the relationships, techniques, and methods for ensuring quality will be stressed.

Large Project Team

The project is organized under a project or program organization with supporting resources matrixed in from engineering and supporting disciplines such as configuration management and quality assurance. This typical structure distributes control of the project to several different places. The project manager "buys" resources from the various resource managers, mainly from engineering which provides the bulk of the resources necessary to accomplish the project development. Resource assignment, in terms of specific personnel is a negotiation between the project manager and the engineering manager. The project manager cannot select specific personnel because the engineering manager assigns personnel based on the job which is being accomplished at the given moment. That is, if the project is in the requirements analysis phase he or she can assign system analysts and when the project is in the coding phase he or she can assign programmers. Thus the basic purpose of this type of organization is to assign the appropriate expertise for the task at hand. The advantages of a matrix organization are:

1. Ensuring that the proper personnel are assigned for the given task and point in the project.
2. Leveling the project manpower loading, thus relieving the project manager from carrying personnel in periods of low manpower loading requirements.
3. Giving the organization at large the capability to efficiently use personnel across a spectrum of projects.

While most managers would prefer direct assignment of personnel, that is not the norm. Rather than treat the various advantages and disadvantages of matrix management (which is not the subject of this book), we will concentrate on how software quality is built into the organization. There are at least two and usually more channels available to report on the project. The configuration management and quality assurance teams report through their respective channels to higher levels, usually to the director (or vice president) of systems (or programs). The chief engineer who is responsible for engineering resources and overall project engineering integrity typically has a separate reporting channel to the director of systems. Of course these channels are not automatically or correctly exercised unless special provisions are developed in the organization to take advantage of this opportunity.

Before discussing how these arrangements can be accommodated, it is useful to understand the requirements for special reporting. Naturally the project manager will resist separate reporting since it involves a parallel inspection or audit of the project. (Needless to say, on small projects where the development team may be dedicated this opportunity may not be present, and other methods are required to accomplish independent review. We will examine these later, but it is useful to point out at this point that this lack of opportunity is usually a major problem on smaller projects because considerations of adequate configuration management, testing, and quality assurance are usually downplayed or ignored.) In any project the mind set of the project manager is towards completion of his or her project and the manager will resist all independent audits or reviews. As a result these reviews are usually forced on the manager when major problems arise in the development. That is exactly the situation that should be avoided. The demonstrated psychology of project management is to hide a disaster as long as humanly possible in hopes that a minor miracle will result. This has nothing to do with project managers, it is endemic to human performance. It is up to the management system to prevent this type of situation. If problems do arise it is advantageous to address them as soon as possible—this has been proven time and time again. As repulsive as it may be to the project manager, the benefit of independent review, if accomplished correctly, is beneficial to the organization as a whole, to the contracting organization or user, and to the ultimate user as well.

The earlier an organization knows about a problem, the earlier it can address funding and scheduling problems that may arise. It is always a danger that bringing the project to higher level scrutiny carries the risk of cancellation; however, this is certainly not the norm—more commonly, all involved will stick to the project because of capital investment. If the project is worth doing, and there are hard requirements for the system under development, it is to everyone's benefit to deal with problems early. Most experience is that projects are finally canceled because they develop into major catastrophes and it is clear that success is unlikely.

The ultimate user benefits because he or she will enjoy the results of the project sooner than if the problem is ignored. If it is his or her money that is being spent, the lower the expenditure, and the better the user will like the system.

Thus, the treatment of separate reporting is an important one in any organization. Merely counting on the availability of separate resource channels is inadequate. The organization must clearly recognize those channels and put into place the mechanisms to exploit this opportunity. We now discuss concepts for accomplishing this.

First line project review is the prerogative of the project manager. The manager should conduct these reviews on a periodic basis, involving appropriate personnel based on the current phase of the project. These reviews should be attended by the key personnel assigned to his or her organization across the disciplines that are required. A partial list includes the configuration manager, the software quality assurance manager, test personnel, chief technical person, and other personnel as required. The purpose of these reviews is for the project team to assess the progress of the project and to address problems that occur. Naturally the solution of these problems is the responsibility of the development team and the project manager. The manager must address solutions and arrange for higher level review or additional resources as determined by the circumstances of the problem at hand.

A next possible level of review occurs outside the project, and is usually conducted at the next level of management, say the person who has responsibility for a number of programs (director of programs). This review is attended by personnel outside the project organization, usually the manager or next line supervisor of matrixed personnel, and is supported by the project team. The viability of this review is dependent, of course, on the accuracy of information presented at the review. Dual reporting channels in matrixed organizations help to ensure that this will be the case. Other techniques are also available. Various reports of progress can be made, consistent with the project schedules and products. Manpower loading is reviewed according to earlier projections. The specific methods of review are set forth in the individual plans that support the project—the software development plan, the software quality assurance plan, and the configuration management plan. The viability of this process is dependent, however, on the organization to set in place and understand the need for the process and the necessary management actions to properly support a positive and "lets get the problem solved" environment. There is no substitute for experienced and competent personnel.

Depending on the size and complexity of the project, additional reviews can be conducted. For large projects, relative to the size of the organization, reviews can be conducted periodically at a higher level, at the director of systems or vice presidential level. While these usually afford more visibility to the project they usually involve personnel who are less familiar with software engineering practice (hopefully this situation will improve in the future) and further removed from the project itself. These reviews usually concentrate on higher level management concerns such as funding, manpower loading, and schedules, and not on the solution of specific technical problems. Of course if a project is having problems these will translate into the above, however, this level can only take macro management action to correct the problem, such as putting additional resources into the project or calling for independent assessments of the problem. These are the type of actions that should be avoided if the project has been well laid out, conducted, and managed.

While the purpose here is not to discuss reviews per se, there can be a number of other reviews depending on the specific project and contracting arrangements. If the project is contracted, the customer will require formal reviews, depending on his or her management desires. These will be specified in the contractual instrument, and supported in the various plans that describe the project development, specifically the software development plan. These reviews are normally formal, in terms that specified procedures are employed, and they are conducted in accordance with the provisions of the contract.

The key documents to this review process are the software development plan and the software quality assurance plan and to a lesser extent the configuration management plan. The software development plan details the project organization, the assignment and control of resources, and the reporting procedures to be used.

If an institutionalized management process is to be used, it should be described. Of requisite importance is what is accomplished at these reviews. The software development plan details the process and products of the development. While the reviews are conducted based on these products, the detail that is reviewed will vary depending on the level of the review—technical reviews are built into the development process as an ongoing process, project reviews assess the results of development, and so forth. The engineering process and its products and the management process within the organization are integrated to support a viable review process.

The major point of all of this is that management organization is not fixed and inflexible, it is the conduit for sound engineering practice and software quality assurance. The procedures that are used in the process of development and the methods employed are the key to success—these are the subject of review—a review process that ensures that the appropriate levels are employed to provide management visibility and cognizance of the project development. Software quality assurance personnel are not outside the organization looking in. They are part of an integral development team dedicated to the successful development of the software project.

Small Project Team

On the other end of the spectrum is the small project, usually managed by a dedicated team. There are usually two reasons that independent software quality provisions are not built into a small project. First, the size of the project and the total resources committed to it are relatively small, thus software quality assurance is often overlooked. Second, the contractor may be small, without a separate software quality assurance team or organization. As plausible as these two cases seem, they do not obviate the need or requirement for software quality assurance.

These cases provide a challenge for software quality assurance—that is, how to provide for an acceptable degree of software quality assurance in small projects and in small contracting organizations. Of course one answer is that the project team, through the use of sound software engineering practice, will instill into the development the practices and procedures that provide for a quality product. That is all well and good, but it does not work well in practice. It does suggest, however, that there are certain projects where it is not economical to provide an independent software quality assurance effort. There certainly is a breakpoint for the application of additional resources and effort to provide for an independent effort. While there is no magical number to apply to cost or size, there are a number of considerations for management to use in assessing the need for an independent effort. These are:

1. *Criticality of the Project.* Is it on the critical path of development? Is the project a development that is associated with a man-critical function, such as a module of a space station?

2. *Size of the Project Relative to the Size of the Overall Development.* Does it represent a major portion of the overall development?

3. *Impact of Slipping Schedule or Increasing Costs.* Are there outside factors that make the development sensitive, such as delivery to a foreign nation or is it a key part of another effort by another contractor?

While it is possible to assign the responsibility of software quality assurance to an individual who reports to the development manager, that is not recommended. We believe that the most effective use and employment of software quality assurance is by personnel who do not report to the project manager.

For small projects, the development team is most likely to be intact. That is, the use of small development teams is usually synonymous with a small contractor that normally does not have the resources to operate in a matrix management environment. How does the small contractor provide for software quality assurance? The answer is through the application of institutionalized software engineering practices and assigned personnel to monitor the implementation of that practice. There must be a consistent software engineering environment that will be employed through the life of the project. The company will normally prepare a software quality assurance plan that will serve as the model for company practice. This plan will be modified with individual project requirements reflected in the project software quality assurance plan and the software development plan. Software quality assurance personnel, whether dedicated to a particular project or charged with monitoring the practice across the company will act in accordance with the specified requirements of the individual project software quality assurance plan and software development plan. Software quality must be an integral part of the project environment. It must be monitored internally and regularly evaluated from the outside.

It is important that the concept of independence be supported so that software quality assurance personnel report outside of the project organization. Whether to a company president or to some intermediate manager is a choice dependent on the size and nature of organization of the specific company. In a small company it may be very hard to structure, but, if the company is serious about developing quality software products, it is a mandatory consideration.

5

QUALITY EVALUATION
OF THE SOFTWARE
DEVELOPMENT PROCESS

The process of software development is the means by which quality is built into the software products.

This chapter examines elements of the system implementation processes, describes the process used for specifying and monitoring quality levels, and discusses the quality evaluation of process oriented factors. The chapter explores how the evaluation process can measure the effectiveness of the software infrastructure and how individual segments of the infrastructure can be evaluated.

There has been a continuing awareness of critical problems encountered in developing systems involving software. These problems include cost and schedule overruns, high cost sensitivity to changes in requirements, poor performance of delivered systems, high system-maintenance costs, and lack of reusability. There has not, however, been a corresponding awareness of the effect that the development process has on product quality and the effects that result from poor integration of the individual process into an effective development infrastructure.

The planning and implementation of process oriented quality factors are the means by which software quality is built into the product.

A quality model for the development process is a hierarchical relationship which describes the overall development environment at the top, and identifies specifics of this environment at the second, third and subsequent levels (criteria and metrics). Software quality may be predicted and measured by the presence, absence, or degree of identifiable software process factors and attributes.

SOFTWARE QUALITY MANAGEMENT

Software quality management has various functional responsibilities during the software development cycle. Software quality management must become involved at the system level; when system functional tasks are allocated to software or to hardware. Once the allocation of functional tasks is completed, specific software requirements can be identified. If the allocation is not correct, the software cannot expect to satisfy the needs of the system. The result can be a set of software capabilities, performance levels, and design constraints which do not meet the needs of the system. Identification of these specific requirements usually involves decisions supported by trade studies. These software trade studies consider life cycle cost, risk, schedule, capabilities, software performance, and final product quality. These activities actually continue throughout the implementation period although the data products are reviewed at several points to ensure the validity of the data.

Once software requirements are specified, quality evaluation emphasis shifts to monitoring the software development. Monitoring continues throughout preliminary design, detailed design, coding and unit testing, CSC integration and testing, and CSCI-level testing, and may continue into the system-level testing that follows. The quality monitoring techniques, other than schedule or cost, determine whether the software process being used for development is sufficiently complete and robust to ensure a quality product. The monitoring procedures provide the visibility of the quality of the evolving product essential to track progress and quality of the development process. This visibility is achieved through an integrated set of reviews, audits, documentation, and product quality gates performed regularly throughout the development. The establishment of criteria and measurement methods for each review and audit, and for all documentation and products, is necessary for tracking progress and product quality. This tracking process enables not only the manager to identify project problems early enough to correct them, but also provides an early warning of productivity and quality shortfalls.

PROCESS QUALITY ATTRIBUTES

The purpose of measuring software process quality is to enable the specification of software project effectiveness and to evaluate the achieved level of quality at specific points during development. These periodic measurements enable an assessment of current status and a prediction of quality level for the final product. The evaluation of software quality should address not only product characteristics but other quality-oriented problems which are rooted in the process being used for development. There must be a means to specify process quality requirements, to quantitatively measure process quality, and to predict a quality level for the development process.

Process assessments measure the degree that the process meets the needs of the project, not the level of software technical performance; for example, how effective is configuration management of the software, not how accurate is the xyz algorithm. However, the process of specifying and measuring process quality is analogous to the process of specifying and measuring technical performance. Both begin with similar activities: system needs are assessed, trade-offs are performed (involving resources and levels of performance or levels of quality), and requirements are specified. Subsequent phases involve evaluations of how well these requirements are being satisfied by the development process.

System adequacy is traditionally evaluated by defining a structure for system and software development process, and by testing to see how the implemented process conforms in later development stages. Product quality has traditionally been evaluated by such methods as reviews, walkthroughs, tests, and audits. This type of quality evaluation ensures that, for example, designs are traceable to requirements, product standards are met by the product, and the products are technically correct.

The evaluation of the software process follows a similar process but is conducted against a different, less visible set of data. A documented structure for the development process is defined and the individual components which comprise it are defined. These are then transformed into a specific set of criteria which indicate progress, and through inspections, audits and reviews, quality and effectiveness are evaluated. The quality management process will enable a quantitative assessment of these process factors at different stages of development, thereby ensuring that specified quality levels are being satisfied in a manner similar to performance evaluation by testing.

Process Framework

Defining hierarchical process relationships is the starting point for evaluating quality of the software development process. High level factors—resource management and control, project planning and management, data production and control, technology application, personnel relations and quality management and test—are at the top level. Lower level criteria detail factors which are the project specific components of the top levels in the hierarchy, and successively lower level measures and characteristics which describe the development process.

This process model must be flexible in that the model must indicate a general relationship between each factor and attribute. Individual elements may be updated to reflect technology advances without affecting the model itself. For example, as new resource management and control techniques evolve, new factors may be added at the lower levels. As monitoring technology evolves, criteria and metrics may be added at the top level; and criteria and metrics can be added, deleted, or modified as necessary. There are top level quality factors and criteria, many second level attributes, and many more elements and lower level measures, factors, and elements that describe the specific techniques and hence the process factors being used for the development.

Quality Specification

When determining and specifying software quality requirements, system development needs are assessed from a quality perspective; the desired quality factors, associated criteria, and applicable attributes and measures are selected and quality-level goals are derived for each separate quality factor. These goals define the required quality levels to be achieved for the factor. In general, choosing a higher quality goal will require more extensive planning, a more disciplined approach to accomplishment and more emphasis in the development process. For example, if the limited resources are available, careful planning of how they will be applied is essential, rigorous monitoring of their application is critical and the entire structure of the project may be centered around the resource problem.

Specifying the evaluations of process quality must be tailored to the project. When assessing and specifying technical performance and development requirements, the environment within which the software project is to take place is the basis for the evaluation. As such, the evaluation techniques must be based on the way that software is developed. This development model must be evaluated against a model of the software process which is provably effective. Balancing the evaluation of the software process against a predefined model is critical if any reasonable assertions concerning process quality are to be derived.

Software Process Monitoring

The evaluation of software process quality measures the discrete components of the development process at different stages of the development cycle. For example, the importance of the resource planning activities diminishes as the project moves through the testing process. The role of configuration management increases in importance as testing complexity increases.

The relative importance of process factors varies as a function of the software application type. The process criteria used to evaluate a real time software development may differ substantially from the criteria applied to a non real time system. The development process differs dramatically between large and small implementations, as do the process criteria used to assess

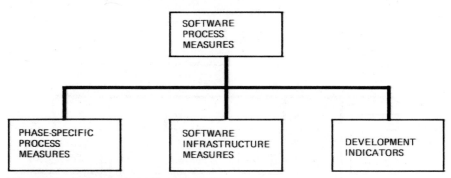

Figure 5-1. Software process measures.

them. The measures of process quality are different for complex versus simple systems. When defining the model to be used for process evaluation, these factors must be considered. The points in the development cycle where data describing process effectiveness is available generally correspond to normal reviews and audits that are conducted to establish or augment a configuration baseline. Before each review or audit, the specific process attributes and criteria selected for evaluation should be defined. The means to be used to score each process area at the review should be defined, and the criteria for acceptability identified.

Besides the formal reviews, the assessment of process factors should be an integral part of the quality management process.

MEASUREMENT OF SOFTWARE PROCESS QUALITY

The measurement of process quality is a more difficult task than the evaluation of product quality. The analysis is not based on a tangible item, but rather on a development function which can only be assessed by an evaluation of effect or by a subjective assessment of effectiveness. The evaluated process component cannot physically inspect a product's attributes; rather, it can only measure the degree that components of the process are consistent with requirements of the planned development environment and are "successful" in the context of the overall project environment.

As illustrated in Figure 5-1, there are three separate factors which may be used to evaluate the effectiveness of the software development process.

1. Software infrastructure measures which are evaluations of the individual components of the software project infrastructure and the degree that each contributes to a software project environment supporting the production of quality software within cost and schedule.

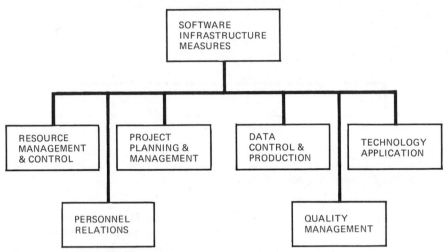

Figure 5-2. Software infrastructure measures.

2. Phase specific process measures which are indicators of process effectiveness and must be resolved before the next phase of development can be initiated.

3. Development indicators which are indicative of project effectiveness and success. These are project characteristics which, if they occur or don't occur, are indicators of project effectiveness or unacceptable performance.

The process measurement parameters indicate the effectiveness of the software development process. These measures, when applied from the beginning of a project, provide a means of defining, evaluating, explaining, and predicting software development production, effectiveness, and project performance.

When applied during a project they can be a means of checkpointing the development process at specific points in the development cycle. These "point" evaluations provide a measure of risk for developing a quality product within cost and schedule.

Software Infrastructure Measures

The measurement of the project infrastructure is the most difficult of all the process evaluations. This is due to the number of diverse components of the infrastructure, the interactions between them, and the differing characteristics of each component. As illustrated in Figure 5-2, the infrastructure components relate to each other in a hierarchal fashion. The components generally fall into six major areas:

1. *Resource Management and Control.* The project policies, practices, tools, techniques, and methodologies which project the need for resources, structure their application to the project, and monitor their effectiveness.

2. *Project Planning and Management.* The techniques used to plan and structure the project environment, and the practices used to control the project, focus the resources and manage project progress.

3. *Data Control and Production.* The project practices, procedures, tools and techniques which control the flow of data, monitor data integrity, structure and organize the data, and report and control the reporting of problems and corrections to approved project baselines.

4. *Technology Application.* The planning of project methodologies, application of the methodologies to the development, effectiveness of the methodologies when applied to the development environment, and the degree that each project methodology is linked with related methodologies to form an integrated project environment.

5. *Personnel Relations.* The relevancy of the personnel mix to the development process requirements, the characteristics of the application, and the environment required or selected for the project. The staff commitment and focus are critical, as are the customer's perception and support of the project.

6. *Quality Management.* The related areas of quality management—quality gates, independent quality assurance, independent verification and validation, and the related areas of test integration of software testing—are critical elements of the software project infrastructure.

Monitoring the software project infrastructure requires that we identify the parts and pieces of each of the six infrastructure areas in sufficient detail to allow their evaluation, analysis, and if necessary redirection to correct discrepancies. From this decomposition, criteria may be developed which will be the basis for evaluating infrastructure quality. Reasonable answers to the following questions which describe the following process attributes are the result of this analysis:

1. *Quality.* Can there be significant quality shortfalls expected? Is there a reasonable potential to correct the problems before the impacts are felt by the project?

2. *Project Performance.* Have the schedule budgets and project plans been developed using accepted project practices? Have they been implemented adequately? Are they being monitored and tracked adequately? Does the project have a reasonable potential for completing the development within the constraints?

3. *Data Integrity.* Is there a reasonable expectation that the software data products will be consistent and controlled, and will describe a software system consistent with the described requirements of the user and/or the needs and expectations of the application?

4. *Realism.* Are the plans for the project realistic. Do they consider the realities of the project technical, administrative, and contractual (organizational) environment? Do they reflect the requirements imposed by personnel, company and the development organization?

5. *Performance Predictability.* Will there be a reasonable expectation that the quality of the software is adequate to meet the needs of all organizations associated with the software? Will the software perform as expected when integrated and deployed into an operational system configuration?

6. *Implementability.* Is there a reasonable expectation that the development staff will be able to execute the implementation as described and develop the software within the technology required of the application? Is there an acceptable probability that the customer will accept and apply the software and system in their operational environment?

The evaluation of these attributes has four segments: (1) identification of the specific components of the project which will be used to measure the process effectiveness; (2) criteria definition which describes the measures to be applied to evaluate each component; (3) data collection phase through use of audits, reviews, or inspections of the data describing the process component; and (4) analysis and evaluation where the results are gathered, interpreted, and evaluated against process criteria and recommendations made.

COMPONENT IDENTIFICATION

There are second, third, and fourth levels which describe the software process. Specific components of these lower levels become less generic and more tailored to the specific characteristics of the project as the lower levels of the hierarchy are developed. A model for this hierarchy is described in the following and questions which evaluate the component against specific attributes are provided.

Resource Management and Control

As illustrated in Figure 5-3, the resource management and control process hierarchy has three components: top down planning, resource plans, and constraint development and monitoring. These three areas describe, at a

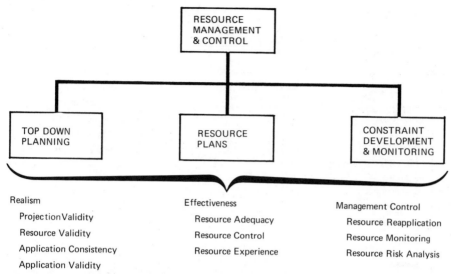

Figure 5-3. Resource management and control measures.

high level, the process used to define resource management and control requirements. Effectiveness in these three areas is measured using the following general sets of attributes.

1. *Realism.* Have the resources projected for application to the project
   been based on a realistic analysis of the true needs of the application
   (projection validity)? Are these resource projections consistent with
   project availability of the resources (resource validity)? Can the resources be applied to the project consistent with funding profiles and
   schedule requirements? Have the resources (application consistency)
   been applied in a hierarchal fashion to the work requirements of the
   project (application validity)?

2. *Effectiveness.* Are the resources projected and applied to the project
   adequate to support the implementation process (resource adequacy)? Can their application be controlled and can the resources be
   applied in a controlled and effective m. nner to deal with development shortfalls (resource control)? Are t. e resources and resources
   mix applied to the project adequate and consistent to the development experience and productivity realities of the project (resource experience)?

3. *Management Control.* Are the resources applied to the project manageable? Can their effectiveness be monitored and are shortfalls recognizable early enough to allow effective correction (resource
   reapplication)? Are there sufficient checks and balances built into the
   development process to evaluate resource adequacy and to suggest

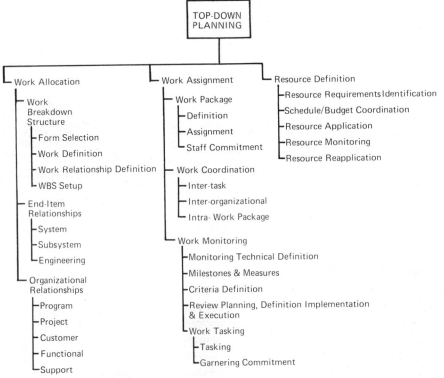

Figure 5-4. Top-down planning structure.

alternative resources to maintain the project integrity (resource monitoring)? Are there adequate risk alternatives in place to permit resource redistribution in the event of unexpected or anomalous project conditions (resource risk analysis)?

Figures 5-4 through 5-6 provide representative lower level process categories which describe the resource areas of the software project model.

The specifics for the model can only be defined after a thorough analysis of the characteristics of technical requirements of the specific project, the development environment planned and implemented for the project, the specific processes to be applied to the project and the expected development experience and risks. The resultant model is, at the lowest level, a complete description of how the project plans, manages, monitors and controls the application of resources to the software development process and serves as the basis for process evaluation.

Project Planning and Management

As illustrated in Figure 5-7, the project planning and management process hierarchy has four components: project planning procedures, project defi-

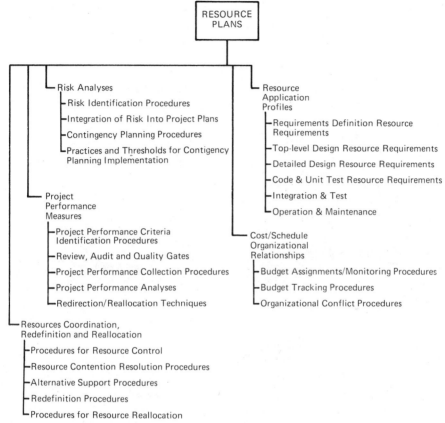

Figure 5-5. Resource plans.

nition procedures, project coordination procedures, and project planning emphasis.

These four areas provide a framework which the many related activities relating to planning and management may be grouped. As illustrated in Figure 5-7, there are eight separate categories of attributes which describe these groupings:

1. *Relevance.* Have the specific plans and management practices been developed after a hierarchal analysis of the specific requirements of the project followed by a decomposition of specific management policies and practices (management hierarchy)? Is the defined management structure consistent with specific identified project technical and administrative needs (management coverage)? Are the plans and management practices scaled to the project characteristics and development requirements (management scope)?

2. *Implementability.* Can the planned or implemented management environment be sustained throughout the life of the project (man-

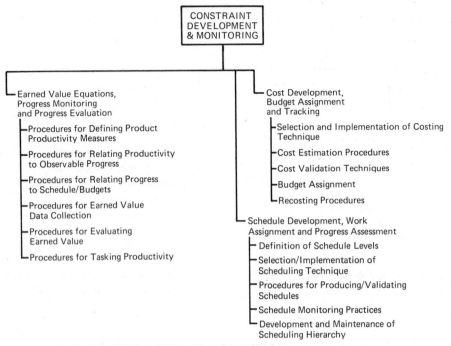

Figure 5-6.   Constraint development and monitoring.

agement sustainability)? Do the plans and implemented management practices limit the management overhead to a degree that can
be supported by the project (management overhead)? Considering
experience and resource limitations, can the planned and implemented management environment be effective (staff capability)?

3. *Achievability.*   Is the planned or implemented project environment
consistent with the realities of the project and are they achievable (realism)? Without a major augmentation of the development resources, can the planned or implemented management environment
be supported (resource compatibility)? Can the planned or implemented management environment be implemented without impacting schedule or cost projections (constraint compatibility)? Are tools,
techniques, methodologies and support facilities available to the
project to support the planned or implemented management structure (implementation capability)?

4. *Scaling.*   Has there been a tailoring of specific, proven management
and control techniques to the specific characteristics of the project
(tailoring)? Has the planning and implementation of a management
and control structure addressed a finite and specific set of project requirements and is the scope of the management environment already defined and understood (management scale)?

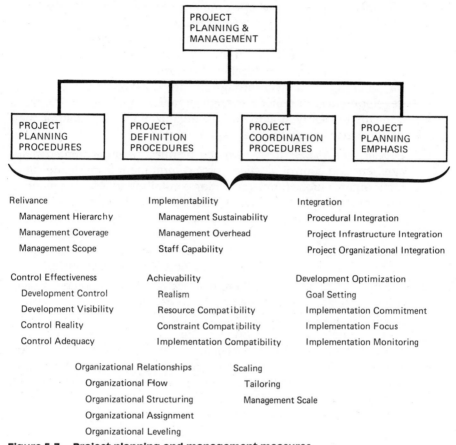

Figure 5-7. Project planning and management measures.

5. *Integration.* Have the planned and implemented management and control procedures been integrated into the overall project environment and has the integration resulted in an effective controlled project environment (procedural integration)? Have the planned and implemented management and control practices integrated the various segments of the project and have they controlled the relationships between them (project infrastructure integration)? Have the management and control practices integrated the activities of the organization of personnel assigned to the project and have they coordinated the organizational relationships within the project (project organizational integration)?

6. *Organizational Relationships.* Has the planned and implemented organizational structure provided a smooth, controlled transition of responsibility and flow of data between organizational components (organizational flow)? Has the organization been structured in ac-

cordance with the project environment and the technical and administrative needs of the project (organizational structuring)? Has the organizational structure included all project functions and can the requirements be staffed within the experience and staff levels identified for the project (organizational assignment)? Is there a plan for transitioning manpower through the organizational structure as the development requirements change (organizational leveling)? Is there a means to clearly assign work to organizations and monitor their performance (organizational assignment)?

7. *Development Optimization.* Do the planned or implemented management and control practices force commitment from the development organizations (implementation commitment)? Has the planned and implemented environment focused the tasks and development organization towards a narrow set of achievable project milestones (implementation focus)? Within the planned or implemented project environment, is there a means to assess progress, identify shortfalls and suggest potential solutions (implementation monitoring)?

8. *Control Effectiveness.* Are there planned and implemented management controls to ensure the organized development of all software products (development control)? Do the planned and implemented management controls provide a minimum load on the project organization while maximizing visibility (development visibility)? Are the planned and complemented project controls achievable within the project environment and framework (control reality)? Are there sufficient controls in place to monitor and structure project performance and control the development process (control adequacy)?

These attributes are applied to the process categories which describe the project planning and management segments of the project infrastructure. The evaluation of these attributes provides an assessment of the management and control integrity of the project, both at a planning level and through the implementation of the management and control environment.

Figures 5-8 through 5-11 provide representative fourth and lower level process factors. The model described for this category and illustrated in the figures is representative. Significant tailoring is required to bring it in line with project requirements, the management and development environment, and the internally and externally specified project constraints which shape the development.

Data Control and Production

As illustrated in Figure 5-12, the third process level of the data control and production hierarchy has three primary categories: control of approved project end items, data standards and production, and control of engineer-

Figure 5-8.   Project planning measures.

ing data products. These areas of the project infrastructure are, perhaps, the critical segment of the p oject infrastructure. Through these areas, project standardization is assured and content consistency is provided when the data is used by different organizations.

The seven separate attribute categories which describe data control and quality at the third level are identified below.

1. *Quality Assessment.*   Are there standards in place for data products and measures in place to assess their quality before they are placed under control (quality standard measures)? Is there a set of formal and informal reviews, walk-throughs and inspections in place to evaluate quality and does the data reviewed go under increased levels of control as it is approved (quality gates and control levels)? Are the initial quality evaluations based on the standards for development and are subsequent evaluations of changes to the products based on the product standards (quality maintenance)? Are the data control levels based on quality checkpoints and does the level of data

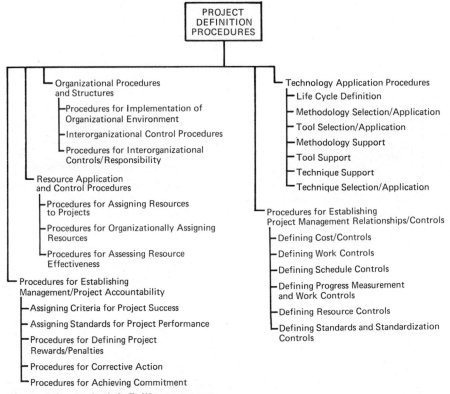

Figure 5-9.   Project definition measures.

control increase as the software data product approvals authorize use by more segments of the project (data approval)?

2.   *Baseline Integrity.*   Are there formal baselines established in the project after completion of a formal customer review (baseline identification)? Are customer baselines maintained on a current basis as changes to the information are made (baseline control)? Is there an evaluation of the operational engineering and product impacts of changes before they are made (baseline analysis)? Is the status of all approved system data products documented and are the released configurations documented and controlled (baseline status control)?

3.   *Data Control.*   Is there a procedure in place to control engineering data as the data is produced and approved (engineering data control)? Is the control integrated with the engineering quality gates and are approved data items maintained on a current basis (data integrity)? Is there a procedure in place to provide controlled, documented releases of all project data (data release)? Is there a procedure in place for tracking the status of releases and providing an audit trail of problems and corrections (data tracking)? Is there a procedure in

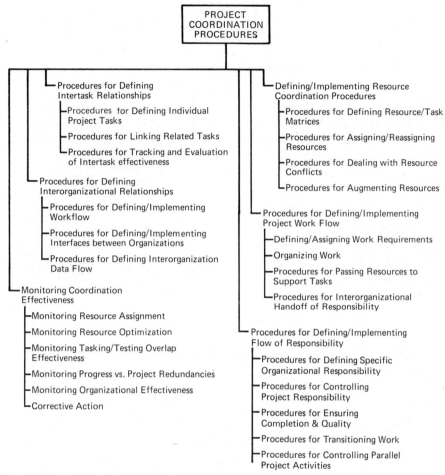

Figure 5-10. Project coordination measures.

place for assessing the engineering and development impacts of changes before the changes are made (data update control)? Is there an effective technique for tasking the functional or development organizations to correct a problem, and a means of monitoring the implementation of the correction and evaluating quality as it is produced (data update monitoring)? Is there a means of assessing the quality of information, and qualifying the update before it is released for use and ensuring its integrity when integrated into a system configuration (data integrity evaluation)?

4. *Data Standards and Control.* Are there standards in place which describe each of the data products which are developed by the project (standards validity)? Are there in place or projected means to minimize the flow of information, control the data products which are

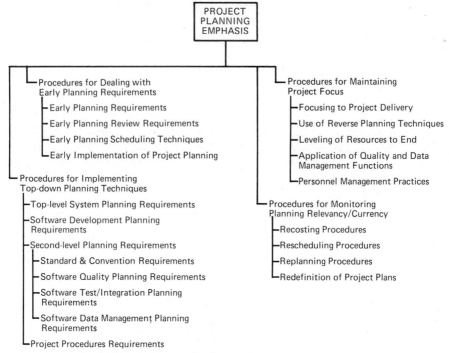

Figure 5-11. Project planning emphasis measures.

part of it and a means to link the flow of data through the various technical methodologies (data linking)? Can the project keep up with the flow of data and control the changes without becoming a bottleneck in the project (data update responsiveness)?

5. *Data Production.* Is there a consistent means for producing data and documentation (data production effectiveness)? Can the project process and control all categories of data developed by the project, both textual and graphical? Is this processing consistent with the development scheduling and project processing requirements (data turnaround)? Are there defined standards for all categories of data used by the project and a means to use this engineering data without major rework in the production of required project deliverables (data transition)? Does the project organization have the resources, the experience and the tools necessary to produce the project data and documentation (data production support)?

6. *Data Release.* Are there procedures in place to release data from the project after project quality has been assured and a structure to ensure their status (data release procedures)?

7. *Post Release Control.* Are there procedures identified to monitor the performance of data released for use and for releasing updated ver-

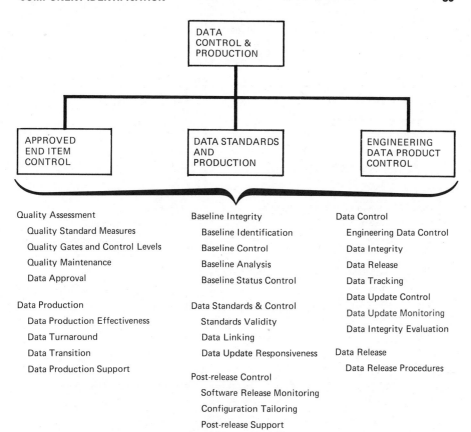

Figure 5-12.   Data control and production measures.

sions (software release monitoring)? Is there a means for integrating documentation or software into specific test or application configurations (configuration tailoring)? Can the software be supportable after it is released from the development organizations (post release support)?

These attributes describe the degree of control of project data. This control is applied as the data products progress through the software life cycle.

Figures 5-13 through 5-15 provide representative lower level data control activities of the project. The specifics for these project areas are highly sensitive to the project structure, organization and technical realities. These project areas are the center of all data flow and control. The effectiveness of these particular segments of the project infrastructure are critical to the effectiveness of the project organization. Unless these segments of the project infrastructure are clearly defined, adequately supported, and effectively integrated into the project environment, the project productivity will suffer and quality will be impacted.

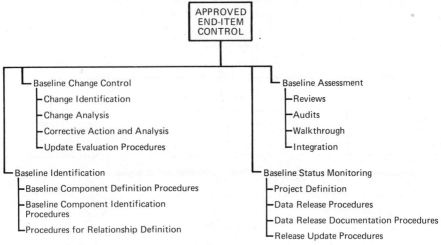

Figure 5-13.   Approved end item control measures.

Technology Application

As illustrated in Figure 5-16, the technology application of the process hierarchy has five primary categories: technical environment definition, technical procedures and techniques, project methodologies, project tools and automated aids, and data linkages between methodologies. The application of technology is the means by which the software is developed. These techniques are the means by which the software project produces the engineering data, validates its correctness and integrates the products into an operational configuration. As previously described, there is not a single technology or methodology involved in the production of software; rather,

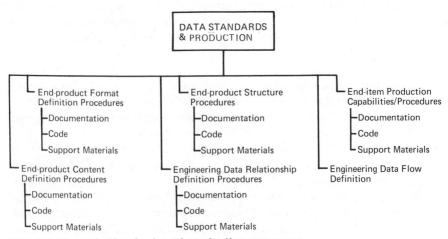

Figure 5-14.   Data standards and production measures.

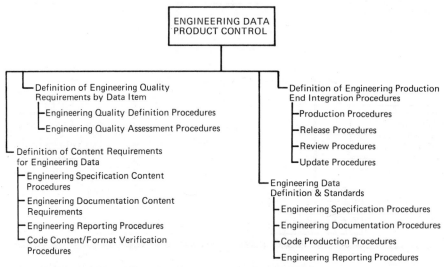

Figure 5-15. Engineering data product control measures.

the process is an integration of many technologies and methodologies, many of which require different support. The process quality attributes measure not only how effectively an individual component of the software technical environment supports the project requirements, but more importantly, how well do the components interact to provide an effective environment for implementing the software within cost, schedule, and technical requirements.

Seven primary attribute categories which describe the software technical environment are:

1. *Realism.*   Does the software project environment utilize tools, techniques and methodologies which are reasonable in light of project technical and administrative realities (technical reasonableness)? Are the components of the software technical environment real or are they based on unproved technologies and tools which are not available (technical availability)? Is the specified technical environment achievable in light of development restrictions? Are there sufficient resources available to support the environment and has the environment been tailored to the specific project needs and constraints (technical achievability)?

2. *Supportability.*   Are the technical areas of the project supportable in the project environment (technical supportability)? Is the project environment sufficient to ensure adequate technical support (technical robustness)? Are there supporting project tools, techniques and methodologies to ensure that the software project environment, when implemented, will be smooth, effective and complete (tech-

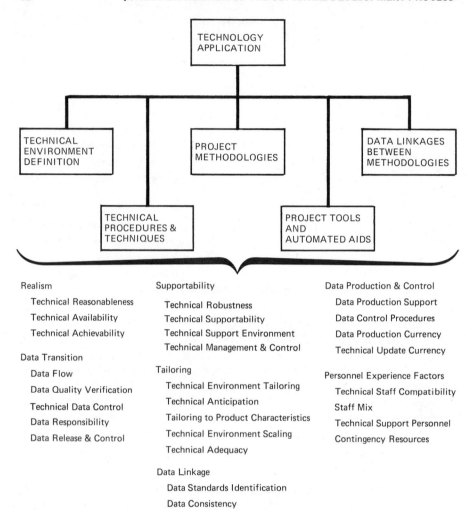

Figure 5-16.   Technology application measures.

nical support environment)? Can the software project management and control practices deal with the complexity of the technical environment? Can sufficient visibility into technical quality and integrity be established to monitor project progress and product quality (technical management and control)?

3. *Data Production and Control.*   Does the project have available the required data production control facilities to support the outputs of the individual methodologies (data production support)? Is there a suite of project procedures, controls, and support facilities which will control the flow of engineering data and will monitor and maintain its

integrity as the data is produced (data control procedures)? Can the project produce current controlled versions of the technical data products without becoming a project bottleneck (data production currency)? Are the controls of technical data and changes sufficiently responsive to allow the timely update of controlled technical information (technical update currency)?

4. *Personnel Experience Factors.* Does the project staff have sufficient technical expertise to implement, support, and sustain the technical environment (technical staff compatibility)? Is there the proper mix of personnel available to support the technical requirements of the project (staff mix)? Are there adequate support personnel available to ensure the integrity of the technical environment of the project (technical support personnel)? Are there personnel conversant with the technical environment and methodologies available for application to the project in the event of contingency or development crises (contingency resources)?

5. *Tailoring.* Has the project technical environment been tailored to the project requirements and is the technology adequate to the technical and specific development needs of the project (technical environment tailoring)? Can the technical project environment control the anticipated data and implementation project needs (technical anticipation)? Have the specific characteristics of the software product been used to tailor the project environment (tailoring to the product characteristics)? Has the project environment been tailored to the realities of the development situation (cost, schedule, personnel, resources) (technical environment scaling)? Have the tools, techniques, methodologies, and project support facilities been scaled to the specific needs of the project and are they adequate to control the project needs (technical adequacy)?

6. *Data Transition.* Is there a defined data flow for the technical products which identifies production responsibility, review responsibility, control, and procedures for dissemination and release (Data flow)? Are there specific gates in place to evaluate the quality of the data products before they are released for use with the project (data quality verification)? Is project control over engineering data applied as the data transitions between development organizations and functions or as data is approved at a gate (technical data control)? Is there a smooth transition of data development and control responsibility which tracks the flow of data and organizational use of the data (data responsibility)? Is there a consistent method for releasing technical data, documenting the release and controlling updates to the data after release (data release and control)?

7. *Data Linkage.* Have the individual engineering data products been described and has the specific format and content of each been de-

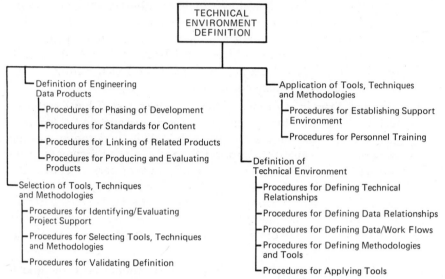

Figure 5-17. Technical environment definition measures.

fined (data standards identification)? Have these technical or engineering data products been tied to the specific methodologies and have the methodologies been linked together (data consistency)? Are the outputs of one methodology tied, on a one to one basis, to the inputs or related as interfacing methodologies (methodology data relationships)?

These attributes describe the effectiveness of the technology which has been applied to the software development project. The measures are irrespective of the specific technologies; rather they are used to monitor and provide control of the development process. The technology model, at lower levels, becomes more specific to the project environment. For example, at the lowest levels, the technology model will detail the attributes of the specific methodologies used and the relationships between them, while at higher levels the attributes detail the project requirements which the methodologies must satisfy.

Figures 5-17 through 5-21 are representative of the technology application process taxonomy. These project areas are primary determinants of the project environment and technical structure.

The technical areas of the project infrastructure are the means by which all data is produced, evaluated, and controlled. In the context of the project environment, the effectiveness of the individual components of the technical environment can only be measured by the degree that each tool, technique, or project methodology supports the goals of the overall project. Quality or productivity measures of individual components without con-

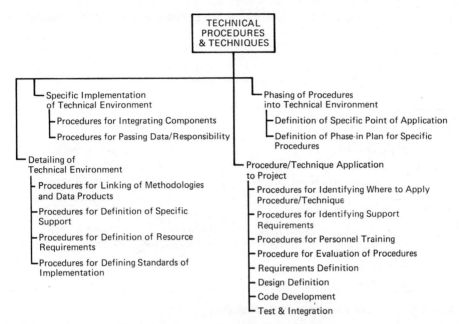

Figure 5-18.   Technical procedures and techniques measures.

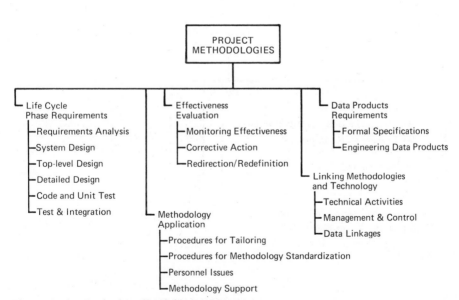

Figure 5-19.   Project methodologies measures.

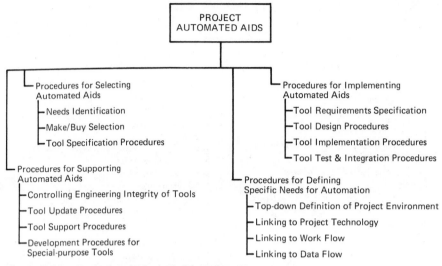

Figure 5-20. Project automated aid measures.

sidering the project needs, environments and peculiar requirements imposed by the infrastructure are not valid from the perspective of the project.

Personnel Relations

As illustrated in Figure 5-22, the personnel relations taxonomy has six subcategories: customer relations, program relations, personnel requirements,

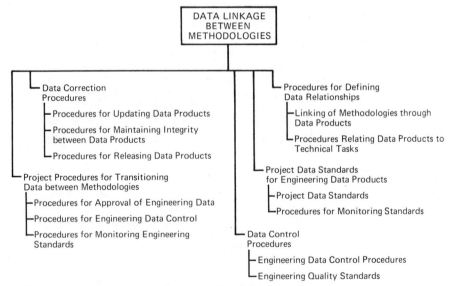

Figure 5-21. Data linkage between methodologies measures.

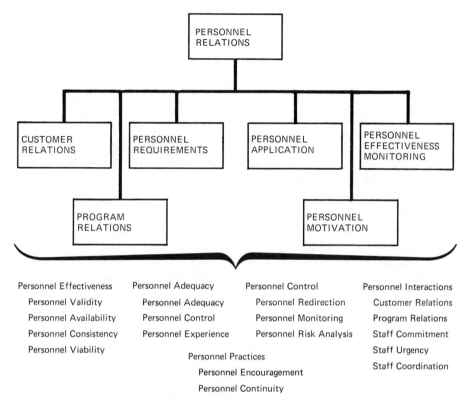

Figure 5-22. **Personnel relations measures.**

personnel application, personnel motivation, and personnel effectiveness monitoring.

These areas detail, at a high level, how the personnel resources satisfy the technical, administrative, and support requirements of the software development process.

The effectiveness of the personnel applied to a project is not measured by how successful an individual is or how high the morale of individuals or groups within the project is. It is determined by how well individuals communicate and work together and the morale within the project. The effectiveness and success of the personnel relations categories of the software infrastructure are measured using the following attributes.

1. *Personnel Effectiveness.* Have the personnel resources projected or applied to the project been based on a realistic analysis of the true needs of the software development project (personnel validity)? Are personnel requirements consistent with projected availability of required software project personnel (personnel availability)? Can the required personnel resources be applied to the project considering

funding profiles and schedule requirements (personnel consistency)? Have the personnel requirements been defined in a hierarchal fashion and have they been considered and layered on to the work requirements of the project (personnel viability)?

2. *Personnel Adequacy.*   Are the personnel resources that have been projected or applied to the project adequate to support the implementation process (personnel adequacy)? Does the project organization control the personnel, focus their activities and force commitment at all levels in the project organization to support the needs and activities of the project in a controlled and effective manner (personnel control)? Are the personnel and personnel mix adequate, and consistent with the development experience and productivity realities of the project (personnel experience)?

3. *Personnel Control.*   Are the personnel resources applied to the project manageable? Can their effectiveness be monitored, and are personnel or productivity shortfalls recognizable early enough to allow effective correction (personnel redirection)? Does the development process provide a smooth transition of personnel responsibility, an assessment of personnel adequacy as data moves through the development cycle and are there checks and balances in place to identify personnel shortfalls before the problems are transformed into productivity and technical impacts (personnel monitoring)? Are there adequate risk alternatives in place to permit personnel redistribution or augmentation in the event of unexpected or anomalous project conditions (personnel risk analysis)?

4. *Personnel Interactions.*   Is the customer knowledgeable about the state of the project, understand its problems, support its development goals and objectives, and committed to its success (customer relations)? Is the program organization supportive of the needs and development requirements of the software organization, committed to its success, knowledgeable of its requirements and shortfalls, and organizationally structured to support its development requirements (program relations)? Is the staff organized according to the needs of the software project, and is there an understanding on the part of all staff members of their role in the project and are they focused and committed to producing a quality product (staff commitment)? Is there a sense of urgency on the part of all members of the staff and is this translated to the timely production of required project data items (staff urgency)? Are the activities of all staff members coordinated and do they understand their commitments and requirements (staff coordination)?

5. *Personnel Practices.*   Does the project have procedures for rewarding good performers, encouraging marginal performers, and punishing inadequate performers (personnel encouragement)? Are there proj-

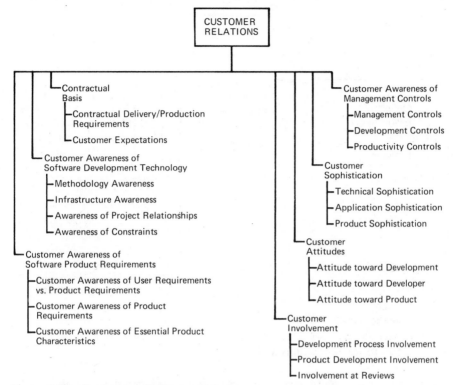

Figure 5-23. Customer relations measures.

ect procedures to retain personnel and will the procedures ensure continuity of personnel assignments in light of changing company or program needs or requirements (personnel continuity)?

The personnel relations attributes are the means by which the adequacy of the staff and their commitment to the project may be assessed. This is a two way street. Without an adequate, competent, and committed staff, the chance of producing a quality product is marginal. On the other hand, if the project environment is not consistent, and structured in such a way as to facilitate the production of quality software, even the most competent staff members will be frustrated in their attempts to produce quality software.

Figures 5-23 through 5-28 provide representative lower level process categories which describe the personnel relations areas of the software project model.

The detailed characteristics of these levels require a complete and thorough analysis of the personnel requirements of the specific project, the customer and program environment both planned and implemented for the project, the specific personnel practices applied to the project, and the expected development experience and risks. The resultant model is, at the

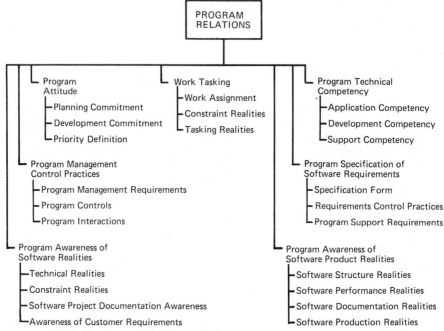

Figure 5-24. Program relations measures.

lowest level, a complete description of how the project will select and apply personnel, control their activities and deal with external organizations to produce and deliver a quality product.

Quality Management

The quality management segment of the process hierarchy has seven primary categories: baseline reviews and engineering reviews and inspections, audits, requirements testing, design testing, development testing, and independent quality techniques (Figure 5-29).

These techniques are the means by which the software quality is monitored as the software products are being built. They provide the facilities to assess the products that are delivered to the customer. These techniques provide the structures by which the software project ensures that engineering data is consistent with the standards of the project. These segments of the infrastructure evaluate product validity and integrate and qualify the products into an operational configuration. The quality management segments establish checkpoints to assess product quality at discrete points. Quality management ensures the integration of development technologies and methodologies to the specific requirements of the project test environment. The quality management attributes consider not only individual components of the quality management environment but how these interact to

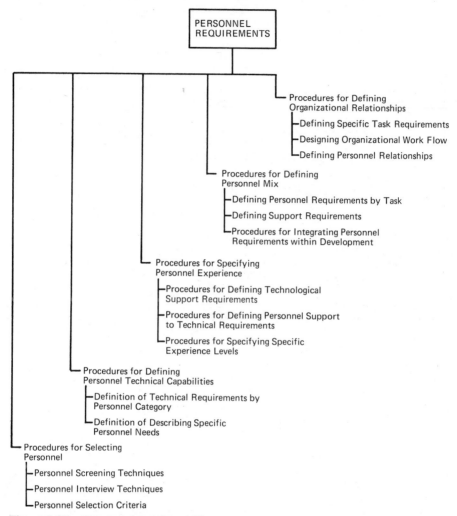

Figure 5-25. Personnel requirements measures.

support the project requirements. The issue that must be addressed by quality management is how well do the individual quality management components interact to provide an effective environment for implementing the software within cost, schedule, and technical requirements.

As illustrated in Figure 5-29, eight primary attribute categories which describe the software quality management environment are:

1. *Data Standards.* Are there standards in place for all documentation which is included in a formal baseline (documentation standards)? Are there standards for all engineering data products that will be evaluated at a quality gate (engineering standards)? Is each piece of

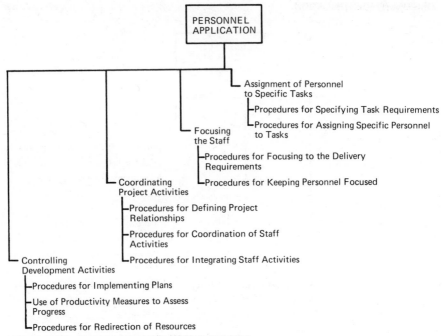

Figure 5-26. Personnel application measures.

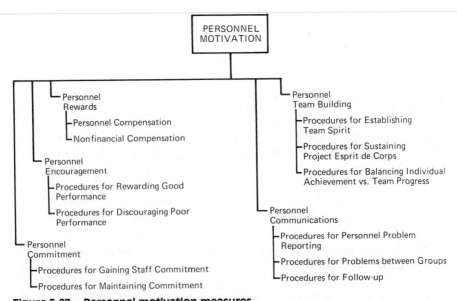

Figure 5-27. Personnel motivation measures.

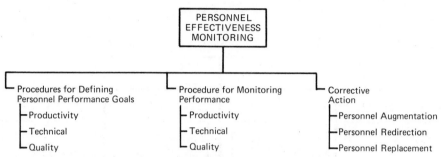

Figure 5-28. Personnel effectiveness monitoring measures.

information, whether it be in a formal document or in a controlled engineering data product described only once and included in a single data product (data uniqueness)? Are the specific relationships between data products identified and are these relationships key to evaluating the quality of all data (data relationships)?

2. *Data Control.* Are the data control practices applied to engineering data products adequate to ensure the quality both as they are produced and after they are released from engineering (engineering control effectiveness)? Are the controls applied to released and approved project baselines sufficient to ensure their quality and integrity (baseline control effectiveness)? Are the procedures used to control all levels of data within the project realistic and efficient in the context of the overall software development environment (data control efficiency)? Are the data control practices applied complete and do they provide control for all data approved at a quality gate or at a formal review (data control effectiveness)?

3. *Review Integration.* Are the baseline reviews iterated as required to ensure the quality, completeness and adequacy of all baselined data (baseline review iteration)? Have the baseline reviews been integrated into the project in such a way as to minimize the impacts on the project while maximizing the quality aspects of the review (baseline review integration)? Are there reviews identified and implemented to checkpoint the quality of all baselined data before it is placed under control and is this checkpointing done by a staff sufficiently knowledgeable to assess baseline quality (baseline checkpoints)? Is the development overhead associated with the planning, conduct, and evaluation of all project baseline reviews consistent with the resource and schedule realities of the project (baseline review overhead)? Are the baseline reviews specifically focused toward a narrow set of objectives, do they evaluate a fixed set of data, is their conduct structured and are they efficiently integrated into the project schedule (baseline review efficiency)? Are the planned and

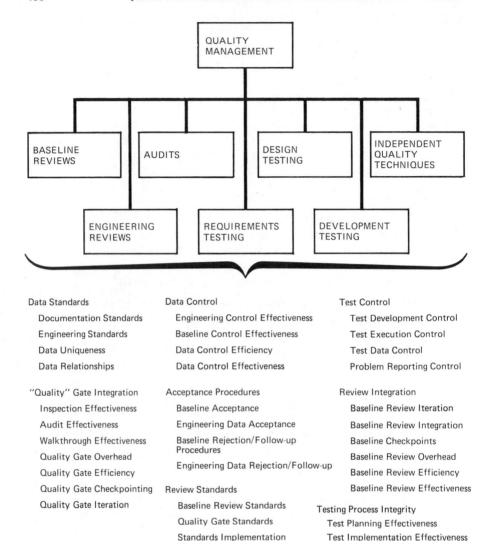

Data Standards
  Documentation Standards
  Engineering Standards
  Data Uniqueness
  Data Relationships

"Quality" Gate Integration
  Inspection Effectiveness
  Audit Effectiveness
  Walkthrough Effectiveness
  Quality Gate Overhead
  Quality Gate Efficiency
  Quality Gate Checkpointing
  Quality Gate Iteration

Data Control
  Engineering Control Effectiveness
  Baseline Control Effectiveness
  Data Control Efficiency
  Data Control Effectiveness

Acceptance Procedures
  Baseline Acceptance
  Engineering Data Acceptance
  Baseline Rejection/Follow-up Procedures
  Engineering Data Rejection/Follow-up

Review Standards
  Baseline Review Standards
  Quality Gate Standards
  Standards Implementation

Test Control
  Test Development Control
  Test Execution Control
  Test Data Control
  Problem Reporting Control

Review Integration
  Baseline Review Iteration
  Baseline Review Integration
  Baseline Checkpoints
  Baseline Review Overhead
  Baseline Review Efficiency
  Baseline Review Effectiveness

Testing Process Integrity
  Test Planning Effectiveness
  Test Implementation Effectiveness
  Test Implementation

Figure 5-29. Quality management measures.

implemented baseline reviews effective in the context of the overall development environment (baseline review effectiveness)?

4. *Quality Gate Integration.*   Is there a set of planned and implemented quality inspections in place to assess product and process attributes of the software and are they effective in performing quality checks as the software is produced (inspection effectiveness)? Are there walkthroughs or informal reviews conducted to assess the quality of all engineering data products before they are released for project use? Are the walk-throughs effective in the context of the project and can they be supported in light of the project constraints (walk-through effectiveness)? Is there a preplanned structure in place to assess the process and product quality? Are the audits effective in the context of the project environment (audit effectiveness)? Is the overhead associated with the quality gates acceptable in relation to project requirements, resource constraints and schedule realities (quality gate Overhead)? Are the quality gates focused towards a narrow predefined objective, is the conduct scheduled and supported by sufficient resources to avoid becoming a project bottleneck, and does each individual quality gate assess a narrow set of data products or concepts (quality gate efficiency)? Are the quality gates integrated into the project such that they checkpoint product quality at discrete points in the project infrastructure just prior to their release for general use in the project (quality gate checkpointing)? Are the engineering data products that are rejected by a quality gate re-evaluated before they are accepted and are problems traced from review to review (quality gate iteration)?

5. *Acceptance Procedures.* Are there predefined standards and procedures in place for accepting approved baseline data and placing it under project control (baseline acceptance)? Are there complementary procedures in place for accepting approved engineering data and placing the data under project control (engineering data acceptance)? Are there specific procedures in place for rejecting unacceptable baseline data and following up corrections (baseline rejection follow up)? Are there specific procedures in place for rejecting unacceptable engineering data and for following up corrections (engineering data rejection follow up)?

6. *Review Standards.* Are there detailed standards in place for all baseline reviews before the review is conducted and are the standards rigorously enforced (baseline review standards)? Are there detailed standards in place for all categories and types of quality gates implemented on the project environment and are they rigorously enforced (quality gate standards)? Have all the standards been implemented in the project environment and are they integral to the project data flow (standards implementation)?

7. *Testing Process Integrity.* Have all levels of testing been adequately defined and is each level traceable to a discrete set of requirements or design? Are the test plans realistic in light of project realities (test planning effectiveness)? Have all test plans been implemented according to the project needs and are the test levels adequately supported in the context of the project environment (test

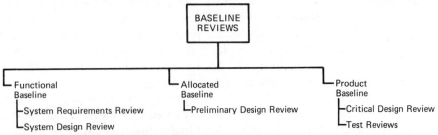

Figure 5-30. Baseline review measures.

implementation effectiveness)? Is the test environment efficient, well structured and characterized by a smooth flow of data and transition of responsibility (test implementation)?

8. *Test Control.* Have the test development activities been controlled and is there a means to ensure the integrity of the plans against the requirements and related project plans (test development control)? Has the execution of tests been structured and controlled, are problems reported and tracked and are corrections to the software requalified before they are installed in a test configuration (test execution control)? Are the data included in a test configuration reviewed and controlled at a project level in order to assure test reproducibility, integrity, and predictability (test data control)? Is there a rigorous discipline in place in the project to ensure that all observed problems are reported, evaluated, tracked, and closed (problem reporting control)?

The need for quality management spans all types of software development: large and small, complex and trivial, real time and non real time. The quality management environment must be scaled to the project characteristics. The environment must be integrated, effective and keyed to the development environment. The quality management model becomes more specific to the project as the model is driven to lower levels of the hierarchy. At the lowest levels, the model will detail specific attributes of the quality management structure and the specific techniques used to evaluate the software and control the integrity of development process.

Figures 5-30 through 5-36 are representative of the quality management taxonomy.

The quality management areas of the project are the means by which quality is monitored as data is produced and provides the gateways to evaluate and authorize the release of baseline and engineering data for project use. The effectiveness of the individual quality management components can only be assessed by the degree that each component provides a discrete function within the overall project environment. Quality measures of in-

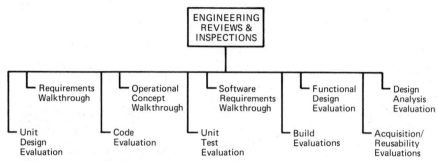

Figure 5-31. Engineering reviews and inspections measures.

dividual components without considering the relationship of the component to other segments of the project is invalid.

This evaluation cannot be made unless there is a clearly defined data and process model for the project, the interfaces between individual segments are defined and the relationships between the individual components understood and used as the basis for the project evaluation.

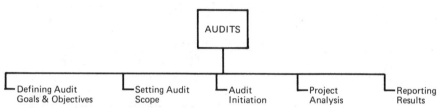

Figure 5-32. Audit measures.

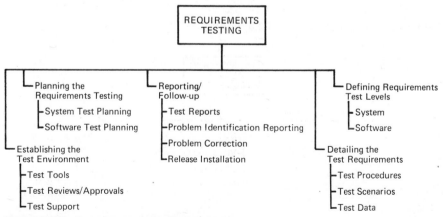

Figure 5-33. Requirements testing measures.

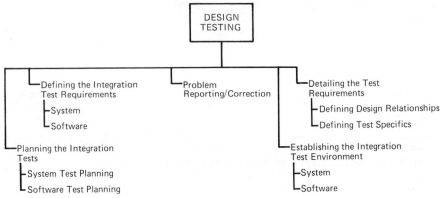

Figure 5-34. Design testing measures.

PHASE SPECIFIC ATTRIBUTES

The previous discussion dealt with the evaluation of the project infrastructure. The complexities of the project infrastructure require that from a quality perspective the evaluation of the development process be complete. The evaluation must be closely tied to the process being used to develop the software and be measurable against a predefined quality model.

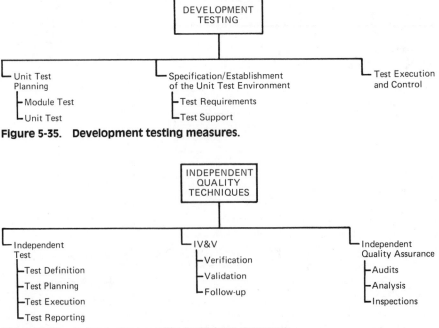

Figure 5-35. Development testing measures.

Figure 5-36. Independent quality technique measures.

Evaluation of the infrastructure, by itself, is not enough. For many reasons the infrastructure may appear to be adequate but, because of schedule creep, project shortcuts that are taken early that have long-term process impacts, or unexpected development problems may not be robust enough to support the next development phase.

There are separate indicators of project effectiveness that indicate the readiness of the project to proceed to the next phase of development. These center around the integrity of the data developed by the project at a particular phase, the adequacy of the project environment to support the anticipated development environment and the support capabilities in relation to current and projected development needs. Before deciding to initiate the next phase of development these factors must be assessed and, if not adequately supported, the project should not proceed unless the risks associated with proceeding are understood and accepted. Depending on the degree of shortfall, these risks can range from significant quality compromises to a complete breakdown in project discipline.

The indicators, expressed as questions in the sections that follow, provide a basis for determining project viability. The individual questions are, in the main, absolutes. Each of them must be addressed by the project or there is an associated risk with attempting to start the next development phase. The degree of impact that can be expected is a function of how well the project has addressed each of the questions.

As with all measures, the phase specific questions must be tailored to the specific characteristics of the project, including size, complexity, application characteristics, and project environmental factors.

System Definition

The purpose of the system definition phase is to define and structure the project environment and establish a clear and consistent set of traceable user and system requirements which are the technical basis for the development.

The data which is produced is primarily textual, reasonably static and can be supported through a simplistic project environment. During this phase, project efficiency is not particularly critical. It is easy to delude oneself because of apparent progress. This is a trap. The project requirements will get more complex and the data flow more difficult to control. The robustness of the project environment that is specified during the project definition phase must be evaluated before the subsequent development phases are started.

Questions which must be addressed during the definition phases before the top level design phase can be started are:

1.   How are requirements to be specified and controlled?
2.   How will functional requirements be defined?

3. How will performance requirements be specified?

4. How will operational requirements be defined?

5. How are environmental requirements specified?

6. How are external interfaces defined and controlled?

7. How are the quality, integrity, and adequacy of each requirement or set of requirements assessed as they are being defined?

8. How will individual requirements be controlled after they have been approved?

9. How are changes to them reviewed and approved?

10. How are the engineering and technical impacts of these changes assessed and integrated into any decision approving a requirements change?

11. What is the exact format for individual requirements specification?

12. How can the individual requirements definitions be translated into a specification which may be approved by the customer?

13. How far from this specification can traceability through design, code and test be ensured?

14. How can the individual requirements be demonstrated so that assurance can be made that what was built was what was contracted for?

15. Exactly how does the data developed as requirements serve as the input to the functional design process?

16. What are the *exact* data links between the project methodologies?

17. What methodologies and automated aids are required to support the development requirements?

18. How much data is involved, how frequently will it change and how will it be organized?

Top Level Design

The purpose of the top level design phase is to synthesize a functional design from the user and system requirements. During this phase a functional design is developed which describes the functional requirements of the software system and application. The amount of project data that must be controlled expands dramatically, fanning out from the requirements. The data is not only textual but has a graphical component as well. The data is used by several project activities in parallel. The data takes on an additional and, if not planned for, disturbing aspect: change. The configuration management problem, the quality assurance requirements, the overall complexity of the project environment and the project interactions which must be supported by the infrastructure become major concerns. If the project cannot support these project complexities during this phase, progress can still be made but the seeds of later disaster will be planted. Specific questions which evaluate whether the top level design phase is adequate to support subsequent phases or data produced during earlier phases are provided in the following.

1. What data is needed to start the functional design process?
2. What is the exact content requirements?
3. What is the level of detail and how is upward traceability ensured as the design is developed?
4. How will the functional design process be accomplished?
5. What design methodologies will be used, how will they be modified to support real-time system applications and how will timing and sequencing data be collected through the design?
6. How will the data dictionary be collected and controlled?
7. What is the *exact* format of this dictionary and how is it controlled?
8. How is design integrity monitored?
9. Who is responsible for the design and how are the impacts of design changes on requirements assessed before the change is made?
10. How are engineering, cost, and schedule impacts of proposed design changes to controlled baselines assessed before the change is authorized?
11. How are functional design parameters evaluated, approved, and controlled as the design is produced?
12. How is the control implemented and how can the project control multiple versions of design simultaneously to support system, software, and test requirements?
13. What is the *exact* format of individual design specifications?
14. How are problems in the released design reported, corrected, and controlled?
15. How will the project store and control this data?
16. If graphical, how will the design data be produced?
17. How does the functional design translate into these requirements?
18. How will the data be generated and reviewed, and how can the design data be produced by the project quickly enough to avoid becoming a project bottleneck?
19. How can correspondence between the graphical design specifications and the internally stored textual data be achieved?
20. How can the project ensure that design changes are reflected in the requirements specifications previously discussed, the code and test requirements in the following, and the affected user's and support documentation?

21. How exactly does the functional design data serve as the basis for the detailed design?
22. What is the *exact* format of the data which is the output from the functional design process?
23. How does this serve as the bridge to detailed design?
24. How are performance budgets carried through the design process?
25. At what level does the functional design process stop?
26. What is the software component described by the lowest level of functional design?
27. How is interface integrity maintained throughout the functional decomposition?
28. How are the interfaces between hardware and functional design documented and maintained, and how are the interface relationships between segments of the functional design maintained and updated?
29. How are the engineering impacts or interfaces monitored and assembled?
30. How are these impacts factored into any functional design decisions?
31. How much functional design information will be produced?
32. What is its exact format when stored in the project files? How frequently will the data change and how can the data integrity be monitored, assessed, and maintained?
33. How does the top level functional design translate into integration and test levels?
34. How are these relationships established, monitored, and maintained?

Detailed Design

It is during the detailed design phase that the complexity of the project interactions, the interfaces between project activities and the data relationships, and control requirements within the project will preclude reasonable progress if not controlled and adequately supported.

First, the detailed design is built on an inherently unstable base. The functional design and supporting data products will change and these changes must be reflected in the detailed design structure of the software. The amount of information to be controlled is significant, the support requirements dramatic and the difficulty in controlling the data products is overwhelming if not planned for and in place. During this development phase, the test planning and development activities begin in earnest and the specific links to integration and test are defined. Poor project control practices, poorly defined quality practices and an undefined or inefficient project environment become apparent during this development phase. Unless the software development environment is sufficiently robust to deal with the complex project interactions and control the flow and integrity of data as it is used by multiple segments of the project, the software development will bog down. There is a high risk that during this phase the traceability links to requirements and design will be lost and, because of the complexity of the project, environment will be lost. Questions which test the integrity of this detailed design environment are provided in the following.

1. What are the *exact* data interfaces between the functional design and the detailed design process?
2. What additional data is required to start detailed design?
3. How is this additional data monitored and controlled?
4. What is the *exact* content of the data items which serve as input to the detailed design process?
5. How is reverse traceability for detailed design maintained through the functional design and to the requirements?
6. How are the relationships among detailed design, the user documentation system interfaces and the contractual requirements maintained?
7. How exactly is the detailed design to be developed?
8. How is it to be described?
9. Is the detailed documentation to be textual or graphical?
10. How is it to be verified?
11. What is the smallest component to be described by blocks in the unit design?
12. How are detailed relationships between these components to be maintained?
13. How are the interfaces between the higher level components maintained?
14. How are the external interfaces described and how are these reflected in the detailed design?
15. How are these relationships maintained?
16. How are the technical adequacy, correctness, and standards adherence of the detailed design assured?
17. How is the data controlled after project approval and release?
18. How are changes in the design made, reviewed, and incorporated in the overall software design?
19. How do the detailed design specifications relate to the "as built" documentation?

20. How will the data be maintained on a current basis and how are changes communicated to all segments of the staff using the data?
21. How does the detailed design translate into unit test, code, and integration testing?
22. How are the relationships between these segments of the development maintained?
23. How are quality relationships maintained?
24. How is the quality of the detailed design assessed?
25. How is it released in subsets to facilitate the implementation of builds for testing?
26. What are the exact format, acceptable content, and structure of the data products which describe the design for coding?
27. How is code and detailed design integrity verified?
28. How are changes in one build or release factored into the detailed design of other builds or releases?
29. How are the data relationships between system and software components maintained?
30. How are the data structures and requirements described in the data dictionary incorporated into the detailed design?
31. How is the integrity between the detailed design, data specifications and functional design ensured and maintained?
32. How are performance budgets allocated, carried through the design and verified?
33. How are problems in performance (or design) verified, reported, corrected, and maintained?
34. How are corrections integrated into the design?
35. How are security provisions incorporated into the design?

Code and Unit Testing

The code and unit testing areas of the project are the most rigorous test of the efficiency and integrity of the software project infrastructure. The project control requirements reach their most critical state when supporting these activities. The manpower is at its maximum developing and testing code. The project data development and control requirements which have been increasing dramatically during the previous phases literally explode during this development phase. The project activity "heats up" during this period with the dramatic increase in walk-throughs, reviews, and software releases. Any project inefficiencies, any required project controls which have not been instituted, or any standards or project organizational relationships that are not smoothed out must be resolved. If not, problems affecting the effectiveness of the infrastructure and, ultimately, the quality of the software will occur. The complexity of the project environment is compounded by the parallelism which reaches its peak during this phase. Software requirements and design are being maintained. Code is being developed and tested. Software is being released for concurrent integration and testing. Documentation is being developed and released. Finally, the integration and test planning and development are in the final stages of implementation.

The project environment must be adequate to support the requirements imposed by the project or the project will grind to a halt unable to produce software of sufficient quality to satisfy the needs of the application. Questions to test the integrity of the project infrastructure during this phase are provided in the following.

1. How is code generated from the detailed design specification?
2. Is the development support machine the same as the target machine?
3. How is developed code tested at a unit level?
4. How is the adequacy of this testing ensured?
5. How are the results verified?
6. How do compilations take place?
7. Are they done interactively or in a batch mode?
8. How does the compiler output code that is testable on the target machine (or in the target system)?
9. How is instrumentation built into the code with assurance that it can be removed?
10. How are security requirements identified in the code and how can their satisfaction be verifiable?
11. What is the *exact* format for code?
12. How are these standards to be enforced?
13. How are problems identified and corrections ensured?
14. How is traceability from code, back through detailed design through the top-level design and to requirements, maintained and ensured?
15. How are code up dates reflected back through the design and requirements and into the user and support documentation?
16. How is access control to the code under development maintained?
17. How are code changes, once made, incorporated into the controlled version of the software?
18. How exactly is software released and incorporated into a system configuration for integration?
19. What is the specific procedure for baselining code elements and ensuring their integrity?

20. What are the exact data requirements for software packages which are released for integration?
21. How are these controlled?
22. How much data relating to code will be produced?
23. How is it organized and how will it be stored on project files?
24. How frequently will the data change, how can the integrity be monitored and assessed?

Integration and Functional Testing

During the periods of integration and testing the entire complexion of the project changes. Until now the project has been focused toward developing many products in parallel that match the design and are consistent with all levels of requirements. Now the project must take these individual products and integrate them into a total software and system capability. There are two primary project modes that the project must support during this phase: software maintenance and software modification. Software maintenance is the addition of functional capabilities to a released version of software. The development requirements for the capabilities implemented as part of a maintenance effort are a subset of those activities used for the development. The infrastructure is the same, the flow of work is a subset of that used for development and the quality assurance checks are consistent with the development requirements. Essentially, all new capabilities implemented during the integration and test period are new capabilities and require development rigor to ensure the integrity of all new releases.

Software modification, on the other hand, is corrections to software already developed to remedy observed performance problems or shortfalls. The environment for these changes is far different than the development environment. There is, in the main, limited need to apply the development methodologies; the quality checks are different than those used during development. Documentation must be updated on a current basis with the code rather than developing new documentation. These project requirements are far different than the needs of the development environment. Questions which test the environment are provided in the following.

1. What are the *specific* test levels to be used to integrate and functionally qualify the software?
2. Is the test machine the same as the support machine?
3. How are the systems built?
4. How are the builds documented?
5. How will the software from one build be maintained on a *current* level with other builds using the software?
6. Will the various levels of software testing be executed serially or concurrently?

7. How will traceability be maintained through the code and design, and finally to requirements for each build?

8. How are systems to be built for testing, through a centralized facility or by the development organization?

9. How are build requirements described?

10. Who controls the technical integrity and who defines and documents the contents?

11. How frequently will these builds take place? (worst case)?

12. How are problems identified, documented, and reported?

13. Who is responsible for the engineering evaluation of problems and authorization of corrections?

14. How is the adequacy of system modifications to be evaluated before they are applied to the system?

15. How are problems assigned for correction?

16. How are problems tracked, corrections monitored, and problems closed?

17. What procedure is used to determine if a level of testing has been completed?

18. What constitutes completion?

19. What are criteria for success and who authorizes completion?

20. What is the *exact* data flow during test?

21. How are test requirements defined?

22. How are the builds generated?

23. Who runs the tests?

24. How do they report requirements and how are test results reported?

25. How are corrections made to the system?

26. How are new systems made and documented?

27. What are the *exact* content and format of data produced during testing and how much data is involved?

28. What is its structure?

29. How is its data organized?

30. What are the levels of data control to be applied?

31. How is the data produced during testing used as input to the build documentation?

32. How is data released to the customer?

33. How are contractual relationships maintained?

6

SOFTWARE PROCESS METRICS

Measuring the process of software development is the qualification and assessment of the project environment in relation to application needs and development requirements.

The previous chapter described the various software development activities for indicators of process quality and a successful software project. These are of little use however, unless data can be observed, collected, or derived indicating the degree the implemented project infrastructure satisfies the specific needs of the application and requirements imposed by the development environment.

Many indicators within a software project can be used as the basic measures of process quality. Indicators fall into two primary categories:

1. Implementation metrics which, when applied to a project evaluation, assess how adequately the project environment was implemented in relation to the project plans, standards and conventions, and implementation requirements.

2. Process metrics, which are observable project conditions resulting from the occurrence of a single project condition, or through the interaction between several related project conditions.

In the case of implementation attributes, the evaluation of the software process will provide an assessment of how well the planned project environment was actually implemented in support of the software development.

Process attributes, on the other hand, measure how well the environment works in the day-to-day support of the project infrastructure.

Both these measures, in fact, are necessary for a clear and complete picture of the software environment. Assuming that the project environment was adequately defined, all components of the plans must be implemented if the integrity of the project infrastructure is to be guaranteed. Often this is not the case. For many reasons; financial, schedule, political, and/or environment, shortcuts are taken in the implementation process without considering the effects of the change on the overall integrity of the project environment.

The two evaluation techniques which are most relevant in evaluating the attributes are inspection and audits. The differences between the two techniques are as follows:

1. An inspection normally has a narrow focus evaluating only a segment of the project environment. The inspection structure is very rigid and the evaluation criteria are predetermined based on a model of acceptability.

2. An audit may also have narrow focus but, in most cases, is used to evaluate the broader aspects of the project environment. Besides checking individual segments of the project infrastructure against plans, audits may evaluate the interrelationships between segments of the infrastructure. When assessing the implementation attributes, audits tend to be more "free wheeling" allowing the auditor to pursue paths not necessarily included in the initial audit.

Whether audits or inspections are used, the evaluation must be based on predefined criteria, or development model. This model must be based on the specific software planning documentation currently in place for the project. These plans can be decomposed into successively lower levels of detail to describe a complete model of the planned software environment. The further down the decomposition of the environment can be driven from the planning documentation, the more valid the evaluation will be.

At the lowest level of the decomposition are the specific project activities, project tools, techniques and methodologies, planned management, project control factors, and development characteristics. The specifics that are detailed at this level represent the inventory that will be used to assess the project implementation of the planned infrastructure.

This decomposition then is used to construct a checklist which will form the basis for both the audits and inspections. For example, in the area of data controlled production, there is a subcategory, engineering data product control. In this category there is a further subcategory, definition of content requirements for engineering data and a further breakdown which defines a process requirement to provide engineering reporting procedures.

At each level of decomposition there is increasing definition of what the planned process hierarchy includes.

Once the project development model is completed, it can serve as the basis for all evaluations of attributes throughout the life of the project. It can be augmented, modified, updated, and clarified as project plans change.

Implementation metric evaluation is based strictly on the definition of factors. The goal is to confirm that the factor has been implemented. Evaluating the effectiveness of the factor and the assessment of the infrastructure and environment is not evaluated by implementation metrics; only verified. Implementation metric evaluation is process confirmation rather than process quality assurance.

Process metrics, on the other hand, assess the effectiveness of the software project environment against predefined attributes of process quality. Process quality, in this context, is a measure of how well the project environment infrastructure provides for the production of software products that meet technical and development requirements. This evaluation is very complex. Not only must the adequacy of individual segments of the project infrastructure be assessed but also the effectiveness of these segments when interacting with related segments of the project infrastructure. This two-tiered evaluation is fundamental to the evaluation of the software process.

QUALITATIVE MEASURES OF SOFTWARE PROCESS

The qualitative measures are an evaluation of the relative "goodness" of specific segments of the project infrastructure. These measures are typically subjective, evaluating specific characteristics of the project environment against a standard of quality. This standard, more often than not, is applied by the evaluator based on experiential factors rather than as a result of a clear definition of project performance requirements. These evaluations, conducted as audits or inspections, answer questions as defined in the previous chapter. The answers are developed after a review of relevant data outputs, support or development characteristics, and observation of project performance. The questions should provide a range of quality for the specific attribute being evaluated. For example, the technology application segment of the infrastructure has many attributes that describe it. One of these, realism, is the degree of conformance that the technology applied to the project addresses the realities of the application and the unique requirements of the development. Under this attribute there are several subattributes. Further detailing of indicators which, when evaluated, will provide an overall assessment of the degree that realism has been considered when selecting and implementing methodologies in the project environment. These lower level indicators, in the form of a questionnaire, structure the evaluation and provide a prespecified set of observations that are to be made. The attributes and subattributes provided in the previous chapter are meant to be representative. When applied to the evaluation of a specific project environment they must be augmented, tailored, and restructured to meet the unique requirements imposed by the software application.

Each of these questions is focused towards a particular project characteristic. These characteristics are indicators of software process quality. They are the measures that an evaluator can use to look at a specific area of a project infrastructure. The questions should force an evaluator to look at specific data products and assess the integrity of a narrow set of project activities. They should allow a relative ranking of quality, not just a yes/no or good/bad rating.

These measures are only as valid as the experience, tenacity, and insight that the evaluator applies to the evaluation. The questions point the evaluator towards specific areas of the project infrastructure. They focus the evaluation but do not provide specific measures of quality. These measures are provided by the evaluator.

How does the evaluator score the results? When faced with a particular question he or she reviews the documentation (if available) that describes how the particular segment of the infrastructure was planned. The evaluator then investigates specific in-process aspects of the project environment that result in the interaction of the area being investigated with the other areas of the project environment. The evaluation should be relative, not absolute. There are ranges of process quality. These range from non-existent, generic (not tailored to the project), adequate, good, excellent, and outstanding. These ranges are the basic score that can be used to rate the answer. Although subjective, the scoring is applied to such a small segment of the project infrastructure described by the question that the effects of subjectivity across the full range of the evaluation are minimized.

The qualitative measures of the project infrastructure are based on observation. They look at the specific activities that are being conducted and, after an assessment of the planned project environment, evaluate the adequacy of the project infrastructure to support the development needs of the project.

Development of the Questionnaire

The process questionnaire is developed through the observation of specific parameters which are indicators of project success. These parameters are a combination of observable and quantitative project indicators. The observable characteristics are non-quantitative, however, they are reliable indicators of the state of the project infrastructure. These indicators are specific to the segment of the infrastructure being evaluated.

Each of these quality attributes, and the subattributes which support them, can be observed by specific indicators that are observable in the project environment. Examples of these indicators are provided in the paragraphs that follow.

Resource Management and Control Indicators

The resource management and control aspects of the infrastructure provide the means by which the software will be built. How do you know when you have enough? How do you know when you have specified the right mix? How can you control the application of the resources to specific project tasks? The answers to these questions are essential if the resources applied to the project are to provide a framework that will support development needs. There are specific indicators that exist in a project when areas of the project are not adequately supported. The following discussions provide one indicator per subcategory. They are meant to be representative indicators. Specific indicators are a function of the project environment, the characteristics of the application, and the development realities of the project.

This infrastructure segment ensures that the resources that are projected as required for a project are based on the actual needs of the project and on the requirements for development. When this is not done there are several indicators which show that the planning of resources has not been adequate. These are related to the individual attributes described in the previous chapter.

1. *Top Down Planning.* Must the resources applied to the project continuously be reassigned or modified to reflect changing development requirements or project needs?

   a. *Work Allocation.* Has the application of resources been characterized by certain areas of the project continously requiring resource augmentation while other areas either never complain or continously underrun?

   b. *Work Assignment.* Is there a lack of understanding on the part of the staff concerning how to satisfy specific assigned tasks, what products to produce, and the schedule and costs that are available to complete the tasks?

   c. *Resource Definition.* Is the project continually running out of certain categories of resources? Is the project plagued by continuous surprises (e.g., running out of critical resources)?

2. *Resource Plans.* Have the resources that have been applied to the project been the proper mix or must they be continuously distributed, augmented, and then redistributed to meet project needs?

   a. *Cost/Schedule Organizational Relationships.* Are there organizational conflicts over resource assignment that have increased as the development has proceeded?

   b. *Resource Application Profiles.* As the project moves through the phases of development, is the phasing of resources smooth and does it track the early projections?

    c. *Project Performance Measures.* Are there repeated unexpected schedule or product quality shortfalls attributable to resource shortfalls?

    d. *Risk Analysis.* Are development crises frequently experienced and are they dealt with through unstructured or reactive management techniques?

    e. *Resource Coordination, Redefinition, and Reallocation.* Is there a smooth sharing of resources between project areas or are the areas of the project protective of the resources assigned to them, irrespective of project needs?

3. *Constraint Development and Monitoring.* Are the costs, schedules, and project performance parameters stable and are they tracked?

    a. *Cost Development, Budget Assignment and Tracking.* Are the budgets that are being used to control the software development resources current and are they based on currently valid size estimates?

    b. *Schedule Development, Work Assignment, and Progress Assessment.* Is the staff aware and committed to the schedules and are they coordinated with the budgets and resource projections?

    c. *Earned Value Evaluations, Progress Monitoring, and Progress Evaluations.* Is the development progress tracked and are trend projections used to forecast schedule compliance?

Project Planning and Management

Project planning and management establishes the environment by which the software will be developed. This segment of the project infrastructure determines how the software will be built. How do you know what techniques to use? How do you know what tools to apply? How do you know when you have specified the right mix? How can you manage and control the development process and translate the development requirements into specific project activities? These are tough questions. Answers to these questions can only be determined if the plans for development provide an environment that is based on development needs and is consistent with the project's ability to apply and control the environment selected. There are project indicators which give early warnings that project plans are inadequate or poorly conceived. As with the previous discussions, the following provides one indicator per subcategory. These are meant to be representative indicators. Specific indicators can only be defined after a definition of the project environment, the technical characteristics of the software application and the realities of the software project environment have been made. The indicators of project planning adequacy are described in the following.

1. *Project Planning Procedures.*   Is there a set of documented project procedures that completely describes the current environment that is being used to develop the software?

   a. *Structuring the Planning Effort.*   Has the project been planned from the top down and can all planned activities be traced to an identified project need?

   b. *Conduct of the Software Planning.*   Were the project plans developed by the individuals responsible for the area of the project being defined and did they have sufficient time to do an adequate planning job?

   c. *Developing Software Development Plans.*   Is the software development plan current and does it adequately describe the current project environment?

   d. *Reviewing Software Plans.*   Have the software plans been reviewed by personnel who are responsible for the various aspects of the software and do they understand the implications of the planned structure?

2. *Project Definition Procedures.*   Has the project structure been modified in a controlled and organized manner to reflect changing project conditions?

   a. *Organizational Procedures and Structures.*   Is there a smooth flow of work between organizations and controlled transition of responsibility?

   b. *Resource Application and Control Procedures.*   Are resource assignments to organizations and tasks made in such a way as to allow tracking of performance and organizational accountability?

   c. *Technology Application Procedures.*   Is the application of specific technologies to the project traceable to specific and identified project needs?

   d. *Procedures for Establishing Project Management Relationships/Control.*   Has the project management environment been scaled to the specific project characteristics and control requirements?

   e. *Procedures for Establishing Management/Project Accountability.*   Are there measurable criteria in place for project performance and is the staff aware of them and committed to meet them?

3. *Project Coordination Procedures.*   Are the activities of all project and organizational elements focused and is there minimal overlap between tasks?

   a. *Procedures for Defining Intertask Relationships.*   Have the tasks that are to be executed during the development of the software been defined from the top down, is the hierarchy current and are all current project activities defined in this hierarchy?

b. *Procedures for Defining Interorganizational Relationships.* Are there documented data relationships between organizational elements that can be verified?

c. *Procedures for Defining/Implementing the Project Work Flow.* Are the flow of data, engineering responsibility and management control defined and are they followed in the production of software data?

d. *Procedures for Defining/Implementing Flow of Responsibility.* Are responsibilities for production of software clearly specified and are all tasks currently being supported by the project under specific and centralized responsibility?

e. *Defining/Implementing Resource Coordination Activities.* Are there project level resource assignment documents and can you verify that they are current and complete, and can you track all resources assigned to organizational elements?

f. *Monitoring Coordination Effectiveness.* Is there obvious project friction resulting from an incorrect assignment of resources to the project organization?

4. *Project Planning Emphasis.* Is there an obvious management orientation towards planning the project before action is taken?

a. *Procedures for Dealing with the Whirlwind Effect.* Was there sufficient time at the beginning of the project to allow adequate planning or were a significant number of planning tasks deferred?

b. *Procedures for Implementing Top-Down Planning Techniques.* Is there a traceable hierarchy that exists through all levels of project planning? Has this hierarchy been followed through when implementing the project environment?

c. *Procedures for Monitoring Planning Relevancy and Currency.* Are the project plans current and do they adequately describe the project infrastructure and environment?

d. *Procedures for Maintaining Project Focus.* Are the scheduling techniques forcing personnel to focus on the deliverable end items of the project or is the emphasis on meeting the next milestone?

Data Control and Production

Data control and production provides the means by which data used concurrently by multiple organizations is maintained, that changes are applied in a controlled manner and that documentation is produced efficiently with a minimum of rework. How do you know when this segment of the project infrastructure is incorrectly implemented? How can you tell if the project environment does not support the data requirements of the project or will result in poor quality outputs? How can you project the data control requirements and establish an environment that will ensure a smooth and controlled flow of data and transition of responsibility?

These questions must be answered if an adequate flow of data is to be maintained and to avoid the data control aspects of the infrastructure becoming a bottleneck within the project environment. In order to be effective, the project data control environment must be the center of the infrastructure allowing a smooth and effective transition of data products between organizational components. Indicators of the adequacy of the data control and production areas of the project are provided below.

1. *Approved End Item Control.* Is there complete control of customer approved project end items and are the baselines that are established between the customer and the software organization current?

   a. *Baseline Identification.* Are all software specifications uniquely identified and are the engineering components sufficiently detailed to allow current maintenance of engineering between the customer and the developer?

   b. *Baseline Change Control.* Is there an audit trail of changes to customer approved end items that reflect all changes made to customer approved specifications or approved data items?

   c. *Baseline Status Monitoring.* Is there complete documentation of all software and documentation releases to the customer and is the status of all approved changes known and tracked?

   d. *Baseline Assessment.* Is there an identified set of formal project reviews and informal project evaluations which assess the quality of all deliverable documentation before it is released to the customer?

2. *Data Standards and Production.* Are all engineering data products being developed against a defined standard and are these standards documented, approved and enforced in the project?

   a. *End Product Format Definition Procedures.* Are there detailed documentation formats defined for all formal documentation and are they enforced in the production and review of all documents?

   b. *End Product Content Definition Procedures.* Is the content of all deliverable data products documented and is the completeness of these documents reviewed before release to the customer?

   c. *End Product Structure Procedures.* Are the end products structured in accordance with predefined procedures and is this structuring reviewed prior to documentation release?

   d. *Engineering Data Relationship Definition Procedures.* Are the relationships between end products defined such that engineering data products are not duplicated across specifications?

e. *End Item Production Capability/Procedures.* Is the production of end items a recurring project bottleneck?

f. *Engineering Data Flow Definition.* Is there a clear definition of engineering activities that controls the production, review, and release of engineering data within the software project?

3. *Engineering Data Product Control.* Is there a definition of the engineering data products to be produced in the project and a separate set of control practices to ensure and control their integrity?

a. *Definition of and Standards for Engineering Data.* Is there a complete set of project standards that describe the format, content, and structure of all individual project engineering data products?

b. *Definition of Content Requirements for Engineering Data.* Is there a complete definition of the content requirements for the engineering data products and are the relationships between the individual data products defined, evaluated, and maintained?

c. *Definition of Engineering Quality Requirements by Data Item.* Are there standards in place in the project that describe acceptable quality levels for each engineering data product in the project, and are these checked through a quality gate before the data item is released?

d. *Definition of Engineering Production/End Item Integration Procedures.* Is there a set of tools, techniques, and project methodologies which will allow the project to produce the engineering data products without essential rework, and are there procedures in place to allow the integration of these into a specification which will be released to the customer.

Technology Application

The application of technology to the development of software is how software products are produced. It is more than just the selection of specific tools, techniques, or methodologies. Rather, it entails the definition and integration of myriad components of an overall project environment into a cohesive project technical structure.

The following are specific indicators which are usable in assessing the integrity and effectiveness of the technical segments of the project.

1. *Technical Environment Definition.* Is there a documented set of project methodologies that are traceable into the software project environment and are they linked together so there is a smooth flow of information?

a. *Definition of Engineering Data Products.* Are there standards in place on the project for all engineering data products and is there an identified means to produce them?

b. *Definition of the Technical Environment.* Has there been an early definition of the technical environment and has this definition tied together all of the individual tools, techniques, and methodologies which comprise it?

c. *Selection of Tools, Techniques, and Methodologies.* Have the individual components of the technical environment been selected after an identification of specific development needs, and is the current application of these components directly traceable to the needs they were originally designed to satisfy?

d. *Application of Tools, Techniques, and Methodologies.* Has the project environment been structured so all essential support facilities for the tools, techniques, and methodologies are in place, and is there sufficient time in the schedules, and resources in the budget to allow training of personnel?

2. *Technical Procedures and Techniques.* Are the various components of the technical environment, their interactions, and the procedures which control their implementation documented? Are there procedures in place in the project which describe their use, and is the staff familiar and supportive of these procedures?

a. *Specific Implementation of the Technical Environment.* Are all components of the technical environment integrated, and are there procedures in place for the transition of data and responsibility?

b. *Detailing of the technical environment.* Is there a detailed level of technical planning in place, and does it describe how the project will produce the engineering data products required to develop the software?

c. *Phasing of Procedures into the Technical Environment.* Have the applications of specific tools, techniques, and methodologies been integrated with the schedule and specific software production needs?

d. *Procedure/Technique Application to the Project.* Are there specific means in place to ensure that all components of the project methodologies environment are supportable and will produce the software engineering items required.

3. *Project Methodologies.* Are there specific methodologies in place to support all technical activities required for the project, are the outputs controllable and is the project capable of supporting the application of each?

a. *Life Cycle Phase Requirements.* Are all of the major phases of the software development life cycle identified, and are they supportable through the software project infrastructure?

b. *Data Product Requirements.* Are there standards and conventions in place that describe all formal specification requirements, and the specific requirements for each engineering data product?

    c. *Linking Methodologies and Technologies.* Is the technical flow of work within the project characterized by a smooth flow of technology, transition of data and flow of responsibility?

    d. *Methodology Application.* Has the project dealt with the personnel, standardization, and support issues essential to bringing new and innovative methodologies into a software production environment?

    e. *Effectiveness Evaluation.* Are there procedures in place to monitor the effectiveness of all project methodologies, identify technical shortfalls, take corrective action and augment the project environment where necessary?

4. *Project Tools and Automated Aids.* Is there an integrated project environment which makes judicious and effective use of automated facilities?

    a. *Procedures for Defining Specific Needs for Automation.* Have all project automated tools been selected after a rigorous top down analysis of project needs, and are these tools specifically linked to the technology, work flow and data flow being used to develop the software?

    b. *Procedures for Selecting Automated Aids.* Have the automated aids being used by the project been selected and applied after a complete and rigorous project needs assessment?

    c. *Procedures for Implementing Automated Aids.* Is there a life cycle defined for the development of project tools, is it sufficiently rigorous to ensure the integrity of these tools and is it uniformly applied?

    d. *Procedures for Supporting Automated Aids.* Are there maintenance procedures in place to ensure the integrity of all automated aids?

5. *Data Linkage between Methodologies.* Are the data products which are outputs from each methodology used by the project paired to the input requirements of the methodologies that interface to it?

    a. *Procedures for Defining Data Relationships.* Do the project standards and conventions define the data relationships between elements of the project environment and are these relationships checked through quality gates before the data transition?

    b. *Project Data Standards for Engineering Data Products.* Is there a complete set of standards for all data products produced by the project and are the standards maintained and current?

    c. *Project Procedures for Transitioning Data between Methodologies.* Are there gates identified to check the quality of data before a transition to the next area of development and, after successfully completing a gate, is the data product placed under project control?

    d.   *Data Correction Procedures.* Are there procedures in place for controlling changes to approved data products and are these procedures rigorously enforced?

    e.   *Data Control Procedures.* Are there procedures in place, scaled to the needs of the project, which will control the integrity of all approved engineering data products?

Personnel Relations

The personnel relations segment of the project infrastructure provides the means by which the software project interacts with the customer, with the program staff, and motivates and controls the staff towards the production of a quality product on time and within budget. How can you project what the customer wants? How do you know when the program is providing you quality inputs? How do you know when your staff is performing adequately or what their degree of commitment is to producing the product? These questions really are the bottom line to software development. If motivation is a problem with your staff, if the customer is dissatisfied with your performance, or if the system organizations are providing less than adequate information or are forcing unrealistic goals, the software project will not be able to produce a quality product. There are many indicators within a project environment which are early warnings that personnel relations existing in a software project are troubled. The questions which follow provide areas which may be investigated in order to assess the adequacy of the personnel relations. These questions are representative of those that may be asked by a software manager. They must be tailored and further developed in the analysis of a specific project environment.

If the personnel relations segments of the project infrastructure are not dealt with properly, a software manager will find that he or she is unable to motivate the staff or deliver a quality product. The areas that are analyzed relate on a one-for-one basis to the discussions provided in the previous chapter.

    1.   *Personnel Relations.* Are all members of the project environment (customers, program management, and staff) committed to the same set of project goals and objectives, are they dealing with a common set of requirements and do they all proceed with the same view of software development?

    a.   *Customer Relations.* Is the customer an active participant in the software development project? Does he or she understand the goals and objectives and does he or she share a sense of commitment in the project?

    b.   *Contractual Basis.* Is there a clear contractual basis for defining the common frame of reference between the customer and the development organizations? Has this frame of reference been translated into a specific set of project requirements that can be measured, produced, and delivered within cost and schedule constraints?

c. *Customer Involvement.* Is there a predefined degree of involvement between the customer and the development organizations and is this involvement phased to the development requirements of the project? Is the degree of involvement adequate to ensure customer visibility and do the levels of interaction minimize development interference?

d. *Customer Sophistication.* Is the customer sufficiently knowledgeable about the application and development techniques being used to provide meaningful input and constructive interaction with the project organization?

e. *Customer Awareness of Software Product Requirements.* Does the customer know what he or she wants, does he or she understand the technical implications of his or her requirements, and is there an awareness of specific delivery characteristics of the system when it is to be turned over?

f. *Customer Awareness of Management Control.* Does the customer understand why specific management controls are in place and does he or she support the disciplines associated with producing quality software?

2. *Program Relations.* Is the program, or system organization knowledgeable about the development process and have they provided adequate input to the software organization to allow the production of an acceptable product?

a. *Work Tasking.* Have specific development tasks been decomposed in a hierarchical fashion and are those assigned to software described in such a way that the products are identified, the production requirements measurable, and the schedules and project interactions reasonable?

b. *Program Specification of Software Requirements.* Has the program specified a clear traceable and testable set of requirements that can be used by the software organization to produce an acceptable product?

c. *Program Technical Competency.* Is the technical staff assigned to the program or system organization technically competent, and are they capable of producing the data products that are required?

d. *Program Management Control Practices.* Has the program or system organization put a set of effective program management controls in place, are they rigorously enforced, and do they provide a tailored, set of controls which do not interfere with the software development process?

   e. *Program Attitude.* Is the primary motivation in the program or system organization the production of a quality system within cost and schedule, and does this motivation filter down through all of the technical and support organizations producing the system?

   f. *Program Awareness of Software Realities.* Does the program or system organization understand the realities of production of quality software, are they knowledgeable about characteristics of software, do they understand the essential relationship that exists between the software and system data products, and are they committed to producing a quality technical product?

   g. *Program Awareness of Software Product Realities.* Has the program or system organization specified a set of product requirements that are achievable, adequate, and producible within the constraints specified for the software project?

3. *Personnel Requirements.* Is there a set of organization and staffing requirements that matches one-for-one the development requirements, and can these requirements be mapped reasonably to the staff assigned to produce the software project?

   a. *Work Flow Procedures.* Are there procedures in place on the project to control the flow of work, the transition of responsibility, and the flow of data between project organizational elements? Are the relationships between these organizations clearly defined, adequately specified, and clearly understood?

   b. *Procedures for Defining Personnel Mix.* Does the mix of personnel match the technical, administrative, and support requirements, and has the mix been phased to the scheduling and production requirements for the software?

   c. *Procedures for Specifying Personnel Experience.* Does the experience level of project personnel match the technical, administrative, and support requirements, and have the staff levels been established to match the technical complexity of the project?

   d. *Procedures for Defining Personnel Technical Capability.* Are there procedures in place for defining individual technical capability requirements for the staff? Have these procedures been translated into staff experience consistent with the project size, complexity, application type, and development environment?

   e. *Procedures for Selecting Personnel.* Have the personnel selection procedures been structured with the consideration of the staffing requirements, the staff phasing, and the availability of personnel?

4. *Personnel Application.* Have personnel been assigned to the project who are qualified to produce the software? Has this application been consistent with the technical, administrative, and support requirements of the software development project?

   a. *Assignment of Personnel to Specific Tasks.* Have personnel been assigned to specific tasks so as to ensure technical consistency, maximize motivation, and engender a personal commitment to produce a quality product within the structure of the software team?

   b. *Focusing the Staff.* Is there a clear staff focus towards a common set of project goals and objectives and has this focus been maintained throughout the software development?

   c. *Coordinating Project Activity.* Have all project activities been coordinated and relationships between tasks been defined and maintained? Do the project management policies and practices force a smooth interaction between separate and distinct organizational segments?

   d. *Controlling Development Activities.* Have the project plans been implemented and is the implementation verifiable? Is project progress and productivity measured against the planned environment?

5. *Personnel Motivation.* Is there visible staff commitment and does this commitment translate into measurable progress according to schedules, budgets, and technical project requirements?

   a. *Personnel Encouragement.* Is there a system of predefined and understood project rewards and penalties for completing or not completing objectives?

   b. *Personnel Rewards.* Are the project rewards consistent with the difficulty of tasks within the environment and have they been effective motivators in achieving staff commitments?

   c. *Personnel Team Building.* Is there visible *esprit de corps* and do staff members act as a team in producing software products?

   d. *Personnel Communications.* Is there effective communication within the project that ensures that issues, once opened, are documented and considered? Are follow-ups enforced through established communication procedures? Is there follow-up available to staff members for issues of project concern?

   e. *Personnel Commitment.* Is the staff committed to producing a software product at the expense of personal convenience?

6. *Personnel Effectiveness Monitoring.* Is there a means in place for monitoring the effectiveness of personnel against productivity requirements and identifying not only the productivity shortfalls but also the specific causes of these shortfalls in the context of the environment?

a. *Procedures for Defining Personnel Performance Goals.* Is there a specific set of performance goals which can be used by personnel to determine what is expected of them and how their performance will be measured?

b. *Procedures for Monitoring Performance.* Is there a technique for monitoring performance against productivity and schedule projection? Do these procedures provide an early warning when productivity slips below acceptable levels?

c. *Corrective Action.* Are there procedures for enforcing corrective actions when productivity or quality shortfalls are recognized? Is there a means to ensure that corrective actions, once implemented, solve the particular problems or issues they were designed to remedy?

Quality Management

The quality management segments of the software project infrastructure are the specific techniques which monitor the production of engineering data products, assess the quality of end items prior to delivery to the customer, ensure the integrity of data before they are used by other areas of the project, and test the software to ensure its design and operational integrity in relation to software specifications. Quality management does not build quality into the product. Rather, it monitors the degree that the quality is incorporated. How do I know that the products I am building meet the needs of the project? How do I know that the interfaces between data products have been adequately supported? How can I be sure that what I am building will ultimately meet the needs of the application and will be consistent with the requirements of the user? These questions must be answered early or the quality problems in the software will not be fixable without a major impact on cost and schedule. Quality management must be an intrinsic part of the project development. It must be integrated into the project structure and provide a system of checks and balances which serve as an early warning, before quality problems become significant. The following questions provide a means to assess the integrity of the quality management segment of the infrastructure. They bear a one-to-one relationship to the discussions in the previous chapter.

1. *Baseline Reviews.* Is there a set of baseline reviews established which will ensure the integrity of end items after they are approved by the customer and before they are used at the next level of development?

a. *Functional Baselines.* Are there specific reviews, the SRR and SDR, to establish a baseline of requirements? Have these been conducted adequately and is the approved data controlled by the customer and software project?

b. *Allocated Baselines.* Are there specific reviews, such as the preliminary design review (PDR), conducted to review the functional design of the software and are there procedures in place, both by the project and customer, to ensure the integrity of this baseline after approval?

c. *Product Baseline.* Are there reviews, such as the Critical Design Review (CDR), in place to establish and maintain the product baseline as the software is developed? These reviews, the critical design review and various levels of test reviews, must be continuously supporting in order to maintain baseline.

2. *Engineering Review and Inspections.* Are there separate and distinct reviews in place that provide engineering quality gates for data products as they are produced?

a. *Requirements Walk-Through.* Are all categories of requirements at each level in the development hierarchy subject to a requirements walk-through to check their form, structure, content, and integrity before requirements are used?

b. *Operational Concept Walk-through.* Is the operational concept for the system checked before it is used as the basis for any design? Has an initial release of the user's manual been made early in the project and reviewed at one of these walk-throughs?

c. *Software Requirements Walk-Through.* Have all categories of software requirements been checked at a walk-through and has the result of this check been used as the basis for definitions of a set of accepted requirements?

d. *Functional Design Evaluation.* Are there evaluations done at each level of functional decomposition to ensure the integrity of the data flow and data definitions? Is the functional design controlled after completion of one of these evaluations?

e. *Design Analysis Evaluation.* Is the top level software design for each CSCI evaluated through a quality gate before the design and definition of software units take place?

f. *Unit Design Evaluation.* Are there walk-throughs of all unit design conducted before coding is authorized?

g. *Code Evaluation.* Are there inspections of code conducted to ensure good practice and standards adherence before the software is released for testing?

h. *Unit Test Evaluation.* Are the results of unit testing independently checked before the software is released for integration?

i. *Build Evaluation.* Are there checks on the integrity and completeness of integration testing before the software is released for functional qualification?

    j. *Acquisition/Reusability Evaluation.* Is all software acquired from outside sources or used from previously developed systems evaluated for standards, relevancy, and technical completeness before a decision is made to use it?

3. *Audits.* Are periodic audits conducted both inside and outside the project to ensure product and process integrity?

    a. *Defining Audit Goals and Objectives.* Are there procedures to define audit goals and objectives before embarking on an audit?

    b. *Setting Audit Scope.* Is there a requirement to set and get concurrence concerning the scope of an audit before proceeding?

    c. *Audit Initiation.* Has the audit been tailored to the specific needs of the audit being conducted?

    d. *Project Analysis.* Are there means to conduct an audit and gain the support of the staff?

    e. *Reporting Results.* Are there specific standards for reporting results and follow-up of identified problems?

4. *Requirements Testing.* Is there an integrated set of testing levels to qualify the software and the system against approved requirements?

    a. *Defining Requirements Test Levels.* Are there separate test levels for the system and software qualification? Are they linked through the test planning documentation and the program and software plans?

    b. *Planning Requirements Testing.* Are there separate test plans for each test level, are they current and do they fully describe how the test will be conducted?

    c. *Detailing the Test Requirements.* Are there test procedures, scenarios, test folders and test data developed and controlled that describe, in a step-by-step fashion, how each of the test cases is to be conducted?

    d. *Establishing the Test Environment.* Is there an integrated environment to support all test levels and ensure a smooth, controlled flow of data?

    e. *Reporting/Follow-Up.* Are there project procedures in place for reporting problems and ensuring appropriate follow-up?

5. *Design Testing.* Is there an integrated set of test levels for qualifying the software against the design and then taking qualified software and integrating it into an operational system configuration?

    a. *Defining the Integration Test Requirements.* Are there requirements to develop system and software integration test plans and will these plans be used as the basis for testing against design?

    b. *Planning the Integration Test.* Is there an integration test plan for the system and is it current? Is there a separate test plan for integrating the software and is it also current?

c. *Detailing the Test Requirement.* Are there build and system test folders for detailing test requirements and have these been translated into specific test cases which are now used to integrate the software?

d. *Establishing the Integration Test Environment.* Is there a smooth and efficient environment for conducting system and software integration tests? Is it supportable through the automated and procedural elements of the project infrastructure?

e. *Problem Reporting/Correction.* Are there procedures for reporting problems and tracking their correction?

6. *Development Testing.* Are the informal test levels (levels 1 and 2) standardized through project standards and conventions and do the teams developing the software rigorously follow these standards before releasing software for integration testing?

a. *Unit Test Planning.* Are there unit test plans developed and reviewed by the task leaders before tests are developed and executed?

b. *Specification/Establishment of the Unit Test Environment.* Is there a consistent project environment for supporting unit testing and is it generally available to all development teams?

c. *Test Execution and Control.* Are there procedures within the project which provide guidance to the technical teams on what is expected for conducting development testing?

7. *Independent Quality Techniques.* Have independent observations of software products and processes been used to objectively check the integrity of the software project?

a. *Independent Testing.* Have critical segments of the software been objectively evaluated through the use of independent testing techniques?

b. *IV&V.* Are there independent verification and validation procedures to assess the integrity of the project and is there follow-up to reported shortfalls?

c. *Independent Quality Assurance.* Are there independent quality assurance procedures to evaluate the project from the outside and provide management reports concerning project strengths and weaknesses?

EVALUATING THE PROJECT INFRASTRUCTURE

Throughout the period of software development there are project conditions which, if monitored, provide reliable early indicators of potential development problems. Some of these indicators are quantitative, others are project conditions which indicate either an existent or potential productivity or quality problem. These conditions result not from any single cause but rather from the interactions between many project problems. They are symptomatic. Correcting the specific condition will not fix the underlying causes. The cause will, if not corrected, result in increasingly severe project problems. The following paragraphs describe these indicators with a brief discussion of their relation to the project infrastructure.

Resource Instability

The project has had to repeatedly add people, automated support, or additional facilities in an unplanned or uncontrolled manner to hold schedules or in response to continual urgent and pressing technical demands.

The keyword in the project condition that indicates a problem is *repeatedly*. Resources needs are often used to mask many project problems. Rather than admit that the project is not proceeding well because of internal problems, the software project often responds by adding resources. The effect is to throw more resources at the wrong problem. The problems are often a direct result of poor planning or project control, technology shortfalls or continued recurrent schedule slips which have not been resolved. The expected benefit will not be realized and the project situation will continue to deteriorate.

Resources should have to be justified based on specific needs, not assumed project improvement. There should be an analysis of how the project condition requiring the resource augmentation occurred, a definition of precisely how the resource will help, and a complete definition of the root causes that are behind the recurring resource problem.

Planning Inadequacy

There is not a current software development plan describing the project environment. The software manager and his or her staff are very vocal in rationalizing why this is not critical.

It's a small project. We've built systems like this before. That's a government requirement; overkill for this project. How can I write a plan like that and hold my current schedules? I've got a quality staff, why do I need this planning garbage?

The fact of the matter is that planning a software project is very difficult. It requires an understanding of the specific technical and development environment to be applied to the project. To plan you must understand the requirements of the project, the constraints that the project must live within and the management, technical, and administrative interfaces that must be supported by the software project. The software project manager must interpret these parameters, develop and document a plan for developing the software, and gain staff commitment to support the planned environment.

Software managers often have difficulty with the planning process. They have been schooled in the technical aspects of the development process, however, the planning, management and control aspects of the project are foreign. They just don't seem as important. Unless this problem is remedied, even simple projects will experience difficulty. The manager (or project leader) must think through and document what he is going to do, how the components of the project infrastructure will relate together, and how the process of development will be managed and controlled if there is to be any reasonable expectation that the project will be successful. From a quality perspective, checks and balances must be built into the project environment if the quality of the products is to be predictable. An unplanned project, or a project whose environment is an accident rather than a predefined interaction of technology, resources, personnel, management disciplines, and data control, is always a high risk proposition.

Schedule Application

The current project schedule spans in excess of 30 days, may not be current, and may not have been statused or updated on a regular basis.

The schedule is the plan for doing the work. It describes not only how long each task will take but also relates development end items to schedule, plans for doing the work and relating the development tasks together. Unless the development is scheduled, or if the schedules do not accurately reflect the state of the development, there is no clear project focus or structure to complete the project.

The schedule span problem is indicative of a specific, and often overlooked development reality; personnel produce more efficiently when focusing on a near-term milestone that they know they will be measured against than on a milestone which is further away. There are many examples of this outside the software environment. Students who develop papers in the last week before they are due, auto repairs put off until right before the car is required, tax returns which are not done until the week before they are due. In the software project this procrastination takes a terrible toll. Instead of only one event being due at a particular point in the schedule, there are several, and the type of activities required to complete the activity do not lend themselves well to the "crash and burn" techniques of software development. In order to meet the development milestone, too often the staff will evaluate and ponder the activity until two weeks before the milestone, then, when faced with an imminent milestone, will attempt to complete the milestone through a herculean commitment of time and energy. Quality suffers, the schedule often slips and the integrity of the milestone is compromised. Schedules, at least at the software production level, that have measurable milestones less than 30 days apart are a much more effective tool than those with longer spans. They force a sense of staff urgency and keep focus towards a near term milestone.

Schedule Performance

The production of major software milestones has been characterized by recurring un-resolved schedule creep where the cause is not attributable to any specific project cause, rather, it seems to be rooted in many factors which are difficult to isolate.

Recurring schedule creep is the most accurate indicator of software development problems. The problem is characterized by many milestones slipping a small amount right before they are due. These slips are recurring and become more difficult to resolve as the development proceeds. These small slips will, eventually, translate into a major project schedule problem. More importantly, they indicate a basic inefficiency in the project which will later affect the overall ability of the project to produce quality software. The causes of this creep are often difficult to resolve. They may be personnel related or they may be based on technology inefficiencies; or perhaps the schedules or costs were invalid to begin with. Most probably the cause is in project interactions and a basic inefficiency in the flow of data and work impacting the transition of responsibility and effectiveness of the project infrastructure. Curing the schedule problem by lengthening or increasing staff spans will not correct the basic project problem.

Technology Effectiveness

The engineering data being developed by the project must be reworked before it is usable in project documentation or by related project areas.

Data rework is time-consuming, frustrating and a sure indicator that the project standards, methodology interactions and project data requirements have not been adequately considered when laying out the project. This rework is not a fact of life, rather is the result of poor early planning, or a lack of planning execution. If allowed to continue, the problems of data incompatibility will surely get worse, eventually resulting in loss of traceability, poor quality of data products and, ultimately may result in development of an unacceptable system. Correcting the problem, especially early in the project, is difficult. It requires fully defining what engineering data products are required, the specific formatted structure of each, how they are tied together, and then tailoring the project technical environment to produce them. This is not easy, however it will result in a smooth transition of data and an application of technology to the specific needs of the project.

Staff Commitment

Even in periods of project stress the staff will not take responsibility for producing to the schedule, for increasing their work hours or for the quality and timeliness of the products they must develop.

The commitment of the staff to the production of quality software is much like a flywheel. Once it gets started, it is not difficult to keep going. Peer pressure, a commitment to schedule, pride in the product being produced, and project esprit de corps all play a part. Getting this started, however, especially early in the development, is difficult. Taking a staff of individuals, especially programmers, and blending them into a focused team committed to meeting a delivery requirement requires establishing a sense of urgency. It requires focusing and coordinating the activities of all project members to a common set of goals and objectives. Most importantly it requires the establishment of a project infrastructure which will support all the requirements imposed by the development. A well planned, complete and robust project infrastructure will tend to consolidate the staff and focus the project towards delivery. A poorly defined infrastructure will be a constant source of frustration, will break down project morale and will result in staff discontent and project inefficiency.

Resource Phasing

The resources applied to the project are characterized by a few resources (such as a suite of automated aids) that are overtaxed (constantly becoming a bottleneck in the project) while others are either not being used or are used so sparingly as to make their utility questionable.

Each project resource, automated aid, support resource and development facility should smooth the productivity of the project, the flow of data and work, and the flow of responsibility. These resources fall into three categories:

1. Those that are used to provide support to one or a small number of specific project requirements and are only applied when these particular segments of the project are active. These resource requirements should be limited and, although important to supporting particular project needs, are normally not critical to project integrity.

2. Those that are specific to a particular phase of development or area of the project infrastructure. These resources are critical to the project integrity since they represent the only means by which specific tasks essential to project success are accomplished. During the phase when they are needed they are heavily used, while not being used much at other times.

3. Those resources that are generally used throughout the development and are critical to the success of the project. These are the backbone of the support segments of the project; as such they must be adequate, scaled to specific project needs and effective.

The resources which fall into categories 2 and 3 are the areas which must be of concern if productivity and quality are to be a byproduct of development. Shortfalls in resource support, bottlenecks in the project caused by resource nonavailability or resources which have been applied in the wrong mix must be corrected or quality and/or productivity compromises may result. When a resource problem is observed, the overall application of resources, automated facilities, personnel, support facilities, and technical support should be assessed and, if necessary, redistributed, augmented, and modified to meet project needs.

Staff Morale

Is there obvious discontent in the staff, a high turnover and an obvious lack of staff support to management and project commitments?

The staff has no sense of accomplishment in producing the software. There is limited, if any, esprit de corps and the staff is not being reinforced by project success. These are symptomatic of project burnout brought about by an inability on the part of the project manager to establish an environment that focuses and rewards initiative and success rather than encouraging unwarranted optimism, poor practices and a lack of general staff effectiveness. These indicators are clearly evident in the project, recognizable when the evaluator first looks at the project environment. A general depression pervades the project. Desks don't fill until late and empty right at quitting time. While at work, the staff lacks enthusiasm and is generally not motivated. This condition, once recognized, must be dealt with. Unfortunately, the correction often is apparently more difficult to deal with than to ride with the problem. It's easy to delude yourself by thinking that things will improve. They won't. Only by correcting the root cause can the motivation or the project be improved. These root causes are poor planning; poor scheduling; lack of goals, objectives and project focus; and a poor flow of work, responsibility and data.

Traceability to Requirements

Can a single unit of code be traced from testing to code through the design to a specific requirement?

Traceability is a basic measure of the effectiveness of the software development process and represents the single most difficult problem facing the development. In order to maintain traceability, all aspects of the project must work together. The requirements, all levels of design, code and test specifications, must adhere to project standards. The project engineering data controls must ensure that all changes to controlled data retain traceability links. The quality gates must ensure that all data developed by the project is traceable upwards, downwards through the test levels, and across to the user and operator specifications. The test cases must verify not only the reliability and design integrity of the software but also the traceability of the software to the requirements.

The traceability link can be lost at any point by poor engineering practices, poor standards, poor controls, or a combination of factors. If not observed early and corrected quickly the link often cannot be re-established. By taking several requirements and tracing them through the system, the integrity of the system links can be verified on a sample basis.

Code Stability

New releases of software don't stabilize after regression testing and do have to be pulled off the floor because of inadequate reliability, incomplete functionality, or unexpected performance problems.

All software which is released for testing should be thoroughly evaluated prior to installation. The testing should have been complete, the performance evaluations rigorous and the quality checked. If there is a problem in software reliability or release integrity, one of three conditions may be present:

1. The project controls and quality checks used to produce the software were not rigorously applied and, as a result the code is of insufficient quality to support testing requirements.
2. The update controls used to modify existent code are not being followed or are being short-circuited to meet short term schedule or release requirements.
3. The project environment is not robust enough to meet the rigorous requirements imposed by software testing.

If any of these conditions exist early, effective action must be taken. The further the software gets into the testing cycle, the more complex the test environment and the more difficult to correct reliability and performance problems.

Problem Reporting

It takes more than 14 days from initial reporting of a software problem to isolating its cause. Often it takes more than 30 days from initial problem report to correction. Oc-

casionally it takes more than 45 days from initial reporting of a software problem to release of a system containing the fix.

This measure of project infrastructure is critical from two aspects:

1. It is a quantitative measure of the effectiveness of the software project infrastructure and indicates its efficiency.
2. It indicates how long the lag will be, from a system release standpoint, to incorporate changes into the system.

During the period of software testing this relationship, report versus correction, is critical. Any delays in finding problems or releasing software can have a devastating effect on project schedules. They can delay test schedules, force work-arounds which compromise quality, and violate the test and release relationships critical to software release integrity.

What can be done if these spans are excessive? The problems generally are in three areas. The first area involves the amount of time required to process and assign a problem report to an organization for correction. This task, although appearing simple, requires an interpretation of the problem to determine the area to be modified and to assign correction responsibility. This process is often difficult to streamline due to bureaucratic overhead and the reluctance of the development organizations to take on more work.

The second area, software update, is the average time required to complete an update once the problem is assigned to an organization. There are two components of this time, one of which is under control of the project and one of which is less predictable. The part which can be controlled is the hold time where the problem sits in a queue waiting for a technical member of the staff to get to it. This is an indication of both update efficiency and staff effectiveness. The second part, update complexity, is determined by the difficulty of the problems being found and the time it takes to correct them. This is difficult to project, however, it impacts the overall correction time significantly. One factor, which can be controlled, is the resources allocated to correct the problems.

The third area is the time required to release a system containing the fix once the software fix has been made. The three components of this area, update acceptance, regression testing, and system release all can be projected and controlled by the project. A smooth transition of software and documentation from the development to the configuration management organizations, efficient regression testing, and a smooth system integration and release procedure will minimize the time required for this processing. The observer should be equally concerned about a process that takes too long as one that is done in too short a time. If this process is too short it could mean that steps in the release process are being ignored or not adequately performed, engineering is being inadequately performed or quality checks and balances are not being done.

Quality Gate Integrity

More than 30 percent of the walk-throughs, reviews or inspections are failing because of poor quality of the data and inconsistency with project standards or a violation of development practices.

There are many reasons why quality gates can reject a product. They are the "first line" in checking quality. Besides being a quality check they also are an early warning of project technical, resource, environment, and experience shortfalls. Excessive quality rejections, for any reason, indicate that there is a fundamental project problem, or series of problems, that are resulting in significant quality problems. Perhaps the standards are unclear. Maybe the staff is unqualified to produce the software. The attitude of the staff may be that the technical quality of the software is not important. Whatever the reason, or reasons, the problem must be resolved. If quality is not a staff priority there is always the uncertainty over how many quality problems are slipping through undetected that will require resolution when time, resources and options are unavailable.

Testing Orientation

The project takes obvious pride in the small number of discrepancies that have been uncovered during testing.

This indicates a critical philosophical project problem. What is the role of software test? In the case described the attitude of the project towards test is to "prove that the system or software works." In this environment, testing is oriented towards isolating the small number of problems rather than aggressive uncovering and reporting of the maximum number of problems to ensure the quality of the system when released.

Early recognition of the problem is critical to the quality of the software when it is released. If caught early in the structure of the project test environment, testing can be reoriented to uncover and report the largest number of problems. The number of problems found then becomes a source of pride.

If not caught early, the project test environment cannot be reoriented without a significant augmentation of resources, a redirection of effort, and a reorientation of project priorities. Often this can't be accomplished and software is released without a thorough analysis of its integrity, reliability or functional completeness.

7

SOFTWARE PRODUCT QUALITY

The products of software development, even at the lowest levels, must be of predictable quality if the end product of the development, the operational software configuration, is to satisfy the needs of the application.

Previous chapters have described the software development life cycle and the software project infrastructure. It is the project infrastructure which provides the framework through which software quality is "built in" the software system product. The attributes and characteristics of the data products, and the degree that they fulfill specific project needs provide an incremental measure of quality of the end product. Product attributes are defined, first, as attributes for each data product produced as the software is developed, and second, as attributes that must be integral to the software when delivered for system integration.

STANDARDS AND CONVENTIONS

Software project standards and conventions provide the basic definition of what is to be produced at each stage of development. These standards describe in detail what is to be included in each individual data element and how it is to appear. Project standards provide specific criteria to measure quality and evaluate the acceptability of software products. They define the format, structure, and content of each individual software data product and ensure product compatibility with those products which either interface with other products, are used in a subsequent phase of development, or use the data product in a higher level project data item or documentation product. Proper definition of project standards provides the link between the data products and aids the integration of project methodologies through the data products each produces.

The standards document is the cornerstone of the software quality management program. This document, commonly termed the programming practices, standards, and convention document, is developed by the software project organization early in the project and is a detailed identification of product and process standards for the project.

The standards contain three major categories of data:

1. Style guides or detailed definitions of the exact content and format of each customer deliverable.

2. An identification of the form, structure, and content of each bridge data item to be produced by the project throughout the development.

3. A description of how each individual development methodology is to be applied to the project and a detailed description of the production data products and the bridge products which link them together.

Style Guides

The style guide contains a detailed annotated outline for each document with examples of acceptable level of detail. The guide should take into account the complexity of the project and the overall requirements for the system. Systems with a single, sophisticated user may require a more general level of detail, while systems which are intended for a wide set of users with varying levels of technical capability may require more detail. If a corporate or company style guide exists, it should be modified according to the specific needs of the project. The style guide should be prepared prior to or at the beginning of the project and negotiated with the customer prior to contract award, or reviewed with the customer early in the project.

Methodology Interfacing

There are, as described previously, many project methodologies used in the development of software. Methodologies are used throughout the development life cycle to specify requirements, aid with top level design, detailed design, coding, test, and integration. These (often individual) methodologies have to be tailored to the project and interfaced together in order to ensure a smooth development process and efficient flow of work and data to develop acceptable quality. Methodologies interface through the data products of the project, thus consistency of data across the project is a requirement for a logical and effective development process. If a quality product is to result, the processes used to produce it must be effective, tailored to the project, consistent with other areas of the project using the data, and consistent with the experience and ability of the technical staff implementing the project.

Data Descriptions

There are many individual data products which link the project together. These data products represent the output from each major development activity and individual methodology used in the development. They also represent the input, or starting point for the next phase of the development and must interface with the methodologies that will be used in that phase. They also form the basis on which product quality is measured. Project audits and reviews are conducted based on these data products and provide an incremental view of quality as the project proceeds. If the data products are developed in accordance with project standards and conventions, software quality will be enhanced.

SOFTWARE ATTRIBUTES

In order to ensure that development products meet a defined quality standard when delivered, standards must be defined early, must be specific to the project and must define *quality and acceptability* attributes for individual data products. There must be quality "gates" identified which will monitor the quality of the data products being produced before they are used by the project. Without a means to measure conformance to standards and conventions, quality cannot be monitored, and standards and conventions are of minimal use.

Specific attributes are defined based on the requirements of the project. These attributes are specific to the application and fall into several categories:

1. *Performance Attributes.* Attributes which describe the execution characteristics of the software when integrated into an operational configuration.
2. *Form Attributes.* Those which describe the form of the product and how it will appear when delivered.
3. *Processing Attributes.* Those which describe processing characteristics of the software.
4. *Functional Attributes.* Those which describe the functionality of the system when integrated into an operational configuration.
5. *Operational Integrity.* Those which describe the reliability, system control, and operational support characteristics of the software and

the degree that the system supports the requirements of the application.

6. *Maintainability.* Those which describe the ease by which the software may be updated to reflect changing system or operational needs or to correct operational discrepancies.

There is a significant amount of ongoing effort within industry, academia, and government, directed towards developing the entire area of what is commonly called software quality metrics—that is, how to describe the overall characteristics of software, namely attributes, and the measurement of those attributes, namely metrics.

Specific attributes, and the measures which evaluate them, vary widely and there is a good deal of controversy over the definition, implementation, and use of software metrics. While this field is still in its infancy and evolving, it does provide a useful means to quantify the status of the software. It is not important that a rigorous scientific basis for software metrics has not been agreed on for general implementation. What is important is that measures be consistently applied across software implementations to develop an experience base that can be used to assess progress and quality in various software projects. This experience base will only result through the application of metrics in actual software projects to develop the knowledge to properly assign attributes and understand specific metric values with respect to the software.

We believe that software attributes will become the primary determinants of software quality. Twelve of these attributes are:

1. *Correctness* Has the software been developed correctly in relation to requirements, design, and documented and approved project standards?

2. *Reliability.* Does the software system execute reliably in accordance with the performance and support requirements of the application?

3. *Efficiency.* Does the software execute efficiently, minimizing overhead, and maximizing software responsiveness and system throughput?

4. *Integrity.* Does the software have built in safeguards to prohibit unauthorized access to software or data, and does it fulfill the requirements of the application?

5. *Usability.* What is the effort required to learn how to operate, prepare input and interpret output, and how usable is the software in relation to the operational and support environment?

6. *Maintainability.* How maintainable is the software system when used in the operational environment—what is the effort required to locate and repair an error?

7. *Flexibility.* How flexible is the software system in the context of the user environment, and how easily do the system capabilities adapt to the changing operational and functional support of the users?

8. *Testability.* Is the software system testable and does it lend itself to thorough design verification, functional qualification, and operational validation?

9. *Portability.* How easily can the software be ported from system to system as needed to meet system requirements and in order to support company or program needs or objectives?

10. *Reusability.* To what degree is the software system, or components of the software system, reusable in different applications or operational configurations?

11. *Interoperability.* How effectively does the software interact with other operational software in the user environment?

12. *Documentation.* How closely does project documentation meet project standards, how well does it describe the system, and how closely does it match the operational capability and configuration of the system?

Project Planning and Requirements Definition

The structuring of the software project and the establishment of the technical requirements for the system are concurrent activities. These activities, and the products which result, initiate the system and software development.

As illustrated in Figure 7-1, during the early stages of the development, three primary categories of data are produced and reviewed.

1. *System (and Software) Requirements.* From system requirements a software specific subset is extracted. This subset, when documented and approved, becomes the technical basis for software development.

2. *System Planning and Technical Data.* Data which describes the system development environment, the constraints of development, and the technical requirements which the system must satisfy.

3. *Software Planning Data.* Data which establishes the software project infrastructure. This data defines the individual components of the infrastructure, the interrelationships between the various developmental activities of the project, how resources will be applied to satisfy identified project needs, and the controls which will monitor progress, quality, productivity, and effectiveness.

Planning Attributes

During the planning phase, software attributes are described which define the characteristics of the development effort. Budgets, schedules, project

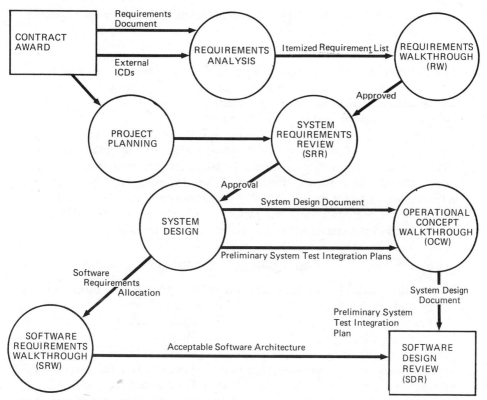

Figure 7-1.   Project planning and requirements definition.

plans, tools, techniques, and methodologies are defined and establish the framework to be used to develop the software. This framework provides the environment for developing quality software and projects sufficient and appropriate resources according to projected manpower loading to afford the development to take place as planned. These attributes should consist of the following:

1. *Completeness*.   Do software plans describe the complete environment to be used by the software project?
2. *Tailoring*.   Have the software plans been tailored to the specific technical, administrative, external, and developmental characteristics of the software development application?
3. *Achievability*.   Are the proposed software plans achievable in light of the technical, cost, schedule, personnel, administrative, and management constraints of the project?
4. *Personnel*.   Do project personnel have adequate experience to implement the planned project environment, and is the proper mix of manpower available to support the needs and requirements of the project?

5. *Realism.*   Are the proposed plans realistic and do they apply proven development techniques?

The individual attributes which describe the usability of project planning data should be predictive in nature; that is, they should describe the usefulness and completeness of project plans in relation to the anticipated development and technical needs of the project.

These attributes should also provide specific criteria for evaluating the quality of project planning on an individual document and data element basis. These evaluation criteria should be based on the requirements of the development and contract, the needs of the program, and be consistent with the limiting factors which will necessarily constrain the development and limit the prerogatives of the software project; for example, those that are set forth in the standards and conventions document (structured code).

Requirements Attributes

The requirements analysis and definition phase is the period during which the system and software requirements are defined.

This phase, as previously stated, is the most important one in any software development. The early data items—concept of operations, user and performance requirements specifications, interface requirements, security and testing requirements—must support the later needs of the project, otherwise the basis of development is not sound and should not proceed.

The attributes of the requirements data products which are critical to the quality of the system and software are:

1. *Nonambiguity.*   Each requirement should be expressed in such a way that its meaning is clear and nonambiguous.

2. *Traceability.*   Every requirement should be uniquely specified, and traceable through the design, code, and test periods of the project.

3. *Testability.*   Each requirement should be expressed in such a way as to facilitate verification by later testing, measurement, observation or analysis.

4. *Implementability.*   All requirements should be implementable—that is, consistent with the technical realities of the project and the ability of the staff to conceptualize and produce the software products.

5. *Completeness.*   The set of requirements should be complete, describing all aspects of the system, and linked together to provide a complete representation of the system.

6. *Reality.*   The requirements should be realistically scaled to the technical characteristics, the technical needs, and the limitations and constraints of the development environment.

7. *Acceptability.* Project requirements should result in a system which is acceptable to the user and consistent with the needs of the application.

8. *User Responsiveness.* The requirements must be responsive to the needs of the user, the operational requirements of the application and the actual documented environment of the system.

9. *Design Free.* The requirements should be free of design. They should specify what the system must do rather than how it will be accomplished.

Software Design Activities

Synthesizing system and software design from the definition of requirements is an iterative process, decomposing requirements into successively lower levels of abstraction until the lowest level, the detailed design, is reached and software coding may begin.

As illustrated in Figure 7-2, the data products which describe the software design are developed concurrently with development of the system design and test specification. The data products which document the design fall into two primary categories: top level design documentation, which details the functional requirements allocated to specific software components; and detailed design documentation, which details the software architecture to the lowest level such that coding may begin.

Top Level Design

The top level design phase is the period during which a functional system and software design is synthesized from the requirements of the system. During this phase, the basic architecture of the system and software, and the functional definition of the system are developed.

The products of the functional design process detail those functions the system must perform and the data and control paths to be supported. The data base definition and structure establishes the data organization and defines the data relationships essential to the software architecture. Data dictionaries detail system data requirements. The functional design must also define software to software interfaces between independently executing components of the software, performance budgets to be allocated as part of the design process, and results in a mini-specification which is a design language representation of the execution requirements at the lowest level of functional abstraction. These components comprise the functional design.

The functional requirements must be specified in accordance with the following attributes:

1. *Completeness.* As with the requirements definition, the functional design must be a complete definition of the system allocated to in-

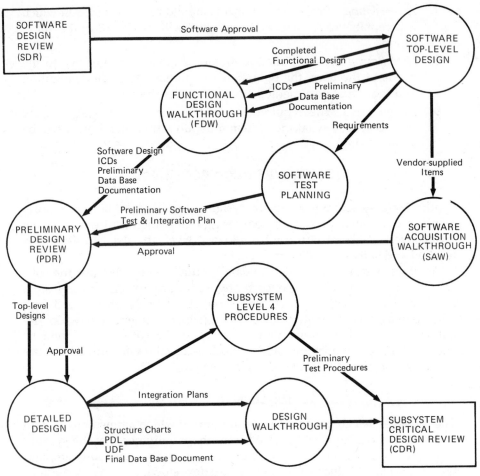

Figure 7-2.   Software design activities.

dividual subsystem or software components. From this detailed functional set, the detailed design may be partitioned into system builds for development and subsequent integration and qualification testing.

2. *Testability.*   All functional requirements must be verifiable through functional qualification testing, functional or performance analysis, or observation. The functional design, as with operational or user requirements, must be testable to be valid.

3. *Traceability.*   All functional design must be directly traceable to the requirements from which they were derived.

4. *Functional Validity.*   All functional design specifications must be clear, concise, and functionally valid in light of operational, system, and hardware realities.

5. *Data Validity.* The functional design must provide a clear definition of the data relationships which exist in the system, the data and control flows which must be supported, and a data architecture which supports an efficient software design.

6. *Achievability.* The functional design must be achievable in light of system performance requirements, development constraints, and implementation realities. The best functional design is worthless if it does not result in a working system capability.

The evaluation of functional design integrity should not only be a static evaluation of the design in relation to project standards and methodological requirements but should also be predictive. The analysis should look at the design utility, application, and adequacy to support future design, implementation and test requirements, and finally soundness in relation to the project need to serve as a foundation for future development and test.

Detailed Design

The detailed design activities translate functional requirements and design specifications into a complete representation of the technical design to a level from which coding can proceed. The primary criteria for successful software design is how well does the design support all segments of the functional design, how easily does it translate directly into code, and how easily does it integrate into a system configuration responsive to system requirements.

The components of the detailed design are the structure charts which define the structural relationships between software components, the control flow and interunit specifications, which link the various elements of the software together, and the unit development folders which document the process of unit design and implementation.

The detailed design components must reflect the following attributes:

1. *Testability and Traceability.* As with requirements and top level design, the detailed design definition must be traceable through the functional design to the specific user requirements.

2. *Integrity.* The detailed design must be developed in absolute conformance to project requirements. Data must support the design.

3. *Implementability.* The detailed design must be scaled to the implementation realities of the project, the resources and experience available, and the technical, schedule, and budget constraints.

4. *Design Characteristics.* The design heuristics, coupling characteristics, and software design attributes must establish a firm basis for development of a quality software system.

5. *Size and Partitioning.* The design must be partitioned into small, modular, and functionally sound units traceable through the func-

tional design to the operational requirements of the system. Partitioning the system into small units affords the capability to deal with the development as a series of small developments rather than as a large, complex implementation.

6. *Structural Integrity.* The design must be structurally sound providing clean interfaces between various design components, a controlled definition and use of data structures, and a predefined, predictable, and controllable execution pattern through the design in response to system stimuli.

7. *Reliability.* The detailed software design must have a complete definition of system error conditions, recovery modes, degraded mode of operation, and system conditions which require special processing to ensure the integrity of the system.

These detailed design attributes are what establish, to a large measure, the quality and reliability of the software. If correct, the detailed design will define a reliable software configuration and will provide an adequate base upon which coding may proceed.

Implementation and Test

The coding, unit testing, and integration and system test phase is a most difficult period from the perspective of quality for the following reasons:

1. The extended time required to successfully complete these activities.
2. The myriad of activities which are occurring in parallel and the long spans of time between the completion of individual events.
3. The many data products that are developed or updated during this period which must relate to each other, be developed in absolute conformance with project standards, and must be technically compatible with higher levels of design and baselined information.

As illustrated in Figures 7-3 and 7-4, during implementation, integration and test the data products are to a large measure informal. They are evaluated through informal reviews or walk-throughs. The two primary categories of data coding and testing are described in the following.

Coding Attributes

Coding attributes describe requirements which detail the environment to be used by the project during coding as well as predictive measures which will forecast code acceptability. These code product attributes include:

1. *Code Structure.* These attributes describe the common architecture to be used by all software components. The structure attributes are

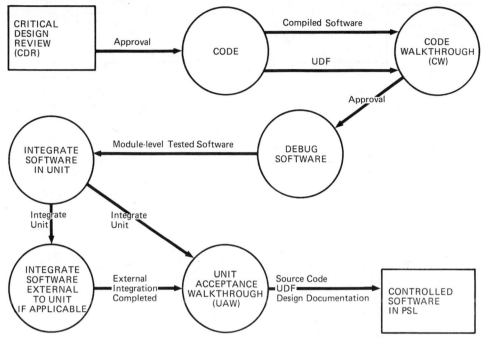

Figure 7-3.   Software Implementation.

specific to each category of software: high order language (HOL),
assembly language, and firmware. The major components of these
attributes include modularity, conciseness, coding style and technique, data commonality and expandability, and application of acceptable practice.

2. *Readability.*   The attributes which describe the form and appear-
ance of all the source code (HOL and assembly language) and firmware. They describe the prologue and commenting requirements,
the use of mnemonics, the software instruction module organization, and the specific application of structured programming conventions.

3. *Program Layout.*   Those attributes which describe how each software code component will be laid out. Rigorous adherence to layout
attributes will ensure consistency of code and acceptability of the
end products.

4. *Code Flexibility.*   These attributes describe how flexible the code is
in response to changing system, operational, environmental or recovery conditions and how well does the code lend itself to enhancement or modification in response to changing software
requirements.

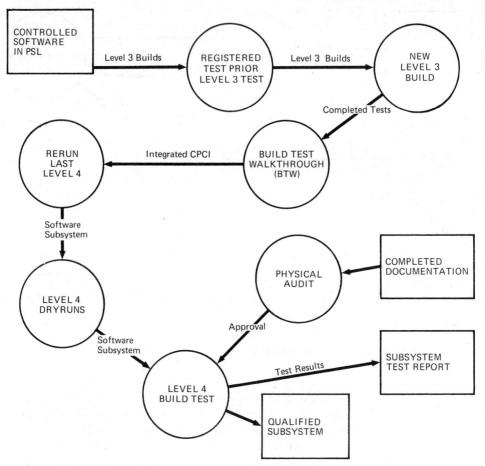

Figure 7-4. Software test.

5. *Code Accuracy.* These attributes describe how closely the code, when implemented, corresponds to the detailed design of the software and how accurate are the data values which result from execution of the code.

6. *Complexity.* These attributes describe how clearly and simply the code satisfies allocated functional and design requirements. Complex programs are more difficult to maintain and are often less reliable than a more straightforward implementation.

7. *Code Documentation Quality.* These attributes describe the quality of the programmer's documentation.

8. *Coding Consistency.* These attributes describe how consistent coding practices and standards are adhered to in relation to other software in the system. The measures of consistency include form, code structure, coding techniques, and code documentation.

9. *Coding Reliability.*   These attributes describe how reliable the software is when executing in an integrated software environment. The components of these attributes include fault tolerance, fault isolation and recovery, and fault containment.

10. *Code Reusability.*   These attributes describe the extent that a given piece of code can be used in other applications. The components of this attribute include generality, hardware independence, modularity, self-documentation, portability, and software system independence.

Quality of code is a complex issue. It is the focus of the planning, requirements, and design activities and represents the first tangible and the most measurable of all software data products. The products of coding are the first products which actually can be put on a computer and cause it to operate in a specific way. As described in later chapters techniques such as modeling, simulation, design verification, or prototyping are effective methods for analyzing design integrity or validity. These are, however, only analytical aids. They test concepts and assimilation but do not tailor an inherent system capability to a user need. Only the code products achieve this end.

The degree that the code products meet the predefined coding standards of the project, and the adequacy of these standards in relationship to the attributes described previously, will, to a large measure, forecast how well the code will support the objectives, goals, requirements, and needs of the application.

Test and Integration Attributes

Poorly specified test requirements, unresolved open issues, incomplete test engineering, or unspecified test tools or data requirements will have a devastating effect on the productivity and quality of the project. Because of the lead times associated with test development, and the fact that most of the effort occurs at the back end of the development when the project has limited resources and options to deal with poorly defined test parameters, early and complete definition of test requirements is critical to project success.

The products associated with test and integration include test plans, test procedures, test scenarios and data, test tooling and environmental support, and test reporting. Generally there are five attribute categories which describe the test and integration products. These are:

1. *Completeness.*   These attributes describe how complete each level of test definition and reporting is, and how completely each individual data product addresses the specific set of test requirements it is designed to satisfy. The intricate relationships which exist in a project as well as the complexities inherent in the project environment dur-

ing test and integration make completeness at each level of planning, in the definition of the test environment and in the reporting of problems and results, critical to the success of the project.

2. *Achievability.*   These attributes describe the achievability of the test program in light of technical realities, cost and schedule constraints and limitations, tooling and support limitations, and issues associated with resource availability.

3. *Traceability.*   These attributes describe the traceability between the various test levels, the design, the software requirements, and the user requirements. All test requirements, plans, and procedures must be clearly traceable to an approved, documented, and controlled set of project requirements if they are to be valid.

4. *Control.*   Test planning must establish a testing environment which must be controlled. Testing tools, techniques, methodologies, and environments must be specified which will act in a predictable manner and which may be controlled to cause specific software paths to be executed or specific functional capabilities to execute.

5. *Reproducibility.*   One of the fundamental aspects of any test environment, and an attribute which must be apparent in all test planning development and reporting, is reproducibility. Test procedures should be sufficiently well defined to allow exact reproduction of the test environment and test execution from test run to test run. Tests and test environments which cannot be easily reproduced or which are structured in such a way as to preclude reproduction will not support all of the objectives of software testing.

SUMMARY

The previously described attributes are characteristics which describe software or data products which are the outputs of each development phase. These attributes "aggregate"; they describe groupings of data, documentation or information rather than individual data items. While it is the hope that the project will be perfect, in reality it never is. Yet the deficiencies represent a cost to the program that has already been incurred. Decisions have to be made on appropriate actions to correct deficiencies or accept the product as is. These decisions are not easy—they depend on numerous factors: significance of the deficiency, cost to correct, program schedule, severity of the deficiency, and so forth. This is the area where management earns its keep.

8

SOFTWARE QUALITY METRICS

Unless a measure is applied to software, and software quality, software engineering will remain an art rather than a science. Commensurately, software quality is extremely dependent on measurement applied through the use of metrics.

In order to achieve a true indication of quality the software must be subjected to measurement, that is the attributes of quality previously discussed must be related to specific product requirements and quantified. This is accomplished through the use of metrics. Without metrics applied to attributes the status of the software is subject to extreme subjectivity, to the point that any statement of quality is suspect and without any real meaning except among members of a small peer group.

While software metrics has not yet achieved a degree of scientific maturity, it is still a valid concept and much work has been undertaken in the field. In order to achieve this status the use of metrics has to be on actual projects—that is, where actual experience will be gathered and a basis developed that can be useful on subsequent software projects. It is important to select metrics that: are useful to the specific objectives of the program; have been derived from the program requirements; and which support the

Intensive use has been made of: RADC technical report RADC-TR-80-109, April 1980 (Volume I, *Software Quality Metrics Enhancements*, and Volume II, *Software Quality Measurement Manual*). The authors are James A. McCall and Mike T. Matsumoto of the General Electric Company; and RADC technical report RADC-TR-85-37, *Specification of Software Quality Attributes*, Feb. 1985, three volumes, by the Boeing Aerospace Company. The authors are Thomas P. Bowen, Gary B. Wigle, and Jay T. Tsai.

evaluation of the software consistent with those requirements. If this is done, the program office and the systems organization will develop a useful experience base to enhance software program resource estimation and attain quality software in successive software development efforts.

This chapter is not intended to be a complete tutorial on metrics. That is a subject that is much too vast for the scope of this book. This chapter provides an introduction to software quality metrics for the software manager and software engineering personnel. It gives the reader examples of the type of metrics that can be applied and how to apply these techniques to manage software quality.

EARLY MEASUREMENT METHODS

Early attempts to measure software concentrated on the product itself, the source and object code delivered. These methods subscribed to the so called black box technique, that is, ignoring the process of development in favor of a quantifiable measure of the end product. Often these measures were in terms of the numbers of errors (or bugs as they are commonly called in the industry) per lines of delivered code over time. The most common descriptor used was reliability. While this may have seemed a simplistic approach, ascribing quality to one definition of the software product, it was an early attempt to achieve engineering control of a difficult and unknown field of endeavor. This led to a number of mathematical expressions of the software product. Two of these are:

1. *McCabe's Complexity Mode 1.*   This model relates a complexity to the measure of the structure of the software and is derived from classical graph theory. The model is described by the formula:
$$V(G) = e - n + 2p$$
where $V(G)$ is the cyclomatic number of classical graph theory, and in this model is a measure of complexity.

   e = the number of edges in the program
   n = the number of vertices
   p = the number of connected components (assumed to be one)

   Figure 8.1 provides a simple example.

$$e = 4$$
$$n = 4$$
$$V(G) = 4 - 4 + 2 \times 1 = 2$$

   Presumably the higher the complexity the more difficult the software will be to design, build, test, and maintain.

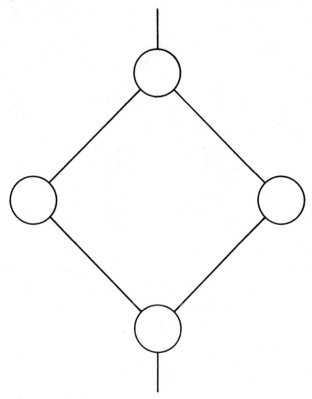

Figure 8-1. Sample control structure.

2. *Halstead Measures.* These measures attempt to provide a measure of quality, or prediction of the software development process by accounting for two factors, the number of distinct operators (instruction types, Keywords, etc.) and the number of distinct operands (variables and constants) used. Halstead defines a number of characteristics that can be quantified about the software and then relates these in different ways to describe the various aspects of the software. For example, the vocabulary of the software is:

$$n = n1 + n2$$

where $n1$ is the number of distinct operators and $n2$ the number of distinct operands. He defines the length of the program by:

$$N = N1 + N2$$

where $N1$ is the total number of occurrences of operators and $N2$ is the total number of occurrences of operands. Halstead then defines a number of relationships that can be quantified using the above characteristics to describe various aspects of the software. For example, the "volume" of the software program is:

$$V = N\log_2 n$$

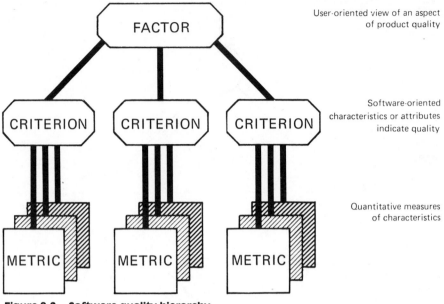

Figure 8-2. Software quality hierarchy.

and "difficulty" is described by:

$$D = n_{1/2} * N_2/n_2$$

While these measures provide historical perspective they have not been accepted for common use and have given way to new methodologies and descriptors for software. Newer metric techniques have been developed that attempt to measure the total process of the software development through a complete set of attribute descriptors. In his book, *Measuring Programmer Productivity and Software Quality*, Lowell Jay Arthur provides a useful treatment of the characteristics of various metrics. He describes the following metric categories: complexity, correctness, efficiency, flexibility, integrity, interoperability, maintainability, portability, reliability, reusability, structure, testability, and usability. While this treatment is useful, software metrics is still an evolving discipline. The treatment presented here represents some of the latest efforts in this area.

QUALITY HIERARCHY

The hierarchy which is achieving a wide degree of acceptance in the software engineering community is illustrated in Figure 8-2. Software (quality) is described through a number of "factors," for example, reliability, maintainability, and so forth. (Arthur calls these metrics.) Each of these factors has several attributes, or characteristics, that describe the factor. These attributes are called criteria. Each criterion has associated with it one, or several metrics which, taken together, quantify the criterion. The criteria for each factor in arithmetic combination provide a value for the factor at the top level.

Depending on the specific taxonomy used, the number of metrics, criteria, and factors will vary. It is not unusual, for example, to have several hundred metrics, quantifying scores of criteria, with a dozen factors at the top level. (This represents a somewhat complex discipline which has accounted for some reluctance on the part of senior management personnel to implement a metrics program.) The specific set of factors, and commensurately criteria, has to be tailored to the project. Criteria can be at cross purposes with one another. For example, in order to achieve maintainability, a high degree of code simplicity would be called for, which could be in contradiction with efficiency of executable code. It is important, therefore, to understand the complete requirements for the software and to specify quality requirements into the project early in the development process.

Until recently, software specifications have largely consisted of performance requirements. Quality requirements were ignored. This was mainly because people did not know how to specify quality and very little was developed in quality metrics. The introduction of software quality metrics now affords the capability to specify software quality in the requirements process. This application must be supported by the customer, allocated in the project through quality requirements, and supported by quantifiable metrics if quality in the software product is to be achieved.

QUALITY FACTORS

A total of 12 quality factors are described for assessing quality. These are based on the perceived quality concerns of the user and program/project personnel. They are grouped according to specific areas depending on the point of view of the user and developer. Table 8-1 depicts these concerns and the commensurate quality factor areas for each concern. The three categories shown relate to specific areas of the software life cycle.

Performance.   The requirements that must be stated and agreed to by the user and that specify how the software will operate.

Design.   The integrity of the design process to implement the software requirements of the user.

Adaptation.   A life cycle concern that affects the user and the maintainer—how easy will the software be to reuse and to evolve to meet new requirements.

Acquisition Concern	User Concern	Quality Factor
Performance How well does it function?	How well does it utilize a resource?	Efficiency
	How secure is it?	Integrity
	What confidence can be placed in what it does	Reliability
	How easy is it to use?	Usability
Design How valid is the design?	How well does it conform to the requirements?	Correctness
	How easy is it to repair?	Maintainability
	How easy is it to verify its performance?	Verifiability
Adaptation How adaptable is it?	How easy is it to expand or upgrade its capability or performance?	Expandability
	How easy is it to change?	Flexibility
	How easy is it to interface with another system?	Interoperability
	How easy is it to transport?	Portabiiity
	How easy is it to convert for use in another application?	Reusability

TABLE 8-1.   Software quality factors.

Table 8-2 tabulates these factors according to these three life cycle areas and provides a brief definition for each factor. Each factor is described in more detail in the following, including a description of the various criteria and examples of metrics that are used to quantify each factor.

1. *Efficiency.*   This factor is primarily measured in terms of the execution efficiency and storage efficiency of delivered code. Execution efficiency can be measured relative to similar existing code if available, or through the use of benchmark programs. Of course, with benchmarks, the chicken or the egg question arises, however, no system is perfect and guidelines are a necessary evil in cases where quantitative metrics do not exist. Storage efficiency of delivered code can be measured by techniques such as examining whether

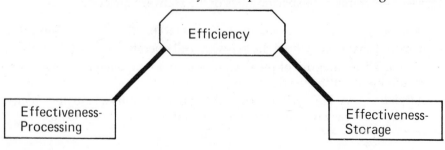

Project/ Program	Quality Factor	Definition
Performance	Efficiency	Relative extent to which a resource is utilized (i.e., storage space, processing time, communication time)
	Integrity	Extent to which the software will perform without failures due to unauthorized aess to the code or data within a specified time period.
	Reliability	Extent to which the software will perform without any failures within a specified time period.
	Usability	Relative effort for training or software operation (e.g., familiarization, input preparation, execution, output interpretation)
Design	Correctness	Extent to which the software conforms to its specifications and standards
	Maintainability	Ease of effort for locating and fixing a software failure within a specified time period.
	Verifiability	Relative effort to verify the specified software operation and performance.
Adaptation	Expandability	Relative effort to increase the software capability or performance by enhancing current functions or by adding new functions or data.
	Flexibility	Ease of effort for changing the software missions, functions, or data to satisfy other requirements.
	Interoperability	Relative effort to couple the software of one system to the software of another system.
	Portability	Relative effort to transport the software for use in another environment (hardware configuration and/or software system environment).
	Reusability	Relative effort to convert a software component for use in another application.

TABLE 8-2. Lifecycle quality measures.

segment length is consistent with available memory, whether data has been packed, and so forth. Efficiency is assessed through data usage measures, storage efficiency measures, iterative processing measures, and performance requirements checks.

2. *Integrity*. Integrity deals with the security and the auditability of the product. Security is an operationally oriented attribute—its metrics are access control and access audit. Auditability is an attribute that helps determine security. It assesses the instrumentation of the

product—how well does the software instrument itself—how well are execution errors recognized, how well are special conditions identified?

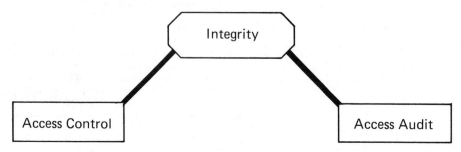

3. *Reliability.* Reliability is concerned with the degree that the software operates without error. This factor is a function of anomaly management, accuracy, and simplicity. Typically reliability has been expressed in terms of error models. There has never been any validation or acceptance of reliability error models and professional software engineers have turned to more practical means of assessing reliability. A simple metric is to assess the numbers of errors per delivered lines of code. Acceptable levels range from one to three errors per thousand lines of delivered code, depending on the complexity and use of the software. Accuracy has to do with the actual performance of the code and the description of the product to provide an acceptable level of precision in processing calculations and outputs. Simplicity is the inverse of complexity. Its measures can be traditional methods, such as McCabe's cyclomatic complexity, or other less rigorous techniques, such as structure of individual modules, that is, minimum number of statements per module, minimum number of module interfaces, and so forth.

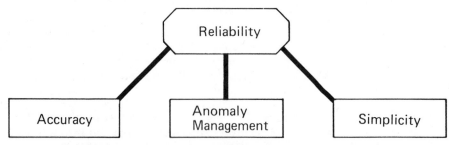

4. *Usability.* This is perhaps the most important factor or measurement area. After all, if the software is not usable by the end user or customer its value is negligible regardless of its capability to score high in other factors. The system may not be user-friendly. It may be extremely difficult to use and require an excessive amount of continuing education for the skill level of the expected user population.

For example, a bank president should not be expected to learn complicated access procedures. The applicable criteria are operability and training.

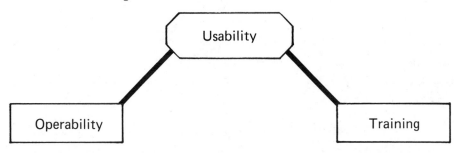

5. *Correctness.* Correctness deals with the extent that the software design and implementation conform to project specifications and standards. Correctness is a function of consistency, completeness, and traceability. Completeness and consistency are attributes that are measured throughout the development process, for example, through product review techniques such as walk-throughs. Traceability assesses the integrity of requirements throughout the development. There are a number of automated tools available, such as PSA/PSL and SREM that assist in the traceability process.

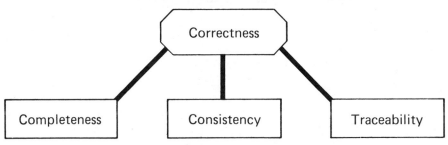

6. *Maintainability.* This is an important area from an economic viewpoint. Consider that of total software life cycle costs, the predominant cost is in the (so called) operations and maintenance (O&M) life cycle phase, as errors are corrected and improvements made to the product as user requirements evolve over time. Estimates for the life cycle cost of maintenance have ranged from 60 to 80 percent of total life cycle costs. A sound development process, resulting in a quality product, is the best insurance for maintainable software. Consistency is the most important criterion for this factor, with modularity, self-descriptiveness, document accessibility, and simplicity as the other attributes. Applicable metrics are consistency checklists, design structure, structured code, coding simplicity, modular construction, quantity and effectiveness of comments, and readability of implementation programming language.

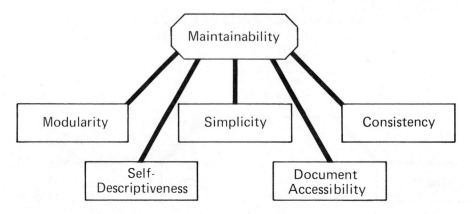

7. *Verifiability.* Verifiability deals with the capability to verify that the software design and implementation is in accordance with program specifications. Verifiability is somewhat analogous to the testability of the code. The key criteria are simplicity, modularity, test, document accessibility, and self-descriptiveness. Metrics that are applicable are design structure, complexity, coding simplicity, test checklists, quantity and effectiveness of comments, and descriptiveness of implementation programming language.

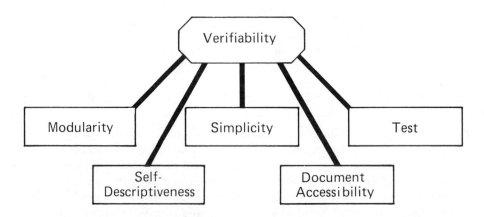

8. *Expandability.* This factor deals with the relative effort involved in increasing the capability of the software. It could take the form of increased or new performance requirements, or enhanced operation to achieve ease of use or efficiency. The attributes of significance are extensibility, generality, modularity, self-descriptiveness, and simplicity.

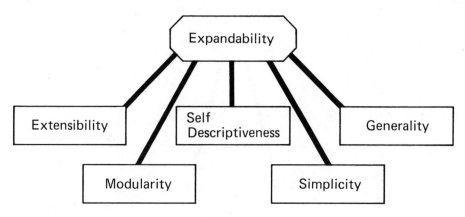

9. *Flexibility.* This factor is extremely important to the life of the software product. The requirement for flexibility is implicit for achieving the introduction of new requirements. The most important attributes are modularity, generality, self-descriptiveness, and simplicity. Applicable metrics are interfaces, generality of structure and data, extensibility, quantity and effectiveness of comments, and description of implementation programming language.

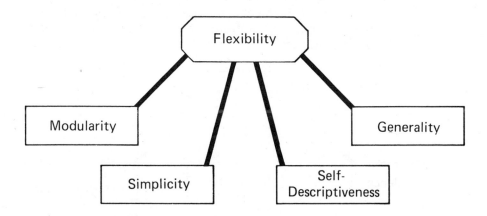

10. *Interoperability.* This factor is important in systems where there will be a high degree of interface with other systems, a condition that is of growing importance as more systems communicate with each other through local and global communications networks. Key factors are modularity, commonality, independence, and systems compatability. Metrics of importance are modular implementation, effectiveness of comments and design structure.

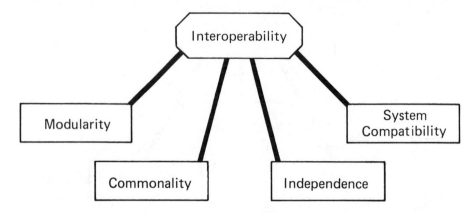

11. *Portability.* This factor deals with the relative ease with which the software can be moved to another environment (e.g., different host machine, operating system, etc.). This factor becomes important when the organization wishes to make an investment in the system such that portions of the system may be reused in new systems. In a system that is unique, such that there is little chance that the code will be "ported" to new systems this factor is of lesser or of little importance. Key attributes are modularity, self-descriptiveness, and independence. Metrics are modular implementation, quantity and effectiveness of comments, descriptiveness of implementation programming language, software system independence, and machine independence.

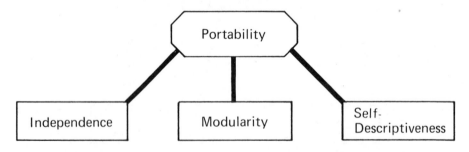

12. *Reusability.* This factor is similar to portability. The distinction is that portability measures the ability to transfer modules of code from one machine (or operating environment) to another while reusability measures the ability to move modules or code to other applications within the same operating environment. It is, therefore, a lesser requirement than portability. The applicable attributes are: application independence, independence, document accessibility, generality, modularity, self-descriptiveness, simplicity, and system clarity. Some of the key metrics are modular interface complexity, quantity and effectiveness of implementation programming language, software system independence, and machine independence.

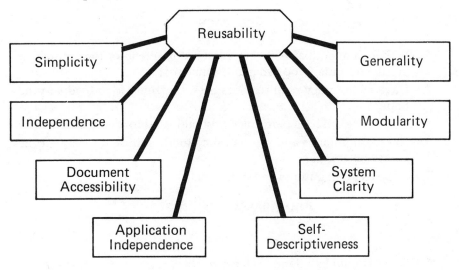

METRICS

The use of the appropriate factors and metrics is determined by the specific requirements of the project. All of the factors do not have to be applied and individual factors/metrics can be modified to customize the quality assessment of the software to the specific demands of the project. The following section provides a list of the applicable metrics. Each of the metrics is described as a set of checklists.

Access Audit

1. Are there provisions for recording and reporting all accesses to the system?
2. There should be provision for the immediate indication of access violation.

Access Control

1. Have user input/output access controls been provided? Are there data base controls? Has memory protection across tasks been implemented?
2. Are there requirements to control user input/output access in the system (e.g., user access is limited by identification and password checking)?

3. Are there requirements to control the scope of task operations during execution (e.g., tasks cannot invoke other tasks, access system registers, or use privileged commands)?

Accuracy

1. Is there a quantifiable statement of requirement for the accuracy of inputs, outputs, processing and constants?
2. Have all accuracy requirements been budgeted to individual functions?
3. Is the error analysis performed and budgeted to the module?
4. Are math libraries and numerical methods sufficient to support accuracy objectives?
5. Are execution outputs within tolerances?

Anomaly Management

Control

1. There should be a definite statement of requirement for the error tolerance of input data.
2. Is provision made for fixing errors and continuing processing? When an error condition is detected it should be passed to a calling routine.
3. Is there a range of values for items and is this checked? Are conflicting requests and illegal combinations identified and checked? Is all input data available for processing and is it checked before processing is begun?

Recoverable Computational Failures

1. Is there a statement of requirement for recovery from computational failures?
2. Are loop and multiple transfer index parameters range tested before use? Are subscripts checked? Are critical output parameters checked during processing?

Recoverable Hardware Faults

1. Is there a definite statement of requirements for recovery from hardware faults?
2. Has recovery from hardware faults been implemented?

Device Status

1. Is there a definite statement of requirements for recovery from device errors?
2. Has recovery from device errors been implemented?

Application Independence

1. Is there a requirement to limit specific references to the data base management schema?

2. Is there a standard for commenting all global data within a software unit to show where data is derived, the data's composition, and how the data is used?

3. Is there a standard for commenting all parameter input/output and local variables within a software unit which includes requirements identifying the data's composition and use?

4. Is there a requirement to localize specific references to computer architecture (e.g., specific device references localized to the executive rather than the application software)?

5. Is there a requirement to limit or avoid the use of microcode instruction statements?

6. Is there a requirement to develop functional processing algorithms such that they are not unique to the system's application?

Commonality

1. A definite statement of requirements for communications with other systems should be included.

2. Protocol standards should be established and followed.

3. There should be a single module interface for input and output.

4. There should be a definitive statement for standard data representation for communications with other systems.

5. Translation standards among representations should be established and followed and a single module should perform each translation.

Completeness

1. All inputs, processing, and outputs should be clearly and precisely defined.

2. All references should be unambiguous.

3. All defined functions should be used.

4. All referenced functions should be defined.

5. All conditions and processing should be defined for each decision point.

6. All defined and referenced calling sequence parameters should be in agreement.

7. All problems reports should have been resolved.

Consistency

1. Is there a standard design representation?

2. Are calling sequence and input/output and error conventions consistently used throughout the development?

3. Is the use of data consistent through the project? Are there standard data usage representations and naming conventions.

4. Are there consistent global, unit, and data type definitions and have they been consistently applied?

5. Is there a requirement to standardize the external input/output protocol and format for all units?

6. Is there a requirement to standardize error handling?

7. Do all references to the same function use a single, unique name?

8. Is there a requirement to standardize all data representation in the design?

9. Is there a requirement to standardize the naming of all data?

Document Accessibility

1. Is all documentation structured and written clearly and simply such that procedures, functions, algorithms, and so forth can be easily understood?

2. Does the design documentation clearly depict control and data flow (e.g., graphic portrayal with accompanying explanations or use of PDL)?

3. Is the documentation adequately indexed such that information can be easily accessed?

4. Does the documentation completely characterize the operational capabilities of the software (e.g., identify all the performance parameters and limitations)?

5. Does the documentation contain comprehensive descriptions of all system/software functions including functional processing, functional algorithms, and functional interfaces?

Effectiveness—Processing

1. Are performance requirements identified and allocated to the design?

2. Are nonloop dependent computations kept out of the loop? Are compound expressions defined more than once?

3. Are the number of memory overlays minimized?

4. Is data grouped for efficient processing? Are mix-mode expressions minimized? Are variables initialized when declared? Is data indexed or referenced for efficient processing?

5. Is there a requirement to use an optimized compiler?

Effectiveness—Storage

1. Are storage requirements allocated to the design?

2. Has the program been segmented for maximum memory utilization and is dynamic memory management utilized?

3. Has the data been packed?

4. Is there a requirement to utilize an optimized compiler?

Extensibility

1. Logical processing should be independent of storage specifications/ requirements by module. Attributes which control processing should be parametric and modules should be table driven.

2. Percent of uncommitted memory should be high—a useful goal is 100 percent availability of committed memory.

3. Percent of uncommitted speed capacity should be high—a goal is 100 percent of committed capacity.

4. There should be a requirement for spare communications channel capacity.

5. There should be requirements for interface compatibility among all the processors, communications links, memory devices, and peripherals.

Generality

1. The extent to which modules are referenced by other modules should be low in relation to the total number of modules.

2. Input, processing, and output functions should not be mixed in a single module.

3. Application and machine-dependent functions should not be mixed in a single module.

4. Processing should not be data value or volume limited.

5. All constants should be defined only once.

Independence

Software System Independence

1. The dependence on software system utility programs should be kept to a minimum. The ratio of three systems references/total LOC should be low.
2. A common standard language should be used.
3. The dependence on software system library routines should be low.
4. The software should be free from operating systems references.

Machine Independence

1. The programming language selected should be a common language available on other machines.
2. The software should be free from input/output references.
3. Code should be independent from code and character size.
4. Data representation should not be dependent on the machine.

Degree of Independence

1. The number of modules that are changed as changes are made to the software system should be minimized. Thus the ratio of number of modules changed/total number of modules should be a minimum across an average of changes.

Modularity

1. The structure of the design and software should be hierarchical in a top down structure (e.g., top down design).
2. All modules should represent one function. Modules should not share temporary storage.
3. There should be requirements among the modules to minimize content, common, and external coupling among software entities.

Operability

1. All steps of the operation should be described.
2. All error conditions and responses should be described to the operator. Have provisions been made for the operator to interrupt, obtain status, save, modify and continue processing?
3. Is the number of operator actions reasonable? Are job set up and tear down procedures described?
4. Are hard copy log interactions maintained?
5. Are there requirements to provide simple and consistent operator messages and require simple and consistent operator responses

(i.e., minimize the number of operator message and response formats; use the same format types throughout the system)?

6. Are there requirements to provide the operator/systems the capability to obtain specific system (or network) resource status information and to reallocate resources?

7. Are there requirements to provide the operator/user the capability to select different nodes for different types of processing or for retrieval of information?

8. Are there requirements to make system implementation details transparent to the user (e.g., the user can access a file without knowing its location in the system/network)?

9. Are there requirements to provide the user options for input media (e.g., terminal, tape drive, etc.)?

10. Are there requirements to provide the user with output control (e.g., choosing specific outputs, output media, etc.)?

11. Are there requirements for all error messages to clearly identify the nature of the error to the user?

12. Are there requirements to establish a standard (common) user command language for network information and data access?

Self-Descriptiveness

1. Modules should have standard formatted prologue comments which describe: module name and version number, author, date, purpose, inputs, outputs, function, assumptions, limitations and restrictions, accuracy requirements, error recovery procedures, and references.

2. A standard format for organizations of modules should be defined.

3. Comments should be set off from code in a uniform manner. All transfers of control and destinations and all machine dependent code should be commented.

4. Comments should be meaningful—they should not merely repeat the language operation.

Descriptiveness of Implementation Programming Language

1. All nonstandard HOL statements and attributes of all declared variables should be commented.

2. The ratio of HOL to non-HOL should be high—preferably the non-HOL usage should be zero.

3. Variable names should be descriptive. Source code should be logically blocked and indented.

4. There should be one statement per line.

Simplicity

Design Structure

1. Is the design organized in a top down manner? Module flow should be from top to bottom.
2. Are all modules independent?
3. Do module descriptions include input, output, processing, and limitations?
4. Does each module have a single entry and exit point?
5. Is the data base properly compartmented?
6. There should not be duplicative functions.
7. A programming standard should be established with the requirement for structured code.

Code Simplicity

1. There should be no jumps in and out of loops and loop indexes should not be modified. The module should not be self-modifying.
2. The nesting levels, number of branches and number of GOTOs should be minimized.
3. The number of variables to executable statements should be kept to a manageable minimum. There should be unique names for variables and single use of variables.
4. There should be no extraneous code or mixed mode expressions.

System Clarity

1. Are there requirements to isolate input/output functions from computational functions?
2. Are input/output functions isolated from computational functions?
3. Top level modules should perform unique functions (i.e., similar functions are not performed within different top level modules which could be restricted to one module).

System Compatibility

1. Are there requirements for this system to use the same communication protocol as the interoperating system(s)?
2. Are there requirements for common interpretation of the content in all messages sent from and received by this system and by the interoperating system(s) (e.g., all variables in the message have the same meaning)?

3. Are there requirements for this system to use the same structure and sequence for message contents as the interoperating system(s)?

4. Are there requirements for this system to use the same data format as the interoperating system(s) (e.g., all real variables as 16 bits in length)?

5. Are there requirements for this system to establish the same data base structure as the interoperating system(s) (e.g., all systems use a relational data base management system)?

6. Are there requirements for this system to establish the same data base access techniques as the interoperating system(s)?

7. Are there requirements for this system to use the same operating system as the interoperating system(s)?

8. Are there requirements for this system to use the same support software as the interoperating system?

Test

1. The number of paths tested should correspond to the number of total paths that exist in the software product. All input parameters should be boundary tested.

2. All module interfaces should be tested. All performance requirements should be tested.

3. All modules should be tested. Test inputs and outputs should be summarized.

Traceability

1. Cross checking of requirements to related modules should be checked. Requirements should flow down into subsequent levels of documentation. Duplicative requirements should not exist, and each lower level requirement should be traceable to the requirements specification.

Training

1. Have lesson plans/training materials been developed for operators, users, and maintenance personnel?

2. Realistic simulated exercises should be provided for.

3. Is there sufficient "help" and diagnostic information available on time?

4. Are there requirements to provide selectable levels of aid and guidance for systems users of different levels of expertise?

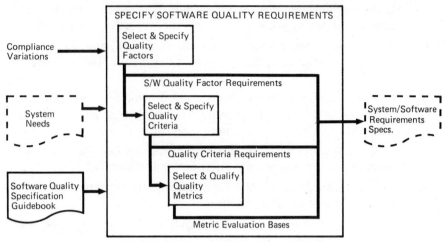

Figure 8-3. Specification of quality factors.

LIFE CYCLE APPLICATION

Evaluating software quality is part of the larger process of software quality management. The process has two major parts: quality specification and software quality evaluation. Quality specification must be introduced early in the development process, in the generation of systems and software requirements. Software quality evaluation is part of the ongoing process of evaluation—through the observation and review techniques that are discussed elsewhere in this book. The planning for software quality metrics is an important part of the planning process and must be undertaken early and with the same vigor as the other phases of planning.

The key to the process starts with the proper selection of quality factors, criteria, and appropriate metrics. Figure 8-3 depicts this cycle. The first step is the selection of quality factors. As previously stated, in all probability each project will not use all the factors. The selection of factors will differ depending on the specific requirements of the program. Table 8-3 indicates the considerations that must be made for different factors. For example, if the system will have an unusually long life cycle use, maintainability and expandability are critical factors, while in a system that may be life critical such as an aircraft avionics system, correctness and reliability are key considerations.

Where all factors are used care must be exercised to prioritize the factors so that they do not represent duplicating requirements. Table 8-4 depicts the interrelationship of software quality factors. For example, if efficiency is a strong requirement, maintainability may be degraded in order to produce a more compact program with minimal storage requirements. Tables 8-3 and 8-4 can be employed to guide the developer in the preparation of quality factor requirements. For example, in a space flight system with hu-

APPLICATION/ENVIRONMENT CHARACTERISTICS	SOFTWARE QUALITY FACTORS
Human lives affected	Integrity Reliability Correctness Verifiability
Longlife cycle	Maintainability Expandability
Experimental system or high rate of change	Flexibility
Experimental technology in hardware design	Portability
Many changes over life cycle	Flexibility Reusability Expandability
Real time application	Efficiency Reliability Correctness
On-board computer application	Efficiency Reliability Correctness
Processing of classified information	Integrity
Interrelated systems	Interoperability

TABLE 8-3.   Quality considerations.

mans onboard, the areas (from Table 8-3) which could be of extreme importance are:

Human lives affected:	Integrity Reliability Correctness Verifiability
Real time application:	Efficiency Reliability Correctness
On-board computer application:	Efficiency Reliability Correctness

ACQUISITION CONCERN / QUALITY FACTOR SPECIFIED	PERFORMANCE				DESIGN			ADAPTATION				
QUALITY FACTOR AFFECTED →	EFFICIENCY	INTEGRITY	RELIABILITY	USABILITY	CORRECTNESS	MAINTAINABILITY	VERIFIABILITY	EXPANDABILITY	FLEXIBILITY	INTEROPERABILITY	PORTABILITY	REUSABILITY
PERFORMANCE — EFFICIENCY	▨					↓	↓				↓	
INTEGRITY	↓	▨										
RELIABILITY	↓		▨	↑								
USABILITY	↓			▨		↑	↑					
DESIGN — CORRECTNESS					▨	↑	↑	↑	↑			↑
MAINTAINABILITY	↓					▨	↑	↑	↑			↑
VERIFIABILITY	↓						▨					
ADAPTATION — EXPANDABILITY	↓	↓						▨		↑		
FLEXIBILITY	↓	↓	↓						▨	↑		
INTEROPERABILITY	↓	↓	↓							▨		
PORTABILITY	↓										▨	
REUSABILITY	↓	↓	↓			↑				↑	↑	▨

↑ = Positive Effect   ↓ = Negative Effect   BLANK = None or Application Dependent

TABLE 8-4. Software quality interrelationships.

Using a simple algorithm the population of factors presents a natural weighting for the factors as follows:

Reliability	3
Correctness	3
Efficiency	2
Integrity	1
Verifiability	1

A further weighting could be applied by determining, for example, that human lives affected is the most important factor, thus the factors associated with this characteristic can be increased in priority, say by an additional increment. Thus, the following order and weighting would be:

Reliability	4
Correctness	4
Efficiency	2
Verifiability	2
Integrity	2

Thus, verifiability and integrity are increased in importance on par with efficiency, while reliability and correctness are double the other factors. Additional weighting may be used to take into account the interrelationships between quality factors. Efficiency appears to be the most affected factor, having a negative effect on integrity, reliability and verifiability. The only other factor that is enhanced is verifiability (by correctness). On the basis of this interrelationship, efficiency could be downgraded in importance, or the relationship could be noted for consideration in the concluding evaluation.

The selection of criteria follows from the factors that have been selected. The following criteria are indicated:

Efficiency—processing/storage
Access control
Access audit
Accuracy
Anomaly management
Simplicity
Completeness
Consistency
Traceability
Modularity
Self-descriptiveness

Note that the only criterion that appears twice is simplicity (in reliability and verifiability). On examination, it could be determined/decided that access audit and audit control are not critical in this system—thus in the interest of cost economy they may be deleted. This has the effect of eliminating integrity, the only model with these two criteria. Other trade-offs should be accomplished to determine the final selection of criteria. The individual metrics should be evaluated in similar manner until a final set is selected. Once accomplished, the quality requirements, including evaluation requirements are recorded in the systems requirements specification.

Metrics may be of two distinct types: predictive in nature or anomaly detecting. While the end evaluation of the assessment of quality is important to benchmark the product for operational and contractual purposes, the predictive nature of metrics is important to the effective development of the

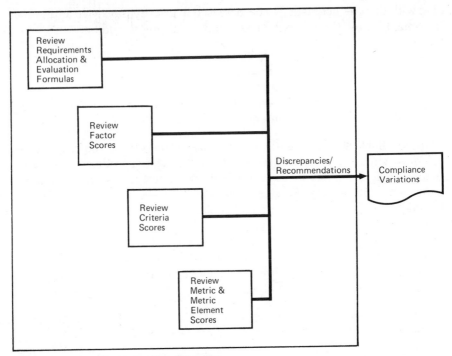

Figure 8-4. Quality evaluation life cycle.

software product. It is important to single out the predictive metrics as a subset of the quality assessment process, for example, if the design has little storage capacity, the end product expandability will be limited. The process chapter intent was to evaluate the "process" and thus this chapter tends to be predictive in nature. As the evaluation proceeds alongside the development a predictive score results at appropriate milestones. As a part of the selection process, those metrics that are predictive should be identified. This subset could then be used to develop a predictive evaluation at appropriate milestones in the development process.

QUALITY ASSESSMENT

Once the evaluation factors, criteria, and metrics are selected, and quality requirements included in the requirements specification, the procedure for evaluation must be put into place. Figure 8-4 shows the life cycle process associated with the evaluation process. It is not critical that the personnel involved in specification be synonymous with those who will be involved in monitoring and evaluation. In fact they should not be identical. The setting of quality requirements is a high level systems function, while monitoring is a life cycle function that should be performed with personnel of appropriate skill level.

Evaluation techniques, discussed in Chapter 10, provide the life cycle activities for collecting metrics. In order to ensure collection and evaluation, a specific organizational element must be charged with the responsibility. This organization could be within the developing organization, however, if this is the case, a degree of independence should be assured. The most likely organizational element is the contractor quality assurance organization or an IV&V activity. In either case the specific responsibility should be assigned early in the systems process so that evaluation is included and will take place along with other development activities. If an IV&V contractor is to be used, contract negotiations should be made early to ensure contractor participation in the requirements analysis process. Several organizations may be involved in collecting data, and their efforts need to be coordinated to ensure a cooperative effort.

Each metric should be reduced to a quantifiable number. A simple example is structured code. A one (1) could be used as an indication that structured code is applied, while a zero (0) could be used if not. Or a range could be established—say from one to six, where six indicates perfect compliance with structured code standards established for the project while a zero indicates just the opposite. The weighted accumulation of these scores provides an overall metric of the software product.

SUMMARY

The use of metrics to arrive at an overall quality score is a dynamic process. As previously stated it depends on the specific requirements of the system and the particular phase of development. While it was not feasible to present a more detailed description of the metrics and the process, the presentation, which has been geared to quality management and general management personnel, will help determine the applicability and specific use of metrics in software development.

PART
III

SPECIAL TOPICS IN SOFTWARE QUALITY MANAGEMENT

9

PROJECT DATA: MANAGEMENT, PRODUCTION AND CONTROL

The effective control of data in the project infrastructure is the means by which quality is "built in" the software. The elements of the infrastructure are integrated through the documentation and data products produced in the project.

DATA CONTROL

Data control focuses on the life cycle "data" products of the development project, including the software product itself which is in a sense "data" or a paper product. Unlike hardware, software is entirely data sensitive, that is, the manifestation of the project is concentrated on visibility into the data products. This is, of course, somewhat true in hardware—based on the various engineering drawings and specifications that must be produced before the first mold is poured or piece of metal cut. Hardware, however, comes together in physical form early in the development process producing physical objects which may be touched, counted, stored, and so forth. Thus, hardware development is much more akin to the industrial history of human experience. Software breaks that development tradition—substituting mathematical form for physical entity. Thus the development of software becomes focused on the expression of that form—the data products of the project.

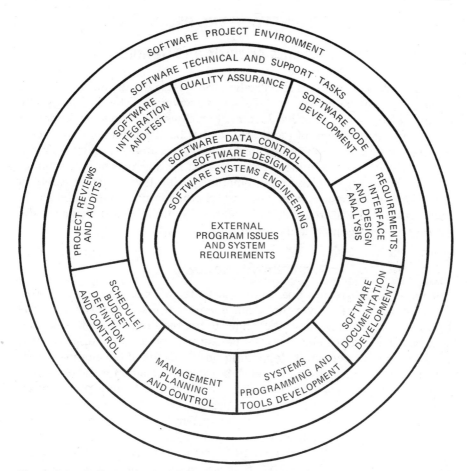

Figure 9-1. Software project infrastructure relationship.

The rigorous control of data within a software project is essential to the production of a quality product. It is the heart of the software infrastructure; the center of all development activity. The effectiveness of the project data flow, as illustrated in Figure 9-1, and the adequacy of the controls in the project technical development and external environment are primary determinants of project productivity and quality.

The software project must provide control over all the data which meets the following criteria:

1. The data product has been approved through an informal or formal review or through a predefined "quality gate."
2. The data product is used by more than one organizational element in the project or in the production of more than one data product.

DOCUMENTATION END PRODUCTS

Requirements Analysis and Definition

The software requirements specification (SRS) is clearly the most important document from the software developer's viewpoint. The SRS is usually compiled from a higher order document, such as a system specification or some form of statement of requirements that has been prepared by a customer (or user). The SRS should be unambiguous and controlled from the very start of the development process. That is, the collection of requirements, and changes to the requirements specification, must be carefully controlled since changes infer cost and schedule impact to the product. In many cases software requirements boards are organized to formalize the process of requirements management.

Requirements Review Board

The requirements review board is a board often used to impose a degree of formality and control over the requirements process. The function of the board is to review and control changes to the requirements of the system. This board is composed of key user personnel, and is often supplemented by development personnel depending on the status of development contract selection. It is extremely useful, if not prerequisite, for the developer to participate in this board since he has the best understanding of the impact of changes to system costs and schedules. This board is most often used in the front end of the system—when the system is being conceived and requirements are being defined—and is most useful in situations where requirements are volatile. The board transitions in responsibility to the Configuration Control Board (CCB) as the system is developed and baselines are defined. The board will not be discussed further in this chapter. It is mentioned here for completeness since it can be an extremely useful tool in large and complex development projects.

In large or complex software development projects, the system specification is the top level requirements document for the development of the system. Software requirements are derived from the system specification and are allocated to specific software and hardware subsystems. In smaller projects the system specification may suffice for the software requirements specification, particularly when the system is predominantly a software system and hardware development is minimal.

The operational concept document describes the way the system will be used in operational practice. Whether an operational military system or a commercial banking operation the "ops concept" will eventually be required. This document is an important one to produce early in the development since it forces the user to come to grips with the sociological implication of automation, for example, the change of procedure for a pilot of an airplane or a teller in a bank. It also has the effect of providing a sobering effect on the requirements specification process. The requirements document can be a wish list and the task of sorting out real requirements from desirable but unnecessary requirements usually falls on the developer and adds time and cost to the development process.

The software development plan which describes the management process that the developer intends to employ in the software development process, describes, in a top level manner, the configuration management concept, the quality assurance approach, the testing approach and possible use of independent testing organizations, development milestones, development organizational resources and structure, types of personnel that will be employed, facilities, software development procedures, controls that will be employed and documentation requirements. The software development plan forces the manager to describe how he or she will manage, what resources he or she will employ, and what procedures will be used. It is a top level document describing what will be accomplished and how the process of software development will be managed and controlled. The software development plan will normally be backed up by more detailed plans depending on the size and complexity of the project, that describe how specific areas of the project will be implemented.

The software configuration management plan begins with the concept in the software development plan and describes the project configuration management system. It contains the description of the organization for carrying out configuration management, a description of configuration management activities of identification, control and reporting (auditing) and more importantly, the process of baselining. Usually there will be a configuration management system in place, and the software development plan will customize the configuration management system to the peculiar requirements of the specific development. The software development plan describes what the CM system must do, the CM plan describes how. In a complex contractual environment where many contractors, or groups, may be involved, the configuration plan should discuss how configuration management will be implemented uniformly across the system.

The software quality assurance plan should relate the procedures that will be employed to ensure a quality product. The plan complements the other plans of the project. The QA plan is used in some organizations to describe the activities of a separate QA group. While this is a useful activity, the approach that is taken in this book (as already stated) is that software quality assurance is endemic to the entire development process and must be the concern of all. As such, QA personnel complement the development team and the rest of the personnel involved in the development. This document focuses on software quality assurance practices that are not already described in other documents.

Interface requirements will be found in any development project to some degree. The extent and complexity of the development environment will dictate whether or not a separate interface document will be produced. Generally there are two reasons for producing a stand alone interface document. First, the system may be a complex one where the interfaces are numerous and separate treatment will ensure effective management and control of the interfaces. Secondly, there may be many organizations involved in the development process and a separate document can be effectively employed to manage the interfaces between the various organizations. In programs that are of a less complex nature, various other documents can be employed (design specifications) to document interface requirements and design implementation. The interface document details the interface requirements to include hardware-to-software and software-to-software requirements and the means by which the interfaces are validated.

The software standards and procedures manual documents the specific software development practices and procedures that will be used in the development process. As such it complements the software development plan and the software quality assurance plan. It details the use of various software tools to help in the design and development process, the use of specific design methodologies, the use of a program design language, programming standards and conventions for high level and detailed design, coding practices, the use of software development folders, and the criteria for the selection of computer software components and units. It will also detail interface conventions for subroutine usage and data base.

Top Level Design Phase

The software top level design document is the primary product of this phase. The top level design is a translation of requirements to a functional design. It decomposes all the requirements and assigns them to specific modules or components of the system for further design (detailed) and implementation. The top level design document considers functional flow, data requirements, interrupts, performance requirements, such as memory allocation and timing, inputs and outputs, interfaces between the top level modules, and special processing requirements, such as control features, error handling, and so on.

The software test plan describes the overall (top level) test plan for a particular software system or subsystem. It may detail the software test for the entire system if the system contains only one major subsystem. If there are a number of major subsystems there will be a commensurate number of individual test plans. The plan details the total scope of software testing including formal and informal testing. Generally informal testing is conducted on the unit and sub-subsystem levels and formal testing conducted on each major subsystem. This approach keeps commitment of resources to a reasonable level as formal testing involves a test team with considerable resources. In addition, informal testing (by the developer) helps ensure that a suitable degree of component integrity is present prior to beginning formal testing. The document details the specific tests that will be conducted, who will conduct the tests, who will monitor and review test results, the methods to document test results, and the criteria to decide when a test is completed.

While the two documents just discussed are the primary products of this phase, there are other documents that may be required and can be initiated at this time. They are the computer system operator's manual and the software user's manual. The computer system operator's manual contains general operating procedures for the operator, such as system start-up, operating procedures, diagnostic procedures, recovery procedures, and so forth. The software user's manual deals primarily with the software of the system and is required when there is a great deal of interaction between the user and the software of the system. It contains information about the software itself, specifically the interface between the user and the software; that is, operating instructions, such as system initialization, operator inputs, options, execution instructions, error instructions, and so on. While it may not be possible, nor desirable, to complete these documents during this phase of the project, it is important to begin them so that important information is captured and these documents are not relegated to the aftermath of development.

Detailed Design Phase

The most important document of this phase is the detailed design document. This document contains all the information about the system so that implementation (coding and unit testing) can begin. If accomplished correctly, it complements the top level design document (in fact, it should build on the top level design document so that an integral design document results) so that taken together they provide an accurate description of the complete software system design. This document details the decomposition of requirements to all levels of the hierarchy, a description of the interfaces between all units and external interfaces, and a description of each unit in terms of its inputs, outputs, interface requirements, performance requirements, data requirements, error handling, and special algorithm requirements.

The data base design document establishes the design of the data base in support of each major software system, usually at the major software subsystem level. The document describes the physical contents and structure of the data base, the relationship between files of the data base, and the interfaces with the DBMS and the other CSCI's. In a less complex system this information can be inserted in the top level design document.

·If a separate interface requirements document was created an interface design document may be used. This document pulls into one place all of the details of the interfaces that are captured in the top level and detailed design documents, and is useful in a large system development.

Detailed test plans and test procedures are prepared for each major software subsystem. This document/documents detail test preparation, inputs, initialization, output data, and the criteria for evaluating results of the test. Test procedures detail procedures for conducting a test, such as the location, time, personnel involved, equipment preparation, software preparation, data collection reduction and analysis, and provisions for reporting the test results.

If the purpose of the software system is to support computer programming, for example a compiler system, then a software programmer's manual is required. This manual details usage procedures for the programmer including the operational structure of the system, the equipment configuration, programming features, such as data formats, addressing schemes, the syntax of the language, special registers and words, program instructions, input/output provisions, and programming examples.

Coding and Unit Testing Phase

The primary product of this phase is source and compiled/assembled code. These are entered into a controlled baseline in preparation for formal integration and testing. At this point all software test plans and procedures should be completed.

Integration and Test Phase

This is the final phase of the development prior to delivering a fully tested and validated product. The products of this phase are all of the documents that have been prepared during the development process which will be delivered with the software product. The two primary documents that are prepared during this phase are the software product specification and the software test report.

The software product specification is a compilation of all of the specifications prepared during development along with the delivered source and object code. These documents include the design documents, the interface design document, the data base design document, and any other appropriate documents that add to the description of the product.

The software test report records the results of a test for each major software system. It should contain the description of the test, the test history, detailed test results, the results of test analysis and evaluation, and any recommendations.

DATA RELATIONSHIPS

As illustrated in Figure 9-2, the relationships between the formal documentation on a project and the development life cycle can be viewed as hierar-

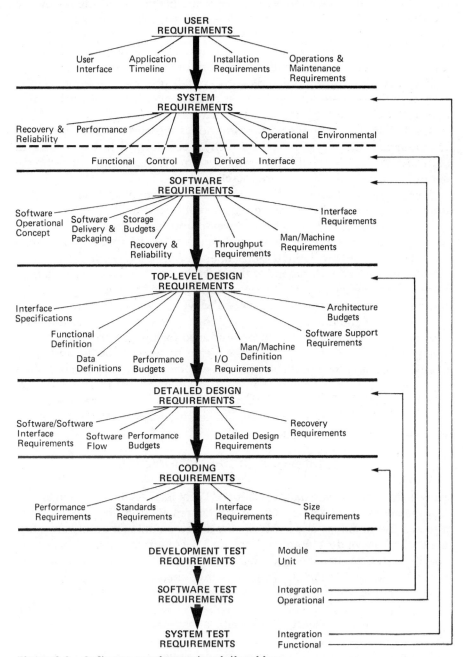

Figure 9-2. Software requirements relationships.

193

chical, tracing the development phases of the life cycle and the review requirements of the contract, and the development relationships in the program.

At the top level, the specification of user and top level project development requirements provides the basic definition of the system. This definition, produced during the early (conceptual) phase of the project is the responsibility of the customer. It must be complete, technically achievable and accurately reflect the needs and objectives of the application. The major product at this level, the system specification, translates user and developer requirements into a system level design to be allocated to hardware and software. At this level, the program, system management and technical control policies and practices are established.

The second level contains the technical, development and planning documents which establish software requirements and define the infrastructure to be used to define design, develop and qualify the software. The tools, techniques, methodologies, and standards to be applied to the software development are defined. Subsequent levels of the hierarchy deal specifically with the development of the software system (and sub-systems). Here the engineering data developed and produced provides the description of the process and end products of development consistent with the software requirements specification and the top level systems specification.

A documentation tree should be produced for the project based on the model of Figure 9-3. It will provide the means by which visibility and traceability into the system and software development process are established and maintained. Poor quality of any document in the chain, or documents which are incompatible with project standards or technical requirements, breaks the "quality chain" and will impact the quality and success of the project.

Engineering Data Relationships

How is this engineering data developed? What is it? As illustrated in Figure 9-4, the engineering data is any output that results from the application of a project methodology and is used in the development of the software. During each phase of development there are a set of inputs which describe the specific technical characteristics that will be used to produce the data products through application of a project methodology.

For example, the system requirements are, in reality, an ordered set of many different categories of requirements. As part of the development process, these must be allocated to specific subsystems and data products of the infrastructure to support an ordered, hierarchical development process.

Once the inputs are ordered, technical analysis results in a set of engineering outputs. During the requirements definition phase a requirements synopsis is produced for each specific set or category of requirements—user, interface, performance, operational, delivery, and so forth. During

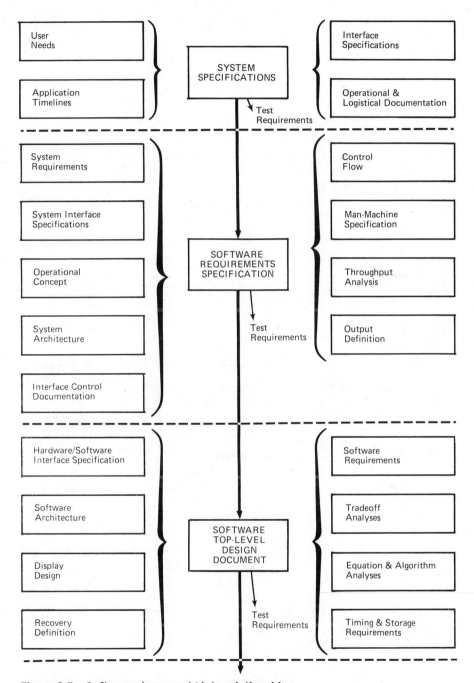

Figure 9-3. Software document/data relationships.

(continued on next page).

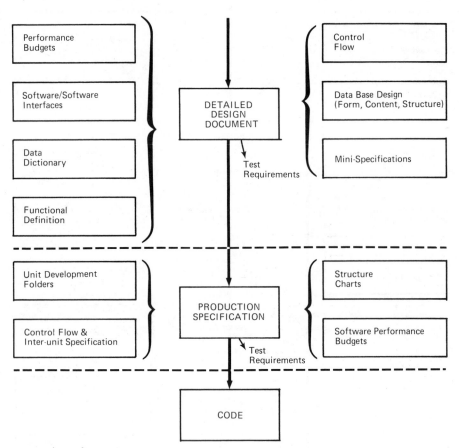

Figure 9-3. Continued.

the top level or functional design stage the requirements are decomposed into a set of functional specifications which may be expressed, at the lowest level of decomposition, as a program design language description of the functional design of the software. The output from these activities is a logical design description, possibly expressed in a program design language. The various levels of integration and test also have specific data products which are used to transition from test phase to test phase.

Data actually exists at various levels of technical development, each of which is used at different levels of documentation. These require that quality standards be flexible depending on the specific data level. The requirements set is an ordered list of requirements described in a specific way according to the standards for the project. The functional design may be described as a "mini-spec," which is a program design language representation of the functional design for the software. The intermediate data products, for example, data flow diagrams, are the means by which the mini-spec is defined. The intermediate data products which lead to a detailed design are the structure charts which are used to describe the design.

The engineering data products which bridge the development activities build-up into the project documentation and are what are used to describe the requirements, design, and as build versions of the software.

The documentation development process is critical to the success of the software project, development productivity, and the quality and usefulness of the software product. From a quality perspective, there are three factors which affect the documentation process:

1. Focusing the software infrastructure towards the efficient production of quality documentation which satisfies specific requirements of the program and the expectations of the document recipient.
2. The predefinition of documentation contents and development of detailed "style guides" which detail the exact requirements of each document section.
3. The control of data quality as the building blocks of the deliverable documentation.

The production of quality documentation taxes all areas of the project and is exercised in all areas of the project. Production of quality documentation requires that each individual segment of the infrastructure be preplanned, tailored to specific project needs; implemented, integrated, and coordinated through program and project level management controls; and that quality data flows smoothly between organizations and development activities.

The document production process starts with development and negotiation with personnel who will use the documentation as well as personnel who will develop the document. This "style guide" negotiation is critical. It ensures that:

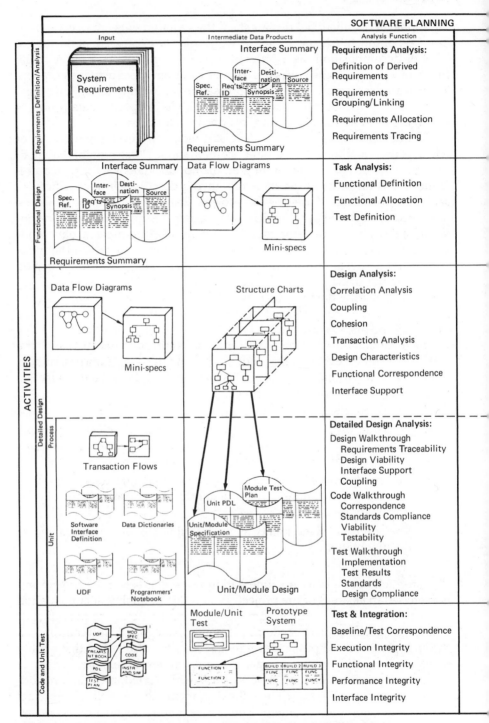

Figure 9-4. Software data and document development relationships.

TASKS		
Outputs	Data Products	Documentation
Requirements Summaries Requirements Allocation Requirements Matrix Interface Definition Performance Summary	**Recovery:** User Requirements System Requirements Interface Software Requirements	Software Test Plan Software Requirements Specification
Data Flow Diagrams Task Sequence Diagrams Mini-specs Mode Analysis Integration Test Plans/Procedures	**Control Flow:** Functional Definition Data Delivery Data Base Design Interface	Data Base Software Top-level Design Document Software Test Plan
Structure Charts Transaction Flows Software Interface Definition Data Dictionaries Module Specification Unit Development Folders Programmers' Notebooks Test Scenarios/Data Build Test Plans	**Mini-specs:** Process Design Control Flow Performance Budget	
Module Specifications Program Design Language (PDL)/Code Unit/Module Test Plans Unit Development Folders Programmers' Notebooks Test Results	Unit Development Folder Programmers' Notebooks	Software Test Procedures Software Detailed Design Specification
Integrated Software Data Base Final Documentation Test Results	**Module Design:** Code Products Test Data	Users' Manual Software Product Specification Software Test Report

1. The specific document content is predefined ensuring that the end document meets the standards and needs of the project.

2. The document recipient is apprised of and agrees with what will be included in the document before any work is done on developing the text.

3. The developer of the document knows what must be included in each of the document "building blocks" and how to integrate these into a section consistent with approved document requirements.

From these approved "style guides" specific quality criteria may be developed for each document. The measure of document quality is how closely the document satisfies predefined project requirements not how complete or esoteric it appears from an engineering perspective.

All approved style guides should be controlled at the project level through the facilities of the program support library.

Based on the requirements of the style guide the tools, techniques, methodologies and specific content requirements to be applied to development and evaluation of each individual component of the document are defined. The specific requirements establish the environment necessary to produce the individual data elements required for each project document. Production of the materials, and control of the process should be in conformance with program configuration management and control practices. All data should be resident in the PSL and subject to the quality gates defined for the project. Under this structure, production of quality documentation compliant with the requirements of the program and software project is a matter of combining and restructuring existing technical and engineering data—not creating new documentation.

SOFTWARE CONFIGURATION MANAGEMENT

Software configuration management and control is the vehicle by which project data is managed and controlled. As illustrated in Figure 9-5, configuration management is the *identification* of all products of development, the *control* of those products, and the *audit* of the project to ensure compliance with the procedures of the configuration management system. It is the means by which all components of the project are brought together through the data being produced. The control disciplines that configuration management provide ensure that approved project data is not violated by uncontrolled and undisciplined updates. It ensures that traceability is maintained throughout the development and that all segments of the project infrastructure use current, valid and controlled data. Without effective configuration management the project infrastructure will collapse.

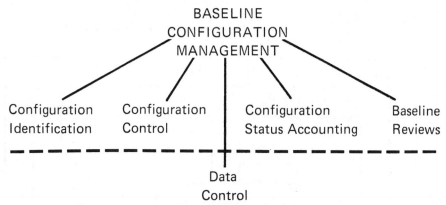

Figure 9-5. Software configuration management relationships.

The configuration management (CM) of software is in two separate segments: baseline and project. Each of these is similar in function, responsibility, control and data control responsibilities.

1. *Baseline.* Baseline configuration management and control ensures that formally approved and released versions of all software documentation, software and test results are controlled and that the application is traceable to the requirements.
2. *Project.* Control of project approved requirements, design, code, build and test parameters which are not necessarily approved by the customer or user of the system.

Baseline Management

Baseline management is the establishment of specific reference points to effect traceability to previous baselines, that is, to ensure that the product being built is, indeed, the product desired. Baseline configuration management is implemented by the program organization rather than the software project organization.

Baseline Management—Identification of Controlled Data

As illustrated in Figure 9-6, the role of baseline configuration management is to establish a common technical relationship between the developer and buyer or end user of the system. This commonality is established through the data products approved by the customer during the development process. The implications of this function to the quality of the end product are enormous. With effective identification of approved data, and careful, controlled changes to these products, assurance that the user's requirements are met is achieved.

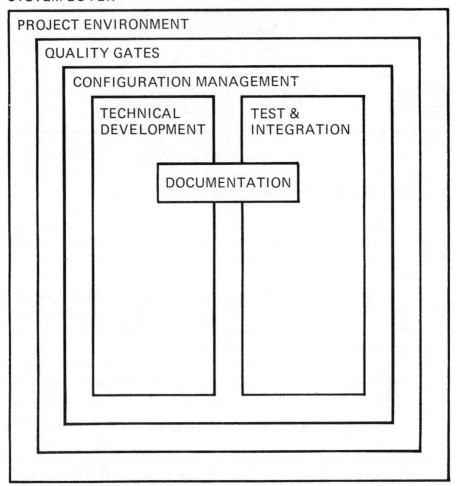

SYSTEM BUYER

PROJECT ENVIRONMENT

QUALITY GATES

CONFIGURATION MANAGEMENT

TECHNICAL DEVELOPMENT

TEST & INTEGRATION

DOCUMENTATION

Figure 9-6. Document relationships.

Accurately identifying what has been approved by a customer through individual data items to ensure that the technical products reflect user expectations is often a complex task. It presupposes an ability on the part of the user to specify in a nonambiguous fashion exactly what is desired. It also assumes that, on an end item basis, the customer and program can accurately relate and trace both data and documentation from baseline to baseline. The third key assumption in implementing baseline management is that there is, in the customer and program organization, sufficient expertise to adequately assess the integrity of data products and proposed changes to these products. This assumption is not always valid.

Baseline Configuration Management—Control of Approved Data

The formal approval of data products at a review establishes the various project baselines or authorizes the incorporation of a series of changes into the approved baselines. The role of baseline SCM is to provide the administrative mechanism for establishing project baselines and initiating, preparing, evaluating, and approving or disapproving all change proposals to customer or program approved data throughout the software lifecycle.

SCM controls software or system end items that have been completed. These end items are in three categories:

1. *Baseline Specification Documentation*   Documentation approved by the customer that specifies the requirements for the software configuration or describes the technical characteristics of the as-built system.
2. *Support Documents*   Documents approved by the customer which describe how the software is to be developed.
3. *Technical Data*   Data approved through either customer or project reviews and require customer approval or review to modify.

SCM systematically controls changes to approved configurations and maintains the integrity and traceability of the approved data products configuration throughout the development life cycle.

Changes to the software system/subsystem may be initiated in response to a variety of events:

1. *Software Deficiencies*   An existing software baseline may be found to be inadequate or incorrect by design, implementation, assumption, or for other reasons.
2. *Hardware Changes*   Problems with hardware components and interfaces among hardware subsystems may yield to solution only through software modifications.
3. *New Operational Requirements*   The ground rules for the software system's operation may be modified; for example, a performance mandate may be reduced or enhanced in scope.
4. *Economic Savings*   Means for effecting cost savings may be determined, or lower development or operating costs may require software modifications.
5. *Schedule Accommodations*   A system/subsystem implementation schedule (for hardware, software, or facilities) may be accelerated or a preestablished implementation schedule may be found to be nonachievable.

Unless a formal means is implemented to control these changes they will quickly cause traceability to be lost. The system being built will not match the approved requirements of the system. The software will be inconsistent with the requirements, and interfaces with other parts of the system will be lost. Formal and effective change control ensures the integrity of program and user support.

Configuration Control Board

The organizational body within the system organization responsible for formal processing of proposed changes to established baselines is the configuration control board (CCB). The CCB reviews, evaluates, approves or disapproves, and releases major technical and nontechnical alterations to system components, both hardware and software, and all baseline specifications. All of these changes will require customer review and acceptance, and could possibly lead to contract changes if the scope of the effort is effected. The CCB consists of representatives from throughout the project.

Changes to documentation, application programs, and support software are reviewed and approved by the CCB before they are made. The CCB interacts with the engineering organization through established project level configuration control practices. These project level practices control released code and documentation that are under investigation and/or being redone but which have not been approved by the program or customer. This joint responsibility should continue until the initiating software performance report, problem report, or change request is officially closed.

Software Configuration Review Board

The software configuration review board (SCRB) reviews and evaluates all the proposed changes to the software or system baselines and the processing/disposition of system problem reports (SPRs). The SCRB differs from the CCB in that it primarily deals with internally controlled data rather than customer or program approved baselines, although on large projects it is conceivable, and even advantageous to have the SCRB act as a subboard. Changes that effect program baselines are transmitted to the CCB after review by the SCRB, unless of course the SCRB is acting for the CCB.

The SCRB is a software board. As required, the SCRB membership may include:

Software technical manager, chairperson
Software development manager
Software technical task leaders
Test and evaluation representative
Systems engineering representative
Project office representative
System software representative

Quality assurance representative

PSL librarian (recorder)

Other representatives, such as product manager and marketing representatives, who have an input to product integration.

Change Control Processing

Formal change control is the means by which correspondence between customer expectations and development realities are maintained. The baseline change control process can be considered to have three basic parts:

1. *Initiation of Change Requests*   Changes to a project's contractual item can be requested by any project personnel, by the customer, or by an interfacing contractor.

2. *Review of Change Requests*   All change requests initiated within a project are initially reviewed at the lowest possible approval level within the project. If the problem described in the request is minor and does not affect other areas of baseline items, corrective action is implemented at the lowest possible level of review. Problems that are more serious and have far-reaching impact require higher levels of review. The precise levels for various kinds of changes depend on the size and structure of the project.

3. *Implementation of Approved Changes*   If approved, a requested change is implemented. This may require changing the software product, its documentation, or both, and may also involve changes to the contract.

PROGRAM SUPPORT LIBRARY

The program support library (PSL) is the administrative mechanism which controls baselines and processes changes. The PSL maintains established project baselines, and monitors and controls the development of project baselines and project data products.

The PSL responsibilities consist of:

1. Technical control and project monitoring of baseline content and quality.

2. Organizational facilities for baselining and controlling the content of structure or software products.

3. Reporting procedures for software design or implementation issues and documentation of library contents of data products.

Software products to be controlled consist of documentation, source code, executable code, and status records for all major software elements. These software elements are categorized and compartmentalized within the PSL. The four levels of PSL compartmentalization are:

1. *Working Data*   All nonapproved software and documentation under development.
2. *Controlled Project Data*   All configuration controlled and approved source codes, test results, and associated documentation.
3. *Configuration Management Data*   The working area for the software project librarian.
4. *Documentation*   All versions of released software documentation, as well as all program reports, action items, and discrepancy reports.

This represents segments of the PSL that are logical groupings of information, each having different project control and support requirements. Access to the data, control of the information within the PSL, and the flow of data throughout the organization are the responsibility of the PSL librarian. The data controlled or supported by the PSL may be either resident on automated files or retained as hard copy files, indexed and controlled through the PSL.

Working PSL Area

The working area is allocated by the librarian to include all project data which has not yet been approved. In format, it is identical to that of the controlled segment.

Each software subsystem has allocated, through the PSL, a hierarchical data organization.

1. At the subsystem level, the PSL working area provides for storage of system functional requirements allocated to the function; system and intersystem interfaces supported by the subsystem; software testing information unique to the subsystem; and subsystem design and transaction flows that define the functional requirements of the subsystem.
2. The next hierarchical level provides for the storage and control of working versions of the data used for the software system design, interprocess interface information, and data dictionary information required for development, test, or integration of the process.
3. The lowest level of the hierarchy, the unit and module level, provides for the storage and control of unit development folders and programmer notebook information. This area contains a copy of the controlled data base for modifications and update.

The working area provides for the storage of utility software developed during the implementation. These utilities are not maintained or supported by the project, but are available through the PSL for programmer application.

The final component is the build area, which is an area within the PSL for storing working copies of software builds and build records for informal version testing.

The working area is assigned by the PSL librarian but is the domain of the individual programmer. It is not normally subject to project control. All items contained in the working area may be modified by the programmer responsible for the component under development.

Controlled Area of the PSL

The controlled area of the PSL is the repository for three categories of controlled software information:

1. *Requirements and Functional Definition* This segment of the PSL serves as the basis for the software development.

2. *Design and Implementation Information* This PSL segment contains controlled software design and coding data that has been released to the PSL through completion of specific software development milestones.

3. *Software Test and Support Facilities* Controlled software test data, tools, and supporting utility software used by more than one programmer in developing, testing, or integrating software.

The controlled PSL area is organized in a hierarchical structure that corresponds to development requirements and phasing of the software production. The controlled structure corresponds to the organization of the working area, facilitating the flow of data from the working segment to the controlled segment as it is approved and transferred under project control. Under this structure, all software data items have an identifier that uniquely identifies the relationship of each data item to the overall architecture and organization of the project.

During integration and test, the PSL will produce and modify software systems from controlled software resident in the controlled library area. This data is documented in version description documents (VDDs). These documents specify the content of each software (build) release, as well as the status of system and software discrepancies. Version description documents data is extracted from the controlled areas of the PSL and is closely integrated with configuration control activities. Library builds utilize the automated facilities of the PSL, selecting the latest version (or selected versions) of each module required in the build, from the controlled area. Modules that are not available in the controlled area are flagged and the librarian has the option of selecting from the working area replacements. The tools then automatically initiate compilation and linking of an executable object system, storing the system in the test area.

Formal software builds are generated at regular, preplanned intervals that track either the build testing schedule or the system release schedule. These software versions are assigned unique version numbers and the contents are formally maintained as the current supported software system. The PSL is responsible for assuring the integrity of the software documentation.

In addition, the PSL releases interim versions of the system software based on current controlled versions. These releases are documented through VDD procedures; however, the releases are considered informal, and the same level of documentation reviews are not applied as required of a major release.

Configuration Management Area

The configuration management area of the PSL is the working area restricted to PSL personnel. The function of this segment is to allow storage of configuration management data essential for PSL functioning as well as storage and control of user-supplied data that describes documentation production requirements or system data configuration. It serves as a holding area for transitioning software project information from the working area of the PSL.

The PSL supported configuration management tools and data are stored in this area and the librarian may approve modifications without additional review or approval.

Documentation Area

This segment of the PSL is used to develop and store released versions of software documentation. This segment is an extension of the controlled area and requires the same level of management and control.

The documentation area of the PSL has two segments: One controlled by the program through the CCB, and the second used to develop deliverable data products from information contained in other areas of the PSL.

The outline for each document and the section-by-section content requirements of each are stored in the documentation area. This serves as the basis for development, production, and evaluation of all project documents, as well as the identification of data control and format requirements collected as the development proceeds.

PROJECT CONFIGURATION MANAGEMENT

The control of software products approved for use by the software project is an integration of manual and automated techniques as follows:

1. *Library Transfer.*   Project data undergoes many internal reviews which assess requirements, evaluate design, inspect code, and evaluate testing and test results. These reviews authorize transfer of data to the controlled PSL area. The reviews confirm that the data, even at low levels, adheres to project requirements. The reviews validate software design then reduce software integration time through identification of design and coding errors early in the development process. They are tied to software schedule milestones. Successful completion of the reviews is required to accomplish schedule milestones and authorize transfer of data from the user area of the PSL to the controlled area.

2. *Changes to Controlled Software.*   The second method of transferring software from project to controlled status is through the software configuration review board (SCRB) action. This action results from processing software problem reports (SPR's). This board will review and evaluate all SPR's, authorize appropriate corrective actions to be taken, track status of all changes in progress, and close the software problem reports after the changes are made. If it is determined that the recommended change affects the approved specification, cost, or schedule, the SPRs are forwarded to the project for resolution.

Library Transfer

When approved by the project, the librarian transfers the information from the working area to the hold segment of the configuration management area. While the data is resident in this area, the librarian reviews it for correspondence in both form and content to the requirements of the data transfer, assembles and reviews all the supporting documentation required by the transfer, and processes all SPRs closed by the transfer. The librarian then generates either a new or interim system release of required data included in the transfer and documents the release in a VDD.

When processed, the data is transferred from the user area to the controlled test area of the PSL where it serves as the new software baseline.

Software Configuration Review Board

The reporting of software or system requirements, design, or development problems is accomplished through the SCRB which is administered and supported through the PSL. This board reviews and evaluates all SPRs, authorizes appropriate corrective action to be taken, tracks status of all changes in progress, and closes the SPR after the changes have been made. These project level practices control released code and documentation that are under investigation and/or being redone but which have not been approved by the program or customer.

The SCRB considers current system problems and project issues which are submitted on SPR forms. The SCRB meets periodically to discuss each SPR which has been submitted and to call in other project members as needed to obtain information concerning a particular problem. The problem may be solved during the discussion, and thus be marked "closed" and signed off immediately. An SPR requiring additional study is assigned to the appropriate individual(s) and the action to be taken and date due are recorded on the form. Such SPRs are considered "open" until the action is taken, a written solution is delivered to the librarian and the solution is approved. The PSL librarian is in charge of keeping these forms up to date and schedules and coordinates SCRB meetings.

Document Update Procedures

An SPR that requires a change in a document will not be approved until the actual change is supplied and marked to reflect the change.

The PSL Librarian files the original of the updated pages, incorporating them with the document original, and releases either the change pages or the new document to the project immediately. An SPR written against the document should not be marked "closed" and signed off until the actual update has been applied and any document changes issued.

Software Update Procedures

Whenever a problem is discovered with controlled software, a software problem report (SPR) is completed and sent to the project librarian. The project librarian processes the SPR, arranges for appropriate review before the SCRB meeting and schedules the SPR for review at the SCRB meeting.

When the SCRB convenes, the SCRB decides if the SPR is out of scope or is strictly an internal software change. Out of scope changes are changes that impact baselined documentation or requirements and require program level or customer approval. Internal changes require only action by the SCRB. If approved for implementation, the responsible person will be assigned to perform the change. If the change involves code changes, the amount of retesting will be determined as part of the tasking. The SCRB reviews the change before the update is made. The project librarian signs the SPR and approves the change for incorporation in the PSL. The SPR is then closed and copies of the completed SPR are given to the originator and responsible programmer.

The procedures that are used to control the integrity of the technical data products and provide traceability to the approved user requirements are the means by which a quality standard is maintained. The baseline software configuration practices implemented by the systems organization provide the assurance to the buyer that what has been approved is, in fact, what is built. Thus, data control and configuration management provide extremely important disciplines for building quality into the project and resulting products of development.

10

QUALITY EVALUATION TECHNIQUES—THE TOOLS OF THE TRADE

The evaluation of software quality is a balanced assessment of the development's process and product attributes.

Software attributes, and the metrics that are used to provide quantitative measurements of them, provide the basis for the assessment of software quality. The review process provides the practices and procedures that enable the capture of this data. This discipline is pervasive throughout the development process, serving many masters and purposes. Reviews are conducted to assess project status, determine software quality, and to decide on the acceptability of the product, and so forth. It is important to use this ongoing and pervasive process to support the quality management program. It is the responsibility of the program and development organizations to provide the necessary management mechanisms to ensure that the review process supports the quality management process, and in the final analysis, provides an accurate overall assessment of the product. This chapter is about the evaluation process itself; that is, how to conduct a meaningful assessment of the software project at various points in time, to determine individual product status; the adequacy of the development process; and whether the development is on schedule, within costs and meeting program requirements.

The process and product attributes described in previous chapters are evaluated through the following methods:

1. *Observation.* The attributes are monitored through observation or inspection of individual development products and formal and informal reviews.
2. *Analysis.* The relationships between products and integration and test activities are observed through exercising and monitoring specific functional, operational, or performance conditions.

QUALITY OBSERVATION AND SCORING TECHNIQUES

Observation is the means by which data is collected to provide an assessment of software development progress and projects and insight into software quality. Observation techniques satisfy different project quality needs according to the level of application within the project, the phase the project is in, and the needs of the specific evaluation. An evaluation to assess project status will collect different data than one to assess specific subsystem quality.

There are several techniques by which quality observations are made. These techniques view the project development and the data being produced, collecting information describing software quality. They define a structure that will provide each organization clear visibility into the specific attributes of software products as they are being developed.

1. *Explicit Observations.* Collection of quantitative data, averages, and other indicators which identify product or process status.
2. *Analytic Techniques.* Observations based on the relationships among software features, product or process characteristics.

In order to minimize the subjectivity associated with an evaluation, different organizations may be employed in the evaluation. Evaluations, when conducted by a group external to the development organization, provide an objective evaluation of the product against the predefined model used to evaluate the product. This independent analysis will provide comparative results. Another example would be to have audits and inspections conducted by more than one organization within the project, each looking at the same information. This duplication of analysis, and the objectivity which results, is critical to the validity of independent analytical activities.

Formal and Informal Reviews

Formal and informal reviews are structured presentations of technical and process oriented data. The review process starts with a definition of the specific goals of the review. Goal setting is conducted by the review chairperson and the leader of the group for whom the review is to be conducted. The goals should include:

1. A statement of review requirements and needs. This should document the expectations of all parties and describe in detail the specific data items to be reviewed. The goals should also define the expected results of the review and what actions will take place.

2. A detailing of how the review will be conducted, the level of detail required, the degree of formality, the representation required by all parties and the decision process which will be initiated at review completion. In addition, decisions should be reached concerning the actions to be taken in the event that the review does not meet its intended goals.

3. A "meeting of the minds" should be reached concerning specifically what will be presented and the criteria which will be used to measure acceptability.

4. An agenda for the review should be developed which will be acceptable to all parties. The agenda should describe what, why, when, and how the information will be presented during the review, when documentation necessary for the conduct of the review will be provided, and when comments must be received to permit their inclusion in the review data before the review.

This early setting of review goals provides a common level of expectation among all parties. Early definition of goals will prenegotiate review conduct and acceptance criteria ensuring that all parties are ready for the review and that the review will be meaningful.

The structure of formal and informal project reviews provides management visibility into the development process and the products which are being produced.

Review Planning

The second stage of review planning is conducted individually by each of the parties who will participate in the review.

The reviewed organization (normally the developing organization responsible for hosting and conducting the review) must establish the expected outcome of the review from their perspective and define a consistent strategy to achieve the desired effect. They must decide what specific data is to be presented to satisfy review requirements. There must be an early definition of who will present the technical content of the review and who is responsible for developing review materials. The organization being reviewed should establish a structure of quality gates to ensure that data used to develop the review is of an adequate and consistent level of quality.

It must be recognized that except in certain limited cases the fundamental reason for conducting a review is to establish a level of confidence in the technical integrity of a segment or phase of a software project, not to meet a milestone. As such, quality issues uncovered during review preparation should be addressed prior to the review or, at least identified and tracked. In the heat of getting ready for a review these issues are often lost. If sufficient information is not available to conduct a review or if the data to be presented is of unacceptable quality or incomplete, the project should face that reality and defer the review.

The reviewing organization (normally, the organization responsible for monitoring the development) should also plan specifically how, from their perception, the review will be supported.

Technical expectations and expected approvals should be predetermined and a qualified team assembled to support the review. Specific data items to be submitted, reviewed, or approved prior to the review should be identified and teams identified to conduct the data evaluation. If document delivery and approval schedules are inconsistent with the review schedule one of the two schedules should be adjusted. Under no circumstance should the review be conducted if essential data has not been reviewed ahead of time.

The five issues which require joint resolution during the planning phases are:

1. The numbers and types of personnel who will attend the review from both the developing and monitoring organizations.

2. The technical information to be presented at each point in the agenda.

3. The criteria to be applied to accept or reject the technical content of the review. This is a further definition of the general criteria defined previously and serves as the basis for all technical analysis. These criteria should ideally be quantitative using a similar rating scale that may be used throughout the evaluation process: audits, walkthroughs, and inspections.

4. Detailing the review schedule. Determining how long will be spent on each presentation, what will be presented, and how the review will be formatted and structured.

5. Go/no-go points, or checkpoints. These should be defined and must be sucessfully achieved if the review is to be allowed to proceed. If these checkpoints are not achieved contingency plans should be predefined.

Review Conduct

The review should be conducted strictly in accordance with the agenda, schedule, and technical requirements. Team leaders for the developing and monitoring organizations should be responsible, from their perspective, for the conduct of the review. They should ensure that the teams meet daily before the review to discuss strategy, and lay out specific responsibilities and agendas. They ensure that the team members attend the review and evaluate the review against the approved criteria and scoring technique. Subjective good/bad or accept/reject determinations are extremely poor practice.

Most importantly, the developing and monitoring organization team leaders ensure that the review follows the agenda schedule and stays on the topic. Even in simple reviews it is possible to drift into "star wars" speculations which defeat the purpose of the review.

The team members should be sure that they understand their specific roles and responsibilities. They must understand the scoring system and how it is to be applied to the evaluation. After each review period each team member should write up his notes, observations and results and submit them to the team leader.

The teams should caucus every day after the review so that individual team members on both sides can provide their written notes, observations, and scoring (whe e used) to the team leaders. A discussion and team debriefing should be held and an action item list developed for the next day.

Postreview Actions

At the end of the review both sides should consolidate their review data into a postreview report. Before this report is finalized as a written conclusion of the review, the team leaders should meet to resolve differences. If a quantitative scoring system was used individual scores should be compared and significant differences resolved. If differences cannot be resolved, the differences should be documented and arbitrated at a higher level. This should take place prior to committing additional resources to areas affected by the differences. If the review is approved the data should be moved to the appropriate level of configuration management. If disapproved, deficiencies must be noted and the review must be rescheduled.

One of the most important actions is to document action items resulting from the review. These should indicate disposition of the item, who is responsible for ensuring that the action is completed, and a schedule for its completion. Action items can take many forms.

1. In some cases, as mentioned previously, differences can be major, or resource impacting, and have to be resolved before additional work can take place in the affected area.

2. Other action items may be considered of lesser consequence in that they are not significant enough to cause a repeated review, however, they have to be resolved before additional work is accomplished in the affected area. These items are scheduled for correction and monitored by the program organization. An example of this type of deficiency is an improper design function resulting from a misinterpretation of requirements. Once detected, the design is changed

without impact to the project manpower projection and the project proceeds.

3. A category of lesser consequence includes deficiencies that are not critical to the orderly proceeding of the project. These may be strictly documentation errors; they are documented and corrected during the normal project support activities. These actions are still monitored by the project team.

Walk-Throughs

Formal reviews provide visibility into the process of system development; however, it must be realized that these reviews are "after the fact" evaluations of end item and milestone developments. Problems found between reviews can significantly impede program performance. Informal reviews, called walk-throughs, augment formal reviews and are conducted at various points within the development by project personnel. Walk-throughs, similar to formal reviews, are interactive in nature. The reviewer interacts with the review audience rather than conducting a one sided evaluation of a single data item. The primary function of walk-throughs is to assess progress.

The objective of walk-throughs is to evaluate application requirements, developing design, code, and levels 2 to 5 test data products. Specific walk-through goals are determined prior to conducting the walk-through and are identified in the notice announcing the walk-through, (Figure 10-1). In preparing for a walk-through, the emphasis is on reviewing the process, and providing constructive criticism. Does it do what it is supposed to do? Does it follow the appropriate standards and guidelines? Secondary objectives may include the identification of style errors, improvement in the quality of the material, and the transfer of ideas and understanding between team members. All data products reviewed and approved at walk-throughs are baselined by the appropriate development group, entered into the program support library and released for use in the next phase of development.

Walk-Through Planning

1. Walk-throughs shall be required for the following types of material: system requirements specifications, top level design documentation, detailed design documentation, source code, and development test documentation.

2. A walk-through should be held for any software development material used by more than one organization. The degree of formality is a function of the approval level of the data.

3. Walk-throughs shall be scheduled well in advance. The reviewee shall send out a *notice*, with the review materials attached, to each reviewer. The *walk-through announcement* (Figure 10-1) should contain

WALK-THROUGH ANNOUNCEMENT

From: _____

Date: _____

To: _____

_____

_____

_____

_____

Subject of Review: _____

_____

A walkthrough will be held on _____

at _____ in _____

to review the material listed above. Please review the attached material before then and prepare your comments. If you cannot attend the walkthrough or will not be able to review the material before that time, contact the reviewee immediately so the walkthrough can be rescheduled.

Current status of the material: _____

The objective of the walkthrough is to: _____

_____

Moderator: _____

Recorder: _____

Design Leader: _____

Attached Material: _____

_____

_____

_____

_____

Figure 10-1. Walk-through announcement.

the following information: the name of the reviewee and the subject of the walk-through; the date, time, and place of the walk-through; the names of the moderator, the recorder, the current status of the material and the design leader; the objective of the walk-through; and a list of the attached materials.

4. The reviewee should check with all attendees before setting the time and date of the walk-through to affix a mutually convenient time.

5. The following people shall attend a walk-through: the reviewee, the appropriate design leader, a peer of the reviewee, and an independent reviewer from outside the development organization (someone from program test, quality assurance, technical support, etc.). The latter two shall be selected by the reviewee. The reviewee shall designate which reviewers will serve as moderator and recorder. It is recommended, but not required, that the moderator and recorder functions be performed by different people. If a follow-up walk-through, it is recommended that the team members of the previous walk-through participate to prevent wasting time reviewing previously discussed material.

6. The reviewee may invite any additional reviewers desired. It is especially useful to invite those who will be impacted by the reviewee's work (other team members who will be working on related material, users, etc.). The number of attendees at a walk-through should be limited to a reasonable number. Members of the development team may be asked to review the material and turn in their comments to the recorder without attending the actual walk-through or review.

7. Supervisors or managers are invited to walk-throughs when their particular skills or knowledge are required. A supervisor may also attend a walk-through if interest is expressed, but the supervisor does not attend in a supervisory role, rather as one member of a team reviewing another member's work.

8. The optimum length for a walk-through is 30 to 60 minutes. If a walk-through requires more than 90 minutes, the subject matter is too large and should be broken into several walk-throughs.

Walk-Through Conduct

The guidelines for walk-through conduct are:

1. The moderator shall determine if the review team is prepared for the review. If they are not, the walk-through shall be rescheduled. For follow-up walk-throughs, the moderator shall verify that the resolution or action list from the prior walk-through is included in the attached materials.

2. The moderator shall be responsible for conducting the walk-through or review. The moderator's function shall be to ensure that

the review meets its objectives in an efficient manner. The moderator shall open and close the meeting, solicit comments from the reviewers, present any of his or her own comments, and monitor discussions to ensure they are relevant to the subject.

3. The moderator shall be responsible for arbitrating disagreements to successful conclusion. Failing that, an action item shall be assigned to the design leader to resolve the issue outside of the walk-through.

4. The recorder shall be responsible for keeping notes of the walk-through. These notes shall be in the form of an action item list consisting of major items that require correction, clarification, or further work. At the conclusion of the walk-through the recorder should read back the action item list to the group to verify that it is correct.

5. The action item list is detailed in Figure 10-2. The recorder fills in the information about the walk-through at the top of the form. The current status field shall contain "NEW" if this is the first review, or "NOT APPROVED" if this is a follow-up walk-through. At the end of the walk-through, the recorder shall note the new approval status of the material (as decided by the review team, to be discussed).

6. Minor comments dealing with style, grammar, punctuation, and so forth, shall be given to the recorder prior to the walk-through and attached to the action item list. The recorder shall place the action item list under control (along with the invitation) and ask that copies be distributed to the reviewee, the design leader, other attendees as requested, and designated program management personnel.

7. During the walk-through, the moderator shall "step through" the material and the reviewers shall identify errors during the reviewee's discourse. Questions raised shall be pursued only to the point at which an error is recognized. The error shall be noted by the recorder and the walk-through continued. No specific solution discussion shall take place during the walk-through.

8. It is advantageous for the reviewee to keep his or her own record of errors, usually on his or her own copy of the material. By using both the formal action item list and his or her own notes, the chances of a problem being overlooked are reduced.

9. At the conclusion of the walk-through, after the action item list has been reviewed, the group shall decide whether to approve the material (with the listed action items) or not approve the material and call for another walk-through (if the group decides the material is incomplete or contains too many errors). The approved/not approved status shall be noted on the action item list by the recorder in the "new status" space.

WALKTHROUGH ACTION ITEM LIST

Subject of Review_____

Material Prepared by_____Date of Review_____

Moderator_____Recorder_____Design Leader_____

Reviewers_____

Current Status_____New Status_____

NUMBER	DESCRIPTION OF ACTION ITEM	RESOLUTION

Figure 10-2. Walk-through action item list.

10. The reviewee shall respond to all action items. The reviewee shall indicate how each issue was resolved in the "resolution" column of the action item list. Copies of this resolution list shall be given to the design leader and placed under control when the material is approved by the team. If the material was not approved, the resolution list shall be handed out with the material for the next walk-through. It shall be the project leader's responsibility to verify that all action items are addressed and resolved.

11. Finally, after a successful walk-through, the product reviewed is baselined by placing it into the project program support library. This marks the project for continuance of development.

Audits

Throughout the development period regular audits of the development process, management and control procedures being applied to the project, project performance and productivity, and technical compliance of the system to standards should be conducted. Unlike project reviews, audits do not result in the baselining of specific data products. Audits act as checkpoints which are "in process" evaluations of developing data or process oriented activities. Audits differ from formal reviews and walk-throughs in that they are not participatory in nature. Audits are close to being a one sided evaluation.

When evaluating a narrowly specified set of project characteristics or product attributes, audits, along with reviews, serve as a first line in assessing quality.

Audits and reviews should utilize checklists. These are predefined identifications of what will be looked at during the audit. These checklists should describe how every piece of information is to be collected at the audit, and identify how the audit or review results are to be evaluated.

Software Audits

The application of audits to the evaluation of software quality is a complex procedure. It must be based on a fundamental premise—the audit is to be a disciplined exercise, using competent personnel to independently evaluate a predefined set of data products against known criteria.

The data collected through the audit must be analyzed and evaluated, and a predefined set of quantitative metrics assigned which rate the quality of the product. The combination of these metrics results in a "quality score." Quality levels can be defined which relate to these metrics or scores to assess quality against levels, thus the quality of the software can be assessed.

Although each audit must be tailored to the specific needs of the project, generically the audit process falls into six distinct phases. These are described in the following.

Defining Audit Goals and Objectives. Before embarking on an audit, the specific goals and objectives to be satisfied must be identified. These goals differ depending on the phase of development, the experience of the project personnel during the implementation, the purpose of the audit, and the use of audit results. These goals must define at least five separate parameters before the audit scope may be defined:

1. Define the specific audit assignment and the desired end products.
2. Define exactly why the audit is being conducted. Is it a routine audit or specifically designed to isolate specific project problems?
3. Define the expectations of the audit recipients.
4. Define the audit audience. Will they welcome or resist a forthright assessment of project status? This should not affect the objectivity of analysis, only the manner in which the audit is approached.
5. Define how the results of the audit will be used and if follow up audits will be conducted to further evaluate the project.

When the goals of the software audit have been defined the scope of the specific audit may be defined.

Setting the Audit Scope.   In determining the scope of the audit, the goals of the audit as well the realities of audit budget, schedule and the experience of available audit personnel must be considered. The audit scope cannot be "pro forma." It cannot be a boiler plate or undefined activity. It cannot apply unsupported techniques or personnel not competent to audit or evaluate the software project. In order to scope the audit effort and define expectations, several activities are critical!

1. Get a fix on the precise nature of the assignment and the desired end product. For example, a software project performance audit which stresses the efficacy of the development may require a compliance check, designed to see if the project is performing in accordance with software development plans. Other audits may require specialized internal review, designed to answer whether development and project control techniques are satisfactory or computer security provisions are sufficient.
2. Obtain related audit reports, permanent files, previous working papers, system and software schedule data, and so forth. Also, follow up on actions taken on prior audit recommendations, as a prerequisite to your audit. If actions were not taken, ascertain why. If actions were taken, inquire or determine whether they achieved the desired objective. If actions were taken that were other than recommended by the prior audit, determine whether these actions achieved the desired effect in the minds of management.
3. Get previously documented program and customer analyses of the software development effort, the integrity and effectiveness of the development process used and summaries or reports which document the integrity of the data products developed or used by the software project.

4. Categorize the software development by application type, size, complexity, and software development phase. Use this categorization to scale the resources, schedule, and budget required for the audit.

5. Establish tentative time parameters for this assignment. These can be changed if conditions warrant, but don't leave the question of time open ended.

6. Determine what staff resources are sufficient to do the job fully.

From this information the individual responsible for the audit should develop an audit plan. This plan should be very brief, highlighting the audit goals and objectives, the way the audit will be conducted, the required software and program participation, the major areas to be assessed, and the expected outputs. In addition, required budgets and schedules should be documented. The auditor should conduct all audits against a predefined set of criteria set by the senior quality engineer. The quality engineer should specify the data to be collected, the relationships between the data products and process attributes, and the form of the data collection. This level of audit planning will ensure that the audit is relevant in the context of the project environment and that the data collected will lead to an appropriate analysis.

Audit Initiation. The initial activities of the audit team establish the relationship between the audit team and the software project staff. Throughout this early period, the team must appear competent, focused and, above all, non-threatening. During these early audit stages several steps should be conducted:

1. Hold an entrance conference with software project management (or whoever authorized the audit) to lay out mutually agreed-to audit objectives, procedures, and target completion dates. These should be documented in a memo of agreement.

2. Request initial working data through the software manager. This initial data can be used to confirm initial assumptions concerning development characteristics. This is critical! The details needed will depend on the size and complexity of the software application, the requirement for the audit and the use to which the data will be put.

3. Reserve adequate staff working space and secure commitments for computer time and for responsive secretarial and duplicating services.

4. Prepare a survey guide that will serve as a broad-based working road map for the staff auditors to follow, based on the preliminary data gathered and the individual characteristics of this particular audit entity. The guide will minimize missing or skimping on important preliminary coverage steps.

Survey Phase—Data Collection. During this period, raw audit data is collected through reviews of project data and supporting documentation, analysis of software project history and progress and interviews with project personnel. The data collection should be in conformance with the agreements between the audit team and management and in accordance with audit questionnaires. The team must be focused due to the vast amount of data which may be required to be reviewed in even a simple audit and the difficulty in determining what will prove meaningful. The data collection steps include:

1. Physically inspect and/or observe the entire organization. This includes facilities, project and support equipment, office layout, computer room and access facilities, filing systems, and scheduling, budget and project monitoring facilities. During this process the initial assessment of the effectiveness of the project environment is made.

2. Compare the observations of physical items to the paper records of the organization. Does the project data inventory compare on a one-for-one basis with the reported milestone and project completion?

3. Review management plans for monitoring and controlling development practices and appraise the process from a conceptual point of view. Consider whether the operating reports appear to be:
   a. Designed to bring operational problems to management.
   b. Properly used by managers to formulate decisions, change policy requirements, and take action on identified problems and not just used for "compliance" or "for show" paper trails.

4. Determine (and this is most important of all) whether all the processes and functions logically relate to the physical aspects of the project that were observed. The clues must all fit. An organizational chart, for example, with numbers of people in each segment should correspond to the direct observation of staff. Some rather elemental items can be easily missed.

5. Prepare flow charts for the development process and organizational relationships. They need not be especially detailed, and may even be preferable, if short and to the point. Flow charts following specific tasks should be made. Those project areas tentatively deemed weak should be verified later and expanded, if necessary, to determine the full extent of the weakness (material or trivial; too much, too little).

6. Pay strict attention to the data interaction between the various organizations within the software project and the organizations external to the software project which interface to it.

7. Ensure that software data products are consistent with project standards. The audit should evaluate data products against predefined

quality attributes for the individual product. All discrepancies and oddities should be noted for later analysis.

8. Consider the software development process. The degree of rigor that planned and documented tools, techniques and development methodologies have been implemented should be noted.

9. When reviewing documentation ensure that it meets project standards and that traceability exists between related documents and technical products. Ensure that all data used by more than one organization, or approved through a review, is controlled.

10. Consider the keepers of the books. Who are they? What are the internal control factors? Who do they report to and who hires, rewards, and fires them? Evaluate the effectiveness of baseline control activities, the program support library and project configuration control practices.

11. Assess the motivation of the staff. Look for punctuality, commitment to making milestones, concentration and focus while on the job, and understanding of the process and product requirements of the development.

12. Keep in mind the critical question; what could go wrong? Don't only consider the current experience but assess potential risks.

13. Decide, and this is more easily said than done, what the objectives of testing are. Look at the specified flow of testing, the relation between the test levels and the project baselines. Determine the relationships among development milestones, project controls, and the development process.

14. Study and know (conceptually) the important differences between what was planned and what was actually accomplished by the project. Consider how and why each change was made and what effect on product and process quality each will have.

15. Consider the "quality gates" used by the project to evaluate developing data. Assess how carefully they were defined, how effectively they support the phase or activity being audited and whether they provide a controlled flow of data.

16. Don't be overwhelmed by the magnitude of the data collection task. Don't let it throw you; it's easier than it seems at first. Does the development process seem logical and is it controlled? Has it been based on prior experience, and is overhead added on a sensible basis? Does it have a method for checking itself and readjusting on a timely basis? Does the project keep accurate books and learn through its own history?

17. Stay alert to the possibilities for project interference with the audit. Consider the charter and responsibility of the auditor. Avoid compromising situations, and attempts to intimidate and give unau-

thorized instructions. Watch for undue pressure and outright threats. The auditor should be prepared to stand behind his or her results and be accountable for the results.

18. Score the data during the evaluation process. Where possible, rate the products being evaluated quantitatively. Use a rating scale to assign a score. All scores should be based on predefined project standards for the data product or development procedures approved for the project which describe the development process. The use of checklists to collect data and provide a vehicle for scoring is desirable.

19. Determine if the data collected during the evaluation is complete, accurate, and provides a sufficient base to assess project status.

Project Analysis. Analysis of software audit results is the means by which the health of the software project is assessed and the quality of the audited data products determined. These determinations are made through:

1. An analysis of the ratings assigned to each of the individual metrics assigned during the evaluation phase.

2. Relating each of the individual items evaluated so an assessment of the project may be made.

3. Weights which assign the relative importance of each data item and component of the development process.

When analyzing the audit information the most critical risks are evaluation subjectivity, improperly drawing a conclusion from conflicting or erroneous data, and not accounting for project trends.

Evaluator subjectivity is a by-product of auditing software projects. Auditors tend to rely on perceptions rather than facts. Often the auditor doesn't know what questions to ask or what data to look at to uncover the state of the software. They investigate most rigorously those areas they feel most comfortable with, and ignore or treat lightly those areas which are not familiar. Critical problems may be overlooked, indicators of health and product status missed, and technical, administrative, and resource shortfalls not recognized. The drawing of conclusions from data is a more critical and difficult problem than the collection of data.

As with any audit activity, a large amount of data of varying complexity is collected. It differs in form and structure and it is difficult to determine trends and project indicators. The evaluation should analyze the project broadly, providing a measure of quality. This measure ideally is an assessment of project risk. The analysis should:

1. Examine the organization to determine development soft spots and project shortfalls.

2. Identify the degree that project objectives will be met and the risks associated with meeting these objectives.

3. Evaluate the effectiveness of the project structure, and the degree that quality checks and project control practices will lead to a quality product.

4. Evaluate the organization's effectiveness, the smoothness of the data flow and the degree that project checks and balances control the development.

5. Determine how effectively the development process supports the implementation of the software.

6. Determine the degree that the products of development meet project form and content requirements, and how from a technical standpoint each satisfies its intended role in the project.

7. Provide a single score which rates the project, blending process and product attributes into a single quality assessment.

Analyzing the software development effort from data collected during the audit should provide an overall picture of the project. There are several steps involved in analysis:

1. The analysis activity should be under the direct supervision of a single individual. All analysis should be narrowly focused and conclusions based on predefined criteria.

2. The analysis should be a reverse pyramid. Raw audit data should be evaluated first and logical relationships between the data defined. From this information, conclusions can be drawn concerning the state of the development. These higher level data relationships are the means by which the software development and product integrity is assessed. The building of evaluation data continues until the final metric, the overall software quality score, is determined.

3. The analysis must be rigorously pursued. An objective posture must be maintained. The evaluator must "keep his or her blinders on," believing the evidence, not relying on perception. Perception can force the evaluation into erroneous directions and avoid meaningful conclusions.

4. More than one evaluator should assess the same audit data. The evaluation criteria and data should be the same for the independent evaluations. The independent evaluations should be compared on a one-for-one basis and major discrepancies between evaluator perceptions analyzed.

Reporting the Results. Findings of the audit should be clearly documented. In the case of software audits, this is especially critical because of the large amount of data, the difficulty of accurately evaluating the information and the often conflicting indications which result. When developing the report, two considerations must be kept in mind:

1. The results will be subject to scrutiny and, as a result must be properly documented. Despite the rigor and care which went into the software audit, if it is improperly documented, the results will be discounted.

2. The auditor will typically have only one opportunity to present his or her findings and, hopefully engender action. If the report is not clear, this opportunity may be lost.

The report must be written for the intended audience and clearly address the audit goals, scope, and findings. The audit report(s) must:

1. Make recommendations fit the report and the reader. Recommendations must be clearly tied to audit results. They must be readily implementable in the context of the actual software project environment. They must be organized by short- and long-term recommendations, and by those which can be implemented without project change, and those which require project modification.

2. Carefully "staff" findings during the course of the audit. Keep people informed as you proceed through the audit. This will ensure accuracy, understanding, and psychological acceptance by management and project staff affected by the audit. Audits which are not staffed will probably be ignored if they are negative or accepted on a selective basis.

3. Ensure that replies are responsive, that they address the issues presented and deal with the recommendations included. These replies must be timely and have the support and concurrence of management.

4. Ensure that there is a complete and explanatory exit conference. If there are any surprises, either management bringing up new issues, new evidence or alternate conclusions, the entire software audit process may be invalidated.

Inspections

The inspections of data products or development process characteristics evaluate the inspected object against a predefined set of criteria for compliance. The conduct of an inspection differs from an audit in that it does not typically involve the developer's staff. They are conducted by an individual or organization different from the developer. They are much narrower in focus and much more rigorously structured.

Inspections are conducted to baseline or control the data product, appraise the effectiveness of a development technique, or evaluate a management or project control technique. The three phases of inspection are goals definition, standards and criteria definition, and inspection and assessment.

Goals Definition

As with audits, the first phase of an inspection is a definition of specific goals to be satisfied. Inspections may be carried out for a variety of reasons and result in several actions being taken. They may be conducted to evaluate data items against project standards. They may evaluate software development practices against documented project plans and/or procedures. They may assess coding or documentation against common acceptable practices. In any event they result in a specific acceptance or rejection of the process or product being inspected, and a corresponding action taken as a result of the recommendations. Before these actions can be defined, and a course for the inspection determined, a set of goals for the inspection must be described. These goals must be defined:

1. The project need that is to be addressed by the inspection.
2. The goals of the inspection. Is it to be part of an audit or review, or will it stand alone? Will it result in approval of a data product or process by itself or will the data be used as a data point for a higher level evaluation? What are the specific data items or process steps to be evaluated?
3. Is the inspection to be based on predefined project standards or must standards be defined?
4. Will the data to be inspected be complete or under development? If the data is undergoing change, identifying how the inspection baseline is to be frozen to avoid a "moving target" is critical to a successful inspection.

This initial setting of inspection goals ensures that the inspection will satisfy the need it is intended for. Unstructured or unfocused inspections, like loose audits, are a waste of time.

Standards and Criteria Definition

The second phase of an inspection defines specific standards for the data product, or development procedures that are to be evaluated, and criteria on which the assessment is to be based. Sometimes these standards exist in approved project plans and procedures or standards documents. Often they do not exist and must be defined before the inspection can proceed. The standards should provide the model on which the process or product is to be assessed. They should define acceptable practice and technical attributes.

Specific criteria should be defined which provide the accept/reject guidelines for the inspector. These criteria should not be pass/fail but rather a relative weight of acceptability. A suggested range is one-to-six. The criteria should reflect several characteristics of the product or process.

1. The role of the product or process in the development and its relative importance.
2. The phase of development in which the inspection is conducted.
3. The type of software being developed and the degree of criticality the process or product plays in the integrity of the application.

The inspection must be defined in such a way that provides nonambiguous guidelines for the evaluator to perform the inspection and assess the results. The model on which the inspection is to be based must be clearly defined. The most effective means to do this is through a questionnaire to be completed by the evaluator. The questions should not be binary, but rather force a rating. The answers should be rated according to the criteria defined for the inspection, and used to derive a metric (through weighted averages) to score the inspection.

Inspection and Assessment

The inspection is conducted offline by an evaluator using the standards for collecting data and the acceptance criteria for assessing results. The inspection process has seven separate steps.

1. It is started by gathering the latest version of the project data to be evaluated or data describing the process to be evaluated.
2. An initial first pass should be made which quickly scans the data and groups it into that which can easily be assessed, and that which requires in depth analysis to properly evaluate.
3. The data most easily assessed should be scored first, providing a rating of the information.
4. The more difficult evaluations should then be made. As much analysis of these data items as possible should be made within basic cost and schedule constraints.
5. Each answer to an evaluation question should be made using the rating scale used for audits. The raw data should then be grouped into logical areas for analysis.
6. Weights should then be applied to adjust the answers against the criteria model. Weighted averages then rate the overall inspection.
7. A final pass over the data should be made to ensure data consistency and inspection validity before the results are turned over to the project for action.

Analytical Evaluation Techniques

Independent analytical techniques are often used to determine the quality of software data items. These analyses provide an independent assessment of the quality of a software system. They are unlike reviews, audits, and inspections in several important respects:

1. They are active; exercising or evaluating software products rather than passively observing their characteristics.
2. They evaluate either through execution or analysis of the technical attributes of the software rather than auditing the products against predefined standards.
3. They are conducted by a team independent of the developing organization. It is important that the team leader does not report to the project leader.

The objective is to establish a level of confidence in system accuracy, performance, operational effectiveness, and long-term reliability under varying operational conditions. They should provide an assessment of each individual software data product against the standards for the project and relate the conformance of the product to the requirements/standards against which it was built.

Analytical evaluation techniques are effective in certifying the operational status and quality of software support. The requirement for this certification becomes increasingly essential as the operational and reliability constraints of the systems become more stringent.

The procedures provide for an evaluation of the internal aspects of a software system to assure that the internal performance characteristics meet operational specifications, and to prove that the system is consistent with long-term reliability requirements of the application.

The procedures also provide an examination of the external attributes of system performance to establish a degree of confidence in the operational integrity of the system. They affirm that actual performance characteristics are in compliance with requirements, and demonstrate that the system will perform adequately under both nominal and extreme execution conditions.

Independent evaluation procedures should be applied to systems before certification for operational use. Independent evaluations will facilitate an objective assessment of operational characteristics, performance, and reliability of the system. Applying these techniques to operational programs that are under development, or modification, or to existing software programs, will provide:

1. An objective analysis of proposed system design requirements.
2. An independent determination and analysis of accuracy and performance characteristics.

3. An analysis of man–machine, hardware, and other pertinent software interfaces.

4. A determination of system long-term reliability.

5. An objective analysis of intermodule relationships and intersystem functional interfaces.

6. An assessment of system execution.

7. Basic source data for determining system operational status for certification purposes.

When made available at the appropriate time in the development cycle, these analyses become a valuable tool for identifying and correcting system discrepancies. Systems that have been modified or are in the process of modification will derive similar benefits. Developing systems should be routinely and periodically evaluated to assess, at that phase of development, performance, reliability, and support requirements.

Requirements Definition

A complete evaluation requires an accurate definition of user requirements and establishment of suitable system performance criteria. These definitions or specifications serve as the comparative basis for analyzing and assessing system structure, performance, and reliability.

This step fixes the analytical baseline for all subsequent evaluation, thereby establishing a set of performance requirements:

1. *Capabilities Definition.* This definition identifies the basic support capabilities, interface requirements, and primary system performance characteristics. These provide a functional basis for subsequent analysis activities.

2. *Structure Analysis.* Structure analysis identifies each critical capability and interface; isolates functional execution and sequence; establishes major mathematical or algorithmic models used; and characterizes major data, peripheral, or processing interfaces supported. Accuracies, timing, and overall performance profiles for each of the minor functional capabilities are ascertained for future analysis.

3. *Establishing Level of Analysis Required.* In order to be able to meet schedules and effectively apply manpower resources, it is necessary to establish, at the outset, the techniques (as described later) to be applied to the various elements of the software system. This decision may have to be modified in accordance with subsequent findings in the analysis of selected areas.

There are two major components to analytical evaluation: verification and validation. Verification asks the question, "Am I building the product right?" Validation, on the other hand, asks, "Am I building the right product?"

Verification

Verification procedures provide an evaluation of system processing functions. This includes:

1. *Specifications Analysis.*   This first-level verification identifies fundamental deficiencies in system structure, basic design criteria, and operational objectives. It also evaluates the software structure to be used in subsequent verification activities. Specification analysis evaluates overall structure from the developer's specifications. It examines overall system integrity and compatibility with system operational requirements. As a final stage, this activity evaluates discrepancies between system specifications and basic functional, system, and user requirements.

2. *Discrepancy Analysis.*   Discrepancy analysis involves identifying effects of, or impacts on, system architecture, timing, accuracy, abnormal conditions, and user/operator interface.

3. *Functional and Architecture Evaluation.*   This evaluation will assess specific attributes of the specified and implemented system architecture from two aspects: structural analysis and code analysis.

4. *Functional Analysis.*   Functional analysis evaluates the flow and integrity of specified software functions and identifies specified and implemented processing "primitives" for further verification analysis. Functional integrity may also be compared to that achieved through independent coding and execution of critical code segments as specified. The analysis will establish the adequacy and integrity of the proposed structure.

5. *Execution Analysis.*   Execution analysis provides stand-alone execution through drivers with known data inputs, in a controlled test environment, in order to monitor particular execution characteristics. Expected results are precalculated (or generated through automated techniques) and compared against the test execution for accuracy, format capability, and so forth. Also evaluated are the effects of anomalous data and alternate computer operation system loads and hardware configurations on the integrity of module execution. The ability to identify and recover from failure conditions will also be examined. Utilizing hardware and/or software monitoring tools and techniques, a timing analysis of the module is conducted identifying timing characteristics for nominal and anomalous execution. This quantitative data provides a comparative basis for evaluating module support against specified system capability and functional requirements.

6. *Primitive Analysis.* Software primitives (i.e., critical code sequences, mathematical models, and processing algorithms) are verified in order to provide a high degree of confidence in their integrity and accuracy.

a. *Code Sequences.* Critical code sequences will be "blocked" (a block is a basic processing structure with a single input and a definable output) and instrumented according to the blocking structure. The instrumented code is executed, providing an examination of interim register settings, critical data, and internal processing characteristics.

b. *Mathematical Analysis.* Mathematical analysis will establish a high level of confidence in the integrity, accuracy, and performance characteristics of critical models. Evaluation is required for all critical mathematics not previously certified for operational use (i.e., any mathematical models not previously verified or having had substantive modification since certification).

The specified model is independently coded and performance and accuracy characteristics are evaluated with varied data values. The structure and accuracy of the model are assessed by hand calculations of the specified equations. Accuracy is verified against known intermediate values to identify mathematical errors.

In order to establish the degree to which specific system and processing requirements are addressed, mathematical formulations are executed in a predefined simulated environment. Included are such considerations as inherent system biases and processing corrections (e.g., refraction, system weighting).

Predefined execution parameters are analyzed to establish confidence in the functional and performance compatibility between the specified model and the application.

Verification assesses compliance of implemented mathematics with specified formulations by independent derivation of equations from system code. The resultant definitions are compared with the specification to assure compatibility of the specified design and implemented code.

Execution of specified mathematical code through test drivers with noncritical or supporting code provides a basis for precisely identifying performance and accuracy characteristics of the model as implemented.

c. *Algorithm Analysis.* The generalized characteristics of processing algorithms require evaluation of the procedures over an average mix of transactions, rather than just for selected data values as with mathematical verification. The verification process entails definition of an analytical model from functional parameters specified for the algorithm. The model is a logical representation of a specified processing function structured so as to provide data about structure and integrity as well as accuracy. The complete algorithm is independently designed from the system listings and compared with the specifications to evaluate accuracy of translation from specification to code. Code is extracted from the listings and exercised using sample data values to establish accuracy and performance of the "as built" algorithm. Results are compared to the specifications and the independently derived basic system requirements to establish compatibility.

7. *Functional Verification.* Functional verification evaluates internal processing characteristics of the implementation. These are evaluated by verification of integrated functional capabilities. Module flow is mapped from system specifications. Input/output interfaces are identified, and major data interfaces to related functions or programs are determined.

   The integrity of specified software relationships and interfaces is assessed by analyzing specified processing flow and interface parameters. In some cases, extremely critical module sequences are independently modeled to establish the integrity of the overall specified functional structure and flow. This analysis does not address the processing adequacy of the function nor the overall interfunctional support in relation to system processing requirements. These are evaluated by procedures described elsewhere.

8. *Interface Verification.* The functional analysis will extract descriptive interface processing parameters from the developer's specifications and compare these parameters against I/O specifications for the peripheral terminal equipment, and other documented hardware interface requirements. Error analysis, recovery requirements, and proper transfusion of I/O techniques from the system must also be accomplished. This evaluation provides a primary analysis of specified interface support, identifying major deficiencies or incompatibilities in the specified support structure.

9. *Operational Verification.* This technique utilizes specific timing, structure, and processing data derived from prior verifications. This data is used to develop a functional model of the application so as to assess overall processing integrity and isolate development bottlenecks.

   The model will utilize specified and verified system functional flow, and either actual or derived timing data in order to reliably predict the performance of the system in the actual system environment.

Validation

Validation analyzes external performance characteristics of the system using nominal and anomalous system performance conditions. The techniques provide an assurance that the overall performance and accuracy requirements of the system will be met under typical operating conditions. The techniques applied include "black box" functional evaluation, system timing analysis, recovery and integrity analysis, and thread analysis.

Functional validation techniques provide identification of accuracy, performance, and interface characteristics of integrated system functions. Drivers are generated that establish the nominal support environment necessary to execute the function. Using either hardware or software monitoring procedures a precise determination of timing and performance characteristics can be made. The resultant data is used to:

1. Provide an analytical basis for comparing actual performance against basic and specified system requirements.
2. Provide data for accurately tuning the system model.
3. Provide exact data for subsequent profile definitions.

Functional accuracies are established by dumping specific values before and after functional execution, and by comparing results against expected values in order to assess accuracies and establish confidence in the ability of the function to execute within operational constraints.

The timing validation process measures subroutine execution time, I/O channel utilization, wait versus execution time, memory usage, and the effects of varying data rates and error conditional functional execution. Timing validation evaluates the software performance in relation to other associated attributes and to overall functional support requirements.

The recovery characteristics of each critical functional capability are identified and evaluated through internal drivers, which intercept and identify functional or system failures. Known error conditions are introduced through drivers specifically tailored to create the condition. System recovery procedures are monitored to identify the parameters that initiate the recovery.

Thread analysis gives assurance that interfunctional relationships and operational system support are properly defined and implemented. The input and output capabilities of the system are mapped to determine the specific outputs resulting from each input. This process thread definition identifies the functional execution profile for each I/O pair in relation to operational requirements.

Operational test techniques include execution in a simulated and live environment to determine system accuracy and timing. They include:

1. *Simulation Testing* To establish a reproducible test environment, a simulation is set up specifically keyed to evaluating the accuracy and performance of the system. Using this simulated input data, along with drivers tailored to establish the required test environment, testing is carried out in a controlled environment with known data val-

ues. The results of the execution are compared against the expected test results to determine variance.

2. *Live Testing*   Collected data samples are "played back" at varying rates into the software system while in a quasi-operational state. Timing statistics, compiled through hardware and software monitoring equipment, are compared to expected and specified timing statistics to determine compatibility. Data rates are varied to establish the effects of timing and variances on system integrity and support.

3. *Failure Analysis*   The previously described elements do not specifically measure the relative merit of the program implementation. Further, they may not fully identify failure thresholds or characteristics. The following additional techniques are applied as requirements demand.

   Failure analysis identifies system performance limits by degrading the system environment through a predefined and controlled procedure. A set of test cases is selected and executed in a nominal environment. Through special programs, system resources can be selectively removed from the support environment. It is possible to limit available CPU cycle time (removed through disabled loops); available system memory (removed through modifications of system tables); and peripheral support (removed through both hardware and software techniques). Execution characteristics are monitored using both hardware and software monitoring techniques. System degradation and system failure points are then accurately determined. The analysis provides a validation of system support characteristics and integrity as the system environment varies, and also gives an accurate determination of the minimum system configuration to adequately support the operational requirements of the application.

Evaluation tools applied in validating external system performance characteristics include:

1. *Hardware Monitors*   A hardware monitor obtains signals from the computer system by attaching directly to the computer's circuitry probes that measure the presence or absence of electrical impulses without affecting system performance. The monitor is a set of counters and clocks that registers the occurrence of certain significant events, such as CPU and channel activity, recording performance figures by measuring the number of impulses, and the timing at each of the probes.

2. *Software Monitors.*   These are provided as asynchronously executing programs that (a) monitor I/O interrupts by device system service calls, (b) provide data describing system execution, and (c) provide

a determination of CPU utilization. Software monitors collect performance data on specific functions of total system execution and identify processing bottlenecks in the system. These monitors require the addition of specific overhead to the system timing and utilization statistics. Thus, they are not as accurate a measure of actual system performance as hardware techniques; however, they are independent of electrical intervention and provide more flexibility.

3. *Drivers.* In addition to monitoring techniques, a generalized set of system drivers is implemented that establishes a controlled execution environment and drives the system with known data parameters. These drivers are sufficiently generalized to readily permit varying the environment in order to test specific performance characteristics.

The verification and validation analysis phases utilize a comprehensive set of evaluation techniques that must be tailored to the specific analytical requirements. The techniques used and the degree to which each is applied is dependent on program characteristics, operational and functional support requirements, the characteristics of the support environment, and available resources to be applied to the effort. A judicious balance must be maintained between the assignment of resources to elements of the software system and the degree to which the respective verification and validation techniques are applied to a given subset. The distribution of effort must take into account factors, such as the accuracy, timing requirements, reliability, interface specifications, and the criticality of operational support. Regardless of the level of the analysis effort, to be most effective it must be totally isolated from the software development process to assure objectivity of analysis and independence of results.

11

ORGANIZATION AND PERSONNEL

The organizational and procedural segments that are used to monitor and assure software quality should be distributed throughout the program organization and should monitor all categories of data: system engineering, hardware and software development, and software test and integration.

QUALITY ORGANIZATIONAL REQUIREMENTS

Quality is the responsibility and goal of the entire project organization. Previous chapters have concentrated on the project infrastructure and the process of, and products of development in order to describe how quality is achieved in a software development project. This chapter describes the organizational and personnel requirements of the project with special emphasis on quality.

The project team organization ranges from a small integrated team of people for smaller projects to a large team of matrixed personnel for a sizable project. Since the matrix organization is the norm for most large companies this will be used as the baseline for describing how quality is built into the organization. The subject of smaller projects and organizations will be treated as a special topic, as will the topic of independent verification and validation (IV&V). The primary emphasis will be on concepts rather than on a specific organization, that is, organizations will not be developed, but the relationships, techniques, and methods for ensuring quality will be stressed.

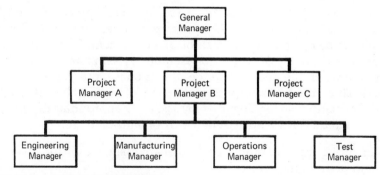

Figure 11-1. Project organization.

Figures 11-1 and 11-2 provide a basic model that is representative of contractor organizations. The project normally reports to a program area manager, or directly to a general manager, depending on the size of the project and organization. Supporting resources are matrixed in from the engineering organization with supporting disciplines, such as configuration management, test, and quality assurance, from a system support or functional organization. This typical structure distributes control of the project to several different places. The project manager "buys" resources from the various resource managers, mainly from engineering, which provides the bulk of the resources necessary to accomplish the project development. Resource assignment, in terms of specific personnel, is a negotiation between the project manager and the engineering manager. The project manager cannot

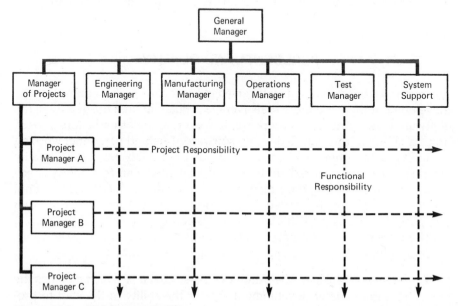

Figure 11-2. Matrix organization.

count on specific personnel that he or she may have preference for. The engineering manager, however, can assign personnel based on the specific task which is being accomplished at the given moment. If the project is in the requirements analysis phase, for example, system analysts can be assigned, and when the project is in the coding phase, programmers can be assigned. Thus, the basic purpose of this type of organization is to afford flexibility in manpower loading, thereby assigning appropriate expertise for the task at hand. The advantages of matrix organization are:

1. Ensuring that the proper personnel are assigned for the given task and point in the project.
2. Leveling the project manpower loading, thus alleviating the project manager from carrying personnel in periods of low manpower loading requirements.
3. Giving the organization at large the capability to efficiently use personnel across a spectrum of projects.

Matrix management actually creates an environment that supports independent assessment, therefore, directly supports software quality assurance. There are at least two channels available to report on the project. For example, the configuration management and quality assurance teams report to their respective functional manager, and if necessary, to the overall (general) manager, if the situation warrants that level of review and arbitration. Thus, separate reporting channels are built into the matrix organization. Of course, these channels are not "automatically" exercised unless special provisions are developed in the organization to take advantage of this opportunity.

PERSONNEL AND QUALITY

If you don't have a qualified staff versed in the technologies required for the development there is a more than average probability that the quality of the software will be impacted. There are, however, many other factors impacting the ability of the staff to develop software. Talented personnel working as individuals rather than a team will not predictably produce a quality product. The unstructured application of a talented staff to a poorly specified requirement does not normally result in a quality product. Talent, if not focused, will become frustrated, lose commitment and eventually drift from the goal of producing a software product meeting quality requirements.

There are many personnel considerations which impact quality and software development productivity. Four of the most critical are:

1. *Personnel Selection.*   Selection of a personnel mix which matches the requirements of development against the ability of the staff to produce it.

2. *Personnel Application.* The controlled application of personnel resources to the technical requirements of development, the constraints of schedule and cost and the needs of the project.

3. *Team Building.* Ensuring that activities of the entire staff are coordinated and that there is clear focus to project delivery requirements.

4. *Personnel Commitment.* Gaining and maintaining the commitment of the staff to the common goals and objectives by forcing a sense of ownership on the part of the organization. Establishing a project environment which will enable open communication between members of the staff, ensure that frustrations and problems are not lost, and providing a communication environment where everyone feels that they are a valued member of the organization. As Don Reifer put it:

I look at personnel problems like a coach. I've got a team to build with less than adequate staff. If I build it, I'll win because each team member will compensate for and help shore up the weaknesses of the others. I've got one or two superstars, five to eight average "Joe's and Jane's and three to four new guys. The concepts of team building and team rewards must be used to mold them into a coherent working group where each cares about the others and all try to achieve a common goal. Give me a person who can communicate and I'll teach him the technical details. Give me three people who can communicate and I'll design a system. Give me 10 people who can communicate and I'll conquer the world.

Personnel Selection

The selection of a staff is analogous to a carpenter selecting tools to build a building. The tools are selected after thorough definition of the steps required to build the building, the schedules and plans for doing the work and, most importantly, a complete definition of the building material requirements. Likewise, the personnel resources are the basic tools which are used to build the software. There is a two edged sword. On the one hand, if the personnel mix is not adequate to support the project the risk is high that they will not have sufficient expertise to complete the development. On the other hand, if the personnel mix is too rich for the project, there will be difficulty focusing their activities, gaining and maintaining commitment and challenging the staff. Getting the best people available is not always the best solution to the software project infrastructure requirement.

In order to match personnel to the project the order of selection is to:

1. Define what will be done from a technical and development perspective.

2. Define how the software project will be implemented and the associated technologies required.

3. Define the specific requirements for numbers of personnel, the experience and expertise by personnel category and the personnel support requirements which provide essential nontechnical services and project control.

Because of a variety of project reasons, too often this sequence of events is violated. Personnel requirements are defined in the flush of the early project, then the personnel acquisition process begins. There is not yet a clear definition of the software technical environment and its implications. There is no reason that total personnel decisions have to be made this early in the project. Categories of personnel can be defined, however, the specific individual personnel requirements need not be defined until the specification for the particular job is complete.

This "phasing of manpower selection" is essential to ensure that the individual staff members fit a staffing profile that matches the project needs. From an implementation perspective, this staffing consistency is critical to project success.

Personnel Application

Even if the optimum staff is selected the problem of applying them effectively to the software project often obviates their potential.

In order to achieve maximum productivity staff members must be phased into the project smoothly, allowing time for training, project orientation, and administrative processing. There must be a clearly defined project structure for the staff members to move into. There must be a documented job with established responsibilities, detailed technical parameters describing the tasks to be accomplished and a clearly defined set of individual and organizational relationships establishing the staff relationships.

The phasing of personnel on to the project must be consistent with scheduled development activities, budget allocations, and predefined development requirements. Everyone must be applied to fill a specific project need. If personnel are applied to the project in an unstructured manner, or worse, brought in to satisfy an undefined or poorly specified requirement, the fabric of the project will be seriously impacted. As they struggle to find their niche, they will be taking time from the productive members of the staff affecting not only their own productivity but the productivity of those around them. To paraphrase Brooks in *The Mythical Man Month*, the addition of staff to an unstructured project will have a negative impact on the schedule required to complete. Everyone working on a software project, whether it be a new employee, a newly assigned staff member, or a long-term project member, must have an assigned task that he or she is accountable for and committed to accomplish.

It is important to plan the organization with phased resources that will meet the requirements of the development project. A number of resource

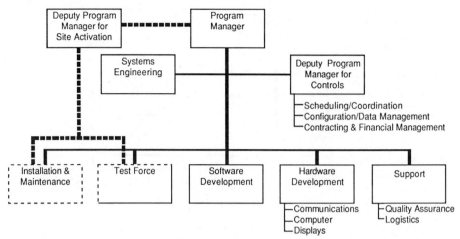

Figure 11-3.   Project organization.

(cost) modeling techniques (e.g., Cocomo) have been developed over the past years to estimate development resource requirements for a large spectrum of development projects. Resource models are not a subject of this book. Rather, it is important to understand that an appropriate mix of personnel should be brought on board to manage the disciplines required to properly support the development project. These disciplines include quality assurance, configuration management, test, and program control.

A simple example illustrates the concept of phasing personnel. Let us assume that we have a program/project that will range around 250K instructions. This is a manageable example, yet can be scaled up or down easily to accommodate smaller or larger projects. Figure 11-3 depicts a prototypical organization for this project. The details of the project are not important; however, in order to set the example lets assume that the project is characterized by a real time application of software to existing (off-the-shelf) hardware interfacing to sensors (e.g., radar) and displaying the results of sensor processing and other data processing functions. Thus, the project incorporates software development, hardware/software integration, test, site installation and checkout, and operations and maintenance.

Figures 11-4 to 11-6 illustrate how these resources may be phased over the life of the project depending on the particular phase of the project. In Figure 11-4 the primary need is for systems engineering. Since the project is software intensive, the software personnel are initially analysts in the systems engineering function. At this point the hardware function is primarily intended to support systems engineering and plan for the acquisition of off-the-shelf hardware. Even at this early phase in the project, support functions are not ignored. The deputy program manager for controls concentrates on the programmatic provisions of the project, including configuration management and documentation control. In the support

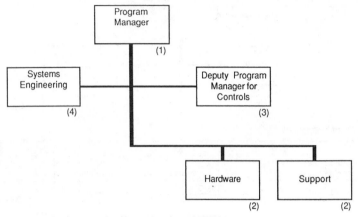

Figure 11-4. Project organization phasing (initial).

function, planning for the important aspects of the project infrastructure takes place, specifically, provisions for quality assurance, computer resources management plans, software development plans, programming standards and conventions, and so forth. Thus the initial program management team includes these essential personnel, or at the very least makes early provision for these activities if the size of the project does not warrant assignment of dedicated specialty personnel at this point in time. Too many projects just start with engineering, and do not include early provision for life cycle activities to include quality assurance.

The peak development organization is shown in Figure 11-5. Notice that the support function has increased to a level of five, representing approximately 7.5 percent of overall project resources. Systems engineering analyst capability has phased down as the bulk of activity shifts to development, and test and initial site activation activities. In Figure 11-6 the project has

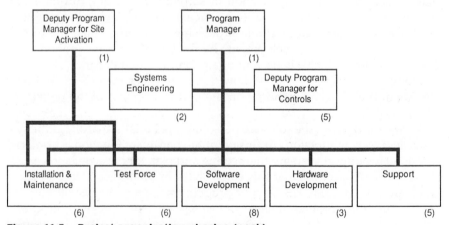

Figure 11-5. Project organization phasing (peak).

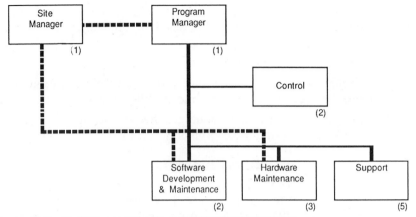

Figure 11-6. Project organization phasing (maintenance).

reduced to a level that would support continuing operations and maintenance. The provisions for support continue with a level of two man years. Naturally this level would depend on many factors; for example, the extent of contractor involvement in logistics tasks, and the level of hardware/software maintenance and modification activity. The important point is that support, including quality assurance, is retained as a continuing lifecycle activity.

Team Building

Team building activities are those that take individuals assigned to a project, coordinate and motivate them towards the production of an integrated product, and focus the activities of the team towards a common set of goals and objectives. Clear staff focus is the single most important component of a team; the staff must all be heading in the same direction.

Even simple software applications require the commitment and interaction of more than one individual to complete. There are requirements to define, a design to develop, code to produce, tests to run, and documentation to complete.

It is too much for even a super programmer. The only way to achieve success is to build a team capable of producing the software, and meeting the needs of development. Depending on the size of the project, the development team can actually be several teams linked together through management polices and practices.

The building of a team committed to the production of quality software requires the presence of five factors.

1. Organizational structures which isolate functional areas of the project, and provide clear organizational tasking and intergroup communication.

2. Clear and understood project goals and objectives that are broken into specific tasks, and assigned to development teams.

3. Measureable milestones that can be used to evaluate team effectiveness and assess performance.

4. Management awareness of the roles and responsibility of each project team, the team relationships, and the allocation of work.

5. A project environment that encourages the satisfaction of individual goals while demanding the completion of team commitments.

Personnel Commitment

There is probably no single component of the project which has a greater effect on development risk than achieving the commitment of the staff towards the production of quality software. What do you look for when assessing the commitment of the development staff? The basic indicator is the clarity and commonality of project goals and objectives, and how well these are understood. For example, if you interview two or more individuals working on the same or related set of tasks within the project, each should understand and be committed to the same, or certainly very similar goals; have the same development objectives, and understand and be working against a common set of constraints. Creative interpretations of the specifics required by each task, license taken with data product form, structure, content and completeness, or an incomplete, inconsistent understanding of development constraints are indications that management is "not in control." If the goals, objectives, and project constraints are not commonly understood, achieving a staff commitment to develop a product is difficult.

The second set of staff commitment indicators includes the visible project signs of staff morale.

1. Overall level of staff enthusiasm and interest in specific problems of software development.

2. Efficiency of the software process and data and responsibility transition effectiveness.

3. Schedule performance and the staff's sense of obvious urgency to meet schedule milestones. The sense of urgency must be from the standpoint of schedule adherence and quality requirements.

4. Staff "esprit de corps". The overall attitude of the individual members of the staff to the project and the overall structure of the organization and the technical, administrative, and organization commitments of the project.

These, and other indicators, are the visible measures of staff commitment.

What can a project do to increase the commitment of the staff? There are four primary contributors to commitment that are under project control: accountability, urgency, peer pressure, and success.

Accountability

Perhaps the most significant contributor to staff commitment is accountability, both from a management standpoint and from the staff perspective. Accountability, when coupled with a project structure of project rewards and penalties, forces a clear focus towards schedule and quality.

A staff member should be measured by specific performance rather than perceived or undocumented performance or "flash." This measure translates directly into dollars, promotion, reinforcement, or increased responsibility. There is a high probability that the staff will be committed to the development, and accept accountability for development performance, if these factors exist. Accountability without reward is not a motivator.

Urgency

Urgency is a second motivator towards commitment. When the overriding staff concern is meeting a milestone that is approaching, and there is a clear commitment to meet the milestone, all other priorities (personal, bureaucratic, project overhead, and management) become secondary. Individual focus becomes meeting the milestone not the development process, nor the analysis, nor the support aspects of meeting the milestone. The blinders are put on and the individual presses forward towards the milestone.

Urgency can be forced by scheduling. If the lowest level schedules have short (2 weeks to one month) milestones, if the milestones are clearly specified and a reward/penalty structure for meeting milestones is in place, a sense of urgency will be the by-product.

Peer Pressure

Peer pressure is a basic component for staff commitment. If there is a feeling that what I do affects the efforts of people I work with, if I care about this, and if my impacts on schedule slips are obvious, the pressures to meet development commitments will be significant. If not, the commitment to perform will be driven by the motivation of individual members of the staff, not by the needs of the project. While individual motivation is necessary, it may not be sufficient.

What are the indicators of peer pressure in the project environment? The first is how well tasks and performance milestones are isolated such that individual responsibility is clear. Poor individual performances can't be masked by project inefficiencies or implementation problems.

The second indicator is the project level rewards and penalties. As described previously, individual commitment is achieved partially by the reward incentives and practices. Likewise, the structure of project reward is essential if peer pressure is used as a means to achieve staff commitment. The software project manager should be responsible and accountable for software schedule, quality, and project performance. Accountability, project commitment, and responsibility should tree down through the organization to the lowest level of the staff. Incentives, rewards, and penalties should be distributed downward through the project organization. It is a mistake for a software manager to shield his or her staff from the effects of their own poor performance.

Finally, the software team must look on the project as a partnership between management, the customer, and the technical staff. Poor performance, by any part of the partnership that affects the software, must be dealt with by the management of the software project. A failure to act and resolve project shortfalls, whether they are management, technical, or personnel issues will cause dissention, project unrest, and will destroy any peer pressure within the project.

Success

There is no more effective motivator, or generator of staff commitment, than sustained and visible project success. Achievement of goals and the production of data products that the team is proud of, and that are recognized as quality, will result in a committed staff, a development team, and a focused and dedicated organization. Success breeds commitment and, ultimately, product quality.

From the other perspective, personnel working in projects that are characterized by failure and frustration quickly lose commitment. Why work hard if, in the overall context of the project, the efforts of the individual won't have any effect? Why break your back if those around you are generating "garbage?" Without project success, staff commitment is difficult, and often impossible, to achieve.

Project success has four observable characteristics.

1. Continued schedule emphasis with a staff commitment to meeting all dates.

2. Engineering data products and end items that generally meet a consistent standard of quality and are approved without major rework.

3. A project environment which makes individual progress and success visible, and rewards or penalizes performance in a timely manner.

4. Frequent and current releases of controlled project information or software systems which are documented, have an identifiable configuration, and have a documented level of quality or operational integrity.

REPORTING AND QUALITY

One of the key provisions of an orderly development is management concern for the progress of the project. This concern is alleviated through reporting procedures that are built into the management process. It is the responsibility of management in general to ensure that appropriate review mechanisms are in place to support visibility into the project at all concerned levels. Naturally, the amount and extent of detail will vary depending on the review level within the company organization. However, without prior planning to ensure that appropriate mechanisms are in place, visibility into the development will be extremely difficult, and could lead to major management problems if the project encounters development difficulties.

The project manager will often resist separate reporting, since it involves a parallel inspection or audit of the project. (Needless to say, on small projects where the development team may be dedicated, this opportunity is not present, and other methods are required to accomplish independent review. It is useful to point out that this lack of opportunity is usually a major problem on smaller projects, and considerations for adequate configuration management, testing and quality assurance are usually downgraded or ignored). In any project the mind set of the project manager is towards the project and he or she will ignore all attempts for what is considered to be undue help, such as independent audits or reviews. As a result, these reviews are usually forced upon the manager when major problems arise in the development, and that is exactly the situation that should be avoided. The demonstrated psychology of project management is to hide a disaster as long as humanly possible in hopes that a minor miracle will result. This has nothing to do with project managers, rather, it is endemic to human performance. It is up to the management system to prevent this type of situation. If problems do arise, it is advantageous to address them as soon as possible; this has been proven time and time again. As disagreeable as it may be to the project manager, the benefit of independent review, if accomplished correctly, is beneficial to the organization as a whole, to the contracting organization or user, and to the ultimate user as well.

INDEPENDENT ANALYSIS—FORCING MANAGEMENT VISIBILITY

The role of independent verification and validation (IV&V) is often confused with software quality assurance. It can be used to support quality assurance, however, it has many other roles. IV&V is the independent (from the developing organization) review of the software project. Independence can be achieved, outside the project organization, by the use of a dedicated team to monitor the project. Before we get into the use of IV&V, it is useful to describe the context within which it will be discussed in this book. There are a number of reasons or methods for the use of IV&V in a software development project.

1. *The SEDA Role.* A software engineering and development activity is sometimes employed by a contracting organization to provide an engineering capability (or addition to an engineering activity).

2. *Independent Testing.* A project may warrant, for any number of reasons, independent testing to assess compliance with system requirements. Usually, these reasons are due to the criticality of the project; it may be a nuclear system, an early warning system or a man-critical system, such as a manned space vehicle. The highly sensitive reasons, in the use of the system, may warrant increased testing resources to provide a higher degree of confidence in the viability of the overall operability of the system.

3. *IV&V.* In this context, IV&V is a practiced discipline to provide an independent assessment of the total project development through the verification of individual development products, and the validation of the delivered product against the stated requirements of the user or system requirements.

In the next several paragraphs we will address each of these practices, relative to the organizational structure of the developing organization or project organization.

SEDA. The relationship of the SEDA contractor to the developing contractor. In some cases the SEDA contractor will be integrated into the contracting organization. In these cases there does not appear to be a difference between contracting personnel and SEDA personnel. The provisions of the contract should dictate how the contracting organization interfaces with the contractor or project personnel. Normally, these procedures are embellished in the various software development plans and have to do with the formal review process. The contracting organization will review the products of the development and participate, or conduct formal reviews, in accordance with prescribed project milestones. In cases where the contracting organization chooses to use the SEDA organization in a special role, or separate from the contracting organization, this relationship should be specified in the contract. These relationships usually involve the interaction of the SEDA contractor with the developing contractor in terms of their roles in reviews, visits to the contractor location, and so forth. These differences are more apparent than real, however, and the SEDA is normally viewed as a part of the developing organization.

Independent Test Organization. This role calls for a careful description of the use of the test organization relative to the project organization. Will the independent test organization be testing the product at the end of the development period or will they be involved in testing throughout the development? In any case, the relationship of the independent test organization with the developing contractor must be specified in the contractual instrument. Access to specifications, test plans, participation in reviews, etc., are all issues that must be clearly defined at the front of the development so that the role and prerogatives of the test contractor are known.

IV&V Contractor. The same considerations are prevalent with the use of an IV&V contractor or organization. The role of, and relationship to, the developing organization must be specified in the contract. This is even more important in classic IV&V, since the IV&V organization is involved in monitoring the process of development as well as products of development. IV&V is like having an on-site inspection team. Their relationship should not be an adversarial one however, and it is up to the contracting organization to carefully define and control this interface so as to maintain a positive environment. Usually, problems arise when the project is going awry, and this is a good indication that there may be serious development problems.

SUMMARY

The provisions of the chapter cover organizational and personnel considerations for building quality into the software product.

The main theme of the management organization should be to build quality provisions into the project during the planning process. It is never too early to start thinking about quality; indeed quality requirements should be incorporated into the systems requirements specification. Management must be concerned with building appropriate review procedures that provide visibility into project status. Visibility should be provided throughout all levels of the organization, with appropriate levels of detail, depending on the level of review in the organization.

Independence of review is a basic tenet of the development process. No matter how it is built into the development process, or whose toes it might step on, it is an extemely important practice to ensure that management gains "honest" visibility into project status. There are many reasons that independence is left out of the project, however, they are often invalid when viewed during a post-mortem attempt to find out what went wrong. Usually this turns out to be the wrong time to discover the problem, and punish the guilty, because it is too late and too expensive to fix the problem.

In any organization people are the key to success. Project personnel must be focused on the goals of the project, supported by a project infrastructure with appropriate engineering practices, and most importantly, properly motivated to accomplish the goals of the program. There must be personal commitment to the goals of the program. Not only must the personnel selected be competent, they also must be phased across the needs of the lifecycle. An example illustrated how phasing manpower throughout the project lifecycle provides for appropriate support resources. Motivation must be supplied through team building, and project personnel should manifest commitment through staff enthusiasm, support of project schedules, and positive individual attitude.

12

THE EFFECT OF RESOURCE AVAILABILITY ON QUALITY

The quality of the software is a function of many factors: technical, administrative, organizational, and management related. Irrespective of the adequacy of these factors in the context of the development environment, there is an obvious and irrefutable quality law that cannot be violated: "If you ain't got the bucks, you can't build the product."

RESOURCE IDENTIFICATION

There are two primary points concerning the law which must be noted:

1. The rule indicates an absolute condition exists: If there are not adequate resources, the product must suffer. This implies that there must be an accurate projection of the resource requirements, an allocation of these to the software project, appropriate phasing of resource requirements to the schedule, and a means to assess resource effectiveness.

2. There must be a sufficiently robust program and systems organization to ensure that the resources and support to the software project are available to provide the higher level support functions (i.e., system integration, program control, system engineering, etc.) essential for system success.

Even in the simplest software development applications, there is a need to project accurately what it will take to develop the software, schedule resource requirements, and establish a smooth working relationship with external organizations supporting or interfacing with the software project. The following sections describe the role of the systems and program organizations in relation to software quality, and discuss software cost and schedule requirements from a quality assurance viewpoint.

RESOURCE AVAILABILITY—THE RIGHT ONES WHEN NEEDED

The nonavailability of critical resources when needed is a common cause of software quality problems, often limiting or precluding implementation success. Consider the project problems resulting from the removal or redirection of a key resource in the midst of the development, such as slippage in a critical hardware schedule or loss of a key employee. Unless anticipated, these situations can be devastating; that is, undermining the ability of the project to develop the software in accordance with predefined budgets and schedules. Because of the nature of the software development process, these crises most often become critical during the integration of the software into an executable configuration. These project crises can be avoided, but only if they are anticipated, solutions planned, and the planned solutions rigorously implemented.

The common resource-related problems which may be anticipated fall into three categories.

1. Hardware facilities essential to the project but not available when needed.
2. Personnel resources required at a given point in the project but, due to conditions outside the control of the software manager, not available when needed.
3. Resource shortfalls in key areas resulting from poor early planning, changing project conditions, or both.

Each of these problems has a significant potential for occurrence. The software manager should recognize their potential and structure the project and allocate resources to avoid these problems and the often resulting quality impacts.

The planning and implementation of the software financial schedule, administrative practices, and early definition of project monitoring practices and procedures, is an essential component of software quality. In order to maintain accurate visibility into the technical and administrative health of the project, the software manager must incorporate these into the project quality gates. These quality gates provide data to evaluate the effectiveness of the software project organization, assess project administration controls and practices, and measure the technical integrity of the project.

Planning and implementation of these controls is often looked on, especially by management, as an adjunct to hardware project development, ancillary to the technical activities of the project and, as a result, of secondary importance. Cost and schedule monitoring requirements are often implemented by personnel with neither project or software development experience. The monitoring approaches are often not tailored to specific project characteristics, and do not integrate the diverse and often conflicting areas of software development. Even when they do, they may not be accepted by software management or project personnel as a constructive, positive source of data.

RESOURCE ALLOCATION

Projecting the resources required to develop a system and allocating them correctly to system engineering, hardware, and software development is a difficult, often impossible task facing the program manager. Estimation techniques are only approximations and are valid only when they have been customized to reflect the realities of the software engineering methodology and company management practices and policies. There is often pressure from both the customer and company management to reduce budgets and shorten schedules. Often the customer does not have a full appreciation of the difficulty associated with the translation of program requirements into program estimates and project delivery schedules. Commitments are often made by management, especially in the heat of controversy, that compromise realistic budgets and schedules. Individual organizations within the program compete for resources, exerting even more pressure on beleaguered management.

Often a systems manager will fail to come to grips with this problem early. He or she will succumb to the temptation to "take the heat off", *and accede* to the demands of functional managers for additional resources. Budget allocation, development schedules and organizational assignments are made to minimize confrontation rather than maintain and support the true needs of the program. This is, of course, the worst case scenario. If it happens, project integrity has collapsed.

The impact of this situation has a devastating effect on the effectiveness of the software project and the quality of the software that is produced. The software manager is forced to schedule and budget to unrealistic goals, and ignore critical planning activities in hope of meeting technical milestones that may not be achievable. Shortcuts are taken to reduce cost and maximize performance at the expense of technical performance. Project emphasis and direction is placed on the next milestone rather than delivery of the system and achieving the end objectives of the program. As schedules become compressed, essential implementation controls and development plans are dropped. The result: the quality of the software not only suffers, but the system may not be deliverable.

RECOGNIZING RESOURCE SHORTFALLS

Software project impacts associated with inadequate resources or schedules must be recognized early if actions are to be taken to assure quality software.

Specification of system and software development resource requirements must take place before beginning development. Like it or not, many times these early projections are the only static factor in the development. Requirements increase, design parameters change, and interfaces are constantly being redefined with the changing systems. Although the budget may be fixed, the basis for the software estimate is not.

At the beginning of system development, system development requirements, development cost, schedule constraints and system operational concepts are defined. The inputs to each development phase are identified and documented and the specifics of each individual product defined. During this phase of development, the foundation is laid for the specification of the system and its ultimate acceptance into the operational environment. As such, the methodologies used to develop and document the cost, schedule, and technical requirements must provide the following:

1. A definition of operational requirements which may be traced through the requirements definition, design, implementation, and test and integration phases.

2. An identification of the technical environment within which the system must operate, including interfaces which must be supported, performance and reliability requirements which must be met, and specific data products and operational data which must be produced if the system is to be operationally sound.

3. Cost and schedule projections which are realistic, based on technical understanding, auditable, traceable and measurable. The cost and schedule projections should be compartmentalized in such a way as to facilitate comparative analyses with independently derived estimates.

4. Technical requirements which are traceable, testable, and which lay the basis for specification of the system architecture and basic system requirements.

5. Risk and contingency analyses which identify the major development risks which must be considered when building the system.

Early in the development the data products are unstable; they change frequently as more information is fixed about system requirements, or the operational characteristics of the application, or user environment. As such, this early phase of the program, in many respects, resembles a study activity and thus employs different management and control practices than the system development. For example, the dynamic nature of the data and the non-operational nature of the end items require a loose configuration management system. Formal project reviews are not as useful as informal walkthroughs conducted by peer groups. This stage of the program is best served by a small, highly motivated team familiar with all aspects of the application and technology, and by very close, informal communications within the organization.

WORK ALLOCATION

Although supporting program functions are not readily perceived by the software development staff, they bear a significant relationship to the success of the project: the ability of the software manager to meet project goals, commitments, and objectives, and to develop a quality product. The software manager must recognize the importance of program control, performance monitoring, and resource management. The prudent software manager recognizes that control over resources during the development period and early recognition of schedule, cost and performance problems will have a positive effect on the quality of the product, and provide a vehicle by which he or she can redirect resources, reallocate work, or modify project parameters to correct development problems.

Within the program environment, the software to be produced is only one of many program elements. These elements include: systems engineering, hardware development, integration and test, installation, logistics, training, etc. The program manager must orchestrate the activities and manage the interactions between them.

The degree to which the manager is successful in this role has a direct relation to how successful the program is and, as a result, the success of the software development.

For the program manager, the overriding concern is to be sure that the activities of these diffuse project elements work together in an effective and controlled manner, and that the program is developed within preallocated schedule and budget constraints.

The initial and possibly the most important step in the program management process is the determination and definition of program objectives for the proposal, contract, and customer documentation. Objectives must be based first on the total program and then extended to the more detailed levels.

A contract summary is often used by the program manager to develop and document initial resource projections and program schedules. This summary is primarily a financial document describing costing and profit projections, schedule commitments, and contract risks. It is the first communication between a program manager and management that commits the program to resource requirements. Based on this summary, the manager tasks the software staff to develop cost and schedule projections, and allocates work throughout the program organization through the program work breakdown structure (WBS).

The work breakdown structure is the primary method of organizing and allocating work throughout the organization. It is the basis for planning and defining a structure for the program, allocating work, and tasking individual organizational elements in a coordinated manner. The WBS is a product-oriented division of hardware, software, services, and other work tasks that organize, define, and graphically display the work elements of the project. Its configuration, content, and detail will vary and will depend on:

1. The size and complexity of the program
2. The organizational structure of participating organizations
3. The arrangement of responsibility for the work to be performed according to the judgment of management

At the top level, the WBS is an identification of the program. From the program, the end items that are major segments of the program or system to be developed are defined. These are then allocated into all required components of the system; the specific work package instructions, and finally, all revisions to work packages and functional planning.

These basic program objectives form the core of the program planning process and, when properly expressed and translated into a WBS structure, provide focus and organization to the program activities. This is accomplished by:

1. Providing a framework to identify project requirements separately from the performing organizations, cost estimating and accounting systems, funding sources, and so on.
2. Providing insight into project element interrelationships and overlaps.
3. Identifying specific work packages for time, cost, labor, and material estimating; pricing; budgeting; work assignment and authorization; accounting; and reporting.
4. Allocating system reliability requirements to subsystems and components.
5. Establishing a specification tree for defining documentation hierarchies and production requirements.

Work Breakdown Structure Development

The WBS decomposes work throughout the project into successively lower levels, resulting in a graphical, hierarchal decomposition of work packages. The WBS is developed by starting at the top level, which provides the program definition, and through an interactive procedure, decomposes work until all levels of the WBS have been satisfied. The number of WBS levels required is a function of:

1. System size
2. Cost accounts and work packages dollar size
3. Personnel requirements for the program and for individual task areas
4. Task duration and schedule
5. Number of milestones in each task
6. Implementation cost
7. Management confidence

The lowest level of the WBS is the point at which the program manager delegates direct management control to the functional or development organizations.

Cost Accounts

Cost accounts represent the effort to be performed by a functional organization in support of a single WBS element. They are used to accumulate summarized project performance data and represent the lowest level in the work breakdown structure at which actual costs are required to be recorded. The planned value of work performed is summarized in these accounts for comparison with actual costs.

Cost accounts are natural points for cost schedule planning control, and is the point at which the organizational structure and the contract work breakdown structure is linked. Planning an appropriate account code structure is essential.

Work Packages

The work package describes the specific requirements, by task, to be used in controlling development.

Work packages are detailed descriptions of work to be accomplished, or required, to complete the contract. A work package:

1. Describes manageable units of work
2. Is unique and clearly distinguished from all other work packages

3. Is scheduled with a start and completion date; has defined, documented scope; and is controlled by budgets (expressed in labor hours, dollars, or other measurable units)

4. Assigns responsibility for performing the work to a single organizational element, with any suballocation of work done by the assigned organization

5. Is integrated with detailed engineering, manufacturing, and other schedules as applicable

A work package is job-specific, resulting in a specific set of products or services, such as a report, a piece of hardware, or a service that is the responsibility of one operating unit within an organization. Work packages plan what must be accomplished, by whom, and provide the basis for the estimation of resources required to accomplish the project.

The size of work packages depends on the degree of management visibility desired and the extent of control to be exercised on the project. Work packages should be small enough to facilitate their management and afford flexibility in the development effort, minimizing the need to redefine them as the project proceeds and program requirements change.

When work packages are defined in great detail, they do not afford flexibility to accommodate changes that arise. If requirement changes or problems are encountered that require alteration of the overall work effort that cannot be reflected in the work allocation, this could cause a disruption of the total program work assignment. The relationship of the technical accomplishment to schedule and budget is a key problem facing program management. Large work packages, covering a major portion of the work, make monitoring of technical progress in relation to budget and schedule projections difficult to determine.

Failure to accomplish assigned tasks on schedule does not become evident until a major milestone is missed, which, in turn, necessitates the readjustment of, and reorganization of, schedule and resource allocations throughout the balance of the program.

PROGRAM PLANNING

When planning the program, generic program objectives are converted to detailed planning requirements and assigned to organization managers for implementation. The managers develop these plans down through the cost account level.

Cost accounts may be summarized to represent the effort to be performed by a major program organization in support of a single WBS element. The program manager ensures that these account summaries are approved by the performing organization before their release for use in the program. Work authorizations ensure that the program manager and supporting organizations have a thorough understanding of the requirements, and that the assigned work has been accepted and understood by the performing group.

After the program manager and performing organizations agree to the budgets for the cost accounts within each area, these are issued as an integral part of the work authorization process and become the basis for cost performance measurement. Resources that have been negotiated, but have not been authorized to the performing organizations, are maintained as planning packages within each organization. The planning process constantly reassesses the work definition against progress and the remaining schedule and resource constraints. Replanning exercises continually result in new or revised work authorizations that modify, delete, or add to tasks, schedules, technical requirements, or resource commitments.

Schedule Planning

Schedule planning is the preparation of project schedules, and includes the development of project master schedules and subordinate schedules, based on the WBS. Schedule planning ensures that all elements of the program are delivered on time and that the activities of program organizations are integrated and focused to specific milestones. Work authorizations clearly identify work statements, schedule requirements, and cost elements to the lowest level of planning and control.

Scheduling is an interactive and dynamic process that, like all planning, starts with a broad plan that is then successively decomposed to lower levels, and then adjusted as more information and facts become available and as changes, modifications, and revisions occur as a result of both in-house and customer action.

Schedules summarize numerous organizational activities into time-phased milestone plans, and provide the project manager an overview of integrated plans for hardware, software, and documentation development and delivery.

Types of Schedules

There are several different levels of schedules by which a program manager controls, orchestrates, and monitors performance. The top level, the master program schedule, identifies the overall goals and objectives for the program. These top level schedules are the schedules that control development of the second-level WBS tasks.

The master program schedule has two major objectives:

1. To provide a technical planning base
2. To smooth the allocation and application of resources

The master project schedule is based on the customer's planning schedules. Its development starts during the conceptual phase prior to contract start, when top level requirements, preliminary cost estimates, and technical requirements are defined and standards set. The schedule is progressively refined during proposal preparation, and in negotiation; and is finalized after customer agreement or contract award.

Through the master schedule, specific project requirements, objectives, and ground rules are established, project deliverables and interim products are defined, and a project logic network is established. This network establishes the task sequences and interdependencies required to satisfy the contract, as well as describe baseline documents, requirements, design, development, facilities, associate contractor, subcontractor, material requirements, fabrication, assembly and checkout, software, and all supporting activities.

From the master schedule, the performing organizations develop more detailed subordinate element schedules, which are integrated into the higher level schedule plans. Informal working-level schedules are developed down to the individual working level and are continuously reviewed and analyzed to ensure that they are compatible with program activities and experience.

Scheduling Detail

After the scope of application has been determined, the optimal level of detail to be included on the networks must be defined. Level of detail refers to the relative number of project events and activities shown on the network, and primarily depends on the degree of project information predetermined to be necessary for adequate programming and control purposes.

As a general rule, the level of detail should be determined beginning with top management information needs and working systematically down through the various organizational levels. This top-down approach reduces the risk of accidental omission of important events that must be monitored. The level of detail may be increased as tighter control is determined to be needed for more extensive planning and control of critical path activities. The relationship among the program evaluation review technique (PERT), WBS, and work packages is direct and is maintained through the charge numbers and program summary number defined through the WBS dictionary.

Milestones

Milestones are the means to measure progress against the program plan. Milestones represent the completion of a total work package, or of a component part that is significant to some other phase of the program. There should be periodic progress reporting against milestone performance by the personnel responsible for the various work packages, and the manager should use these reports to make the necessary management decisions and actions. In order to provide this data, it is desirable, on the PERT schedule, to have at least one milestone per work package per reporting period.

SOFTWARE COST ALLOCATION AND ITS RELATION TO QUALITY

Much work has been done, within the industry, in the areas of software sizing, productivity estimation, cost derivation, and work and resource allocation. Unfortunately, unlike other industries where the costs associated with development correlate to some quantifiable measure such as square feet, software product costs correlate to functional attributes, which are difficult to size.

The software industry, unlike older more established industries, has not yet developed standard tools, techniques, and methodologies for projecting or validating software development resource requirements.

When estimating software, the typical base unit of measure for the sizing of a software product, and hence the basis for estimating resources required to develop it, is the line of code.

Secondly, most programmers do not know how to estimate lines of code. Most programmers have not done the same work over and over again, and do not have a reference point from which to measure.

Finally, there are any number of ways a set of specifications can be coded to achieve the same basic result, even when the input and output formats are fixed.

Even if we could estimate lines of code with any accuracy, this quantity would only be clearly useful when the functions to be coded are defined with regard to input, processing, and output. Specifying the job itself is a major part of the work to be done.

The customer cannot always provide a detailed software specification, nor can the cost and schedule projection wait until the specifications are complete. Like it or not, the project must estimate not only how long it will take to build the product, but also how long it will be before we determine exactly what the job is to do. A cost relationship must be established between user requirements and the work that must be done to meet these requirements.

Often these critical and early estimates are made by personnel unfamiliar with the unique requirements of software development and the complex project interactions essential for software development success. They are often caught in a whirlwind of activity focused towards satisfaction of critical short term milestones. Meeting an early program review schedule, with whatever is available, often becomes more important than laying a nonambiguous, testable, and traceable foundation for the program responsive to user needs. Staffing the project frequently takes precedence over defining the organizational structure and requirements. Defining budgets and schedules, and negotiating resource requirements, many times becomes more critical than defining and understanding the tasks to be accomplished and the relationships between them. Short-term program success is often paid for by long term program difficulty.

What is the relationship between software costing and planning, and what is the relation to software quality? Early in the project software costing is done to develop estimates on which the software resource requirements are based. These estimates, despite their importance, are based on incomplete information, and often subject to unrealistic cuts in order to meet a predetermined commitment. The initial software cost estimate does not correlate exactly to program requirements. There is not a clear work plan early in the project nor is there a firm technical basis upon which an estimate can be based; therefore, the relationship to the program planning activities is, at best, loose. Until the program environment is established, software technical requirements are fully developed, and the WBS is complete, software cost estimates are largely a guess.

From a quality standpoint, the initial estimates must have a functional basis. The only way that any early estimation validity can be established is if the costs are traceable to requirements. The estimate must be verifiable at least to a preliminary set of software functional parameters, be based on documented, validated productivity projections, and be validated through an expert opinion, through analogy to an existent system and/or by use of a software cost model. Most importantly, there must be a program and software commitment to recost at regular intervals especially when additional detail concerning the program environment or software technical or design becomes available. Unless these steps are incorporated into the software cost procedure, there is too high a probability that early cost estimates will become frozen, and there will not be sufficient available resources to produce a quality software product when more detail is known about the product.

APPENDIX

SOFTWARE REPORTING METRICS

PROJECT IMPLEMENTATION CONSIDERATIONS

This appendix written by the U.S. Air Force and the Mitre Corporation, entitled "Software Management Effectiveness," provides illuminating material on the use of "high level" management metrics and rules of thumb. Their use can provide management with visibility of the status of the software development. They do not provide an indepth evaluation and are provided because they may be of interest to the reader.

These parameters should not be the only parameters collected; they should be augmented by more detailed reports appropriate to the specific project. For example, a project with multiple CSCI's being developed by multiple subcontractors on multiple processors should have each CSCI independently tracked for size, resource, utilization, and development progress. The successful use of these metrics depends on the program manager's enforcement of serious technical review of the monthly numbers. It is only through these reviews and the related interpersonal communication that the accuracy and relevance of the contractor's estimates can be ascertained.

SOFTWARE REPORTING METRICS

This section presents metrics from two perspectives. This discussion relates to the charts that follow in this section. The first perspective describes the intent of the metrics, lists some comments related to the profile presented when data is collected and plotted, and gives a definition of what data should be collected. The "definition" is intentionally loose. The definition of what data will be collected should be formally established and tailored for each software development program.

The second perspective shows a sample plot of the metric data. The metrics are plotted and show current month plus the previous 10 months of

267

activity. This allows room for the next five months' data to be predicted. Milestones, such as Preliminary Design Review (PDR), Critical Design Review (CDR), may be indicated on the abscissa. In some cases, planned values are plotted. Where planned *data is shown*, it should be the data derived from the first plan submitted. For example, the personnel profile is usually provided in the proposal, so the personnel profile from the contract is shown. (In the case of personnel, an additional planned profile may be included if the contractor is reporting his current anticipated profile). Another example is shown under test progress. The planned profile should be that established when the contractor's test plan was approved. (The plots shown are independent examples chosen to illustrate the type of data that may be collected. They do not represent data from one program).

Below the example plot, some rules of thumb are presented. The rules are intended to help interpretation of the metric data.

PROGRAM SIZE

The computer program size indicators are intended to show the magnitude of the software development effort. Software machine language instruction count affects the requirements for processing capability, and source lines of code (SLOC) affect the software engineering effort necessary to build the system. Growth in machine instruction count can lead to a conflict with hardware capacity; growth in SLOC can lead to schedule slips and management problems due to understaffing. The values presented in this metric may be used to check consistency in later metrics.

Most programs exhibit rising estimates of SLOC machine instructions. The development effort for a system may be reduced if some of the SLOC can be reused from other programs. There is some effort associated with integrating lifted code (i.e., borrowed from some other source without change, e.g., operating systems or an application previously completed) and even more effort when modifications are needed. The degree of effort must be estimated for each system. An "effective" count of to-be-developed SLOC is often useful for comparing proposed schedule and staffing estimates against program size. The "effective" count may be derived from the reported data by adding the new code to be developed to weighted counts of the lifted and modified code (i.e., since the effort required to incorporate a line of lifted and modified code is different from the effort to build a line of new code, the numbers of lifted and modified SLOC are weighted before determining an effective value for SLOC to be developed).

The count of machine language instructions, total source lines of code, SLOC to be lifted from other programs, SLOC to be modified from other programs, and SLOC to be developed as new code for this program, should each be updated and reported at the end of each calendar month. The term "SLOC" is often interpreted to exclude non-delivered support software

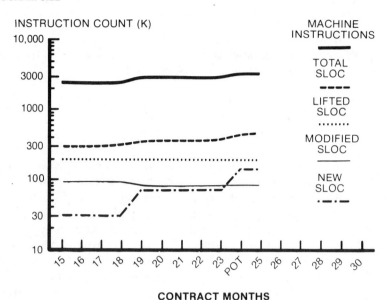

Graph A-I.   Program size.

such as test drivers. However, if new support software programs are being developed, then they should be included in the program size counts.

The lines of code to be counted should include all source instructions that are used by preprocessors, compilers, and assemblers to generate machine code. It excludes comments, but includes format and data type statements.

Rules of Thumb

1. The estimated instruction counts for one month should not vary from the previous report by more than 10 percent without explanation. (Note: a change in the estimated instruction count does not necessarily imply trouble—it implies the contractor has a new (improved?) understanding of the requirements and his design approach). If any instruction count changes by more than 50 percent, the software development management approach should be reviewed for adequacy.

2. Expansion ratios between machine language instruction count (MLIC) and SLOC vary from 3:1 to 8:1.

3. Typical weights for deriving "effective" to-be-developed SLOC are:

New Code	100 percent
Modified Code	50 percent
Lifted Code	10 percent

4. SLOC is one of the factors that directly affect number of staff-months

required for software development. Since development effort is related to the number of SLOC, implement higher order language (HOL) wherever feasible. Using HOL has other benefits too (e.g., reusability, maintainability, testability, etc.).

SOFTWARE PERSONNEL

The software personnel indicators are intended to show the ability to apply resources to the program and maintain staff towards completing the program. The software staff includes the engineering and management personnel directly involved with software system planning, requirements definition, design, coding, test, documentation, configuration management, and quality assurance. Experienced personnel are defined as those individuals with a minimum of five years experience in software development for applications similar to the system under development.

The staffing profiles for total software staff and for experienced software staff should be plotted as the contract begins. A normal program may have some deviations from the plan, but the deviations should not be severe. A program with too few experienced software personnel, or one which attempts to bring many personnel onboard during the last stages of the project's schedule, is in trouble. The normal shape of the total software staff profile is to start at a moderate level, grow through the design phases, peak through the coding and testing phases, and then to gradually taper down as integration tests are successfully completed. The normal shape of the experienced staff profile is to be high at the initial stage of the project, dip slightly through coding and then grow slightly through testing.

The number of software staff, in each experience category, expected onboard at the end of each calendar month should be plotted at the beginning of the contract. The count, of total software staff onboard and experienced software staff onboard, should be reported at the end of each calendar month.

Rules of Thumb

1. The ratio of total to experienced personnel should never exceed 6:1 (3:1 is a typical ratio for most real-time systems).

2. The time required for software development depends on the staff-months delivered.

    a. Under-staffing is an early indication of schedule slippage and, potentially, causes an ever-accelerating rate of slippage.

    b. Adding manpower to a late project will seldom repair the schedule.

PERSONNEL

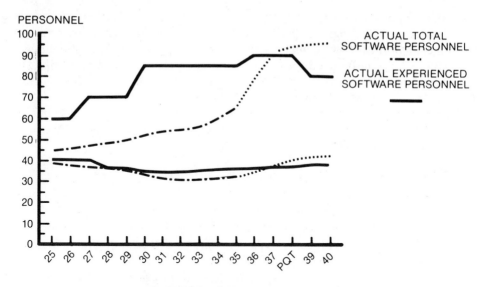

CONTRACT MONTH
Graph A-II.   Software development personnel.

3.   A program which is maintaining the staffing profile, but which is experiencing a high personnel turnover rate, is not maintaining needed continuity among the design and implementation staff.

SOFTWARE COMPLEXITY

The software complexity indicator is intended to show the degree of sophistication expected to be present in the software. It does not include development constraints (such as schedule) and is, therefore, not a full measure of software development difficulty. The complexity indicator is calculated to be an overall indicator. This overall complexity indicator is intended to be derivable from the information used to estimate complexity in B. Boehm's *Constructive Cost Model* (COCOMO). (See *Software Engineering Economics*.)

The complexity of the software should not change through the life of a program. Changes may occur, however, in response to requirements changes, or a reallocation of software functionability among processor resources. (It may also change in response to knowledge gained as the design is developed.) Changes in the complexity rating should be interpreted as an indication of important changes in the program.

The software complexity indicator is calculated by combining the weighted average of the complexity ratings for each computer software configuration item (CSCI) and all nondelivered (but developed for this program) support software. Weighting is established according to the percent of the total software (SLOC count) contained in each CSCI or necessary support software programs (SSP). Note: lifted or modified code that may be included in the CSCIs will be included in the calculation. The guidelines in Table A.1 will be used for determining complexity. A CSCI's complexity should be the highest complexity rating appropriate for the CSCI's commonly performed operations.

The total of the weighted complexity ratings will result in a number between 100 and 400. This number will be updated and reported at the end of each calendar month of the contract.

Rules of Thumb

1. The complexity rating for one month should not change from the preceding report by more than 10 percent without explanation.
2. Programs with complexity ratings over 300 should have more than 40 percent experienced software staff.
3. Wherever possible, employ mature off-the-shelf operating systems, compilers, database management systems, and support software.
4. For programs of similar size, real-time applications are generally more complex than non-real-time applications.

DEVELOPMENT PROGRESS

The development progress indicator is intended to monitor the contractor's ability to maintain development progress. It will measure the degree to which the contractor can keep module test and integration on schedule. After CDR, the next traditional milestone which reveals the status of software development is the test milestone. This is much too late in a program to recover, if significant problems are discovered. An earlier indication of success or problems in a program is the degree of adherence to a planned schedule for module design, development, and test.

The design of modules usually begins around PDR. Data to monitor the design progress is rarely delivered as a contractual obligation, but if it is available, a count should be plotted of the number of module design packages that have been closed. For example, the design has passed internal review and is considered "frozen" by the contractor's software development methodology. After CDR, when the contractor begins developing software modules, a healthy program will experience a steady progression of new modules. If the modules are being developed in spurts, it indicates problems with managing the software. Sporadic module development can be caused by factors such as over-utilized development machines or under-experienced staff. It results in a high pressure environment where all the software is due at once. For a normal program,

Rating	Control	Operations			Data Management	Display
		Computational	Device Dependent			
Low (1)	Straightline code. Few special operators.	Evaluation of simple expressions (A = B+C).	Simple formats , dedicated devices.		Single file(s) structure.	Single output.
Nominal (2)	Simple nesting. Some intermodule control & queue control.	Use of standard math & standard routines, matrix, vector operations, ordinary differential equations.	Device selection, optimized I/O overlap.		Multifile structure, single output.	Simple query, limited choice.
High (3)	Reentrant, fixed priority interrupt handling.	Matrix equations, partial differential equations.	Communications line handling.		Special purpose sub-routine activated by data streams.	On-line interactive, screen driven.
Very High (4)	Multiple resource scheduling, dynamically changing priorities.	Highly accurate analysis of stochastic data.	Device time independent, optimization of devices.		Generalized file structures, search optimization structures.	Tutorial, AI assisted, full range of graphics.

TABLE A-1.   Software complexity rating.

273

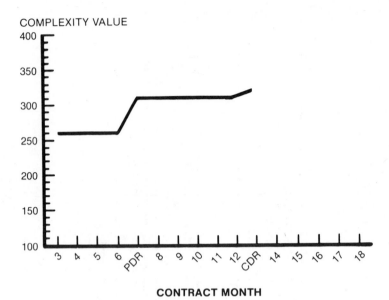

COMPLEXITY VALUE

CONTRACT MONTH

Graph A-III.   Software complexity.

the total number of modules which have passed module test (sometimes called "unit" test) should be continually increasing, and the total number of modules that have been integrated should be similarly rising with a constant slope.

The module test and module integration schedule should be reported by the contractor at CDR. The number of modules whose design packages have been closed, the number of modules passing module test, and the number of modules passing integration tests and accepted into the contractor's configuration control system as integrated software will be updated at the end of each calendar month of the contract. For example, modules that have been integrated are modules that have been tested and found to work together acceptably as a functioning element that is equivalent to a computer system component (CSC).

Rules of Thumb

1. Between CDR and PQT, monitor the modules tested and integrated as indications of development progress.

2. Modules tested and integrated should progress at a reasonably uniform rate and according to plan.

3. The development plan should take into account the interactive nature of test and integration (i.e., the test program should begin and continue throughout the software integration activities).

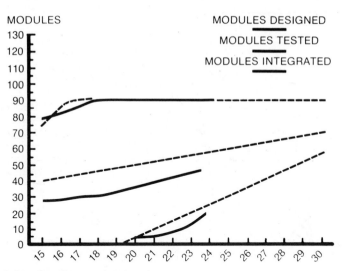

Graph A-IV.   Development progress.

TESTING PROGRESS

Preliminary qualification testing (PQT) is the earliest time during which the customer (Government) can officially determine whether or not the desired functions are being provided. The testing progress indicators are intended to show the degree to which the contractor's implementation of the design is meeting program requirements. The testing progress indicators also show whether the test program is going to be severely extended or whether it may be concluded on a reasonable schedule.

The test schedule line should show the cumulative count of tests planned to be completed for PQT and formal qualification test (FQT). A plot of tests that have been successfully passed should overlay the schedule if all tests were passed on schedule. Most programs will experience schedule slip or failed tests, and, therefore, the tests passed line can be expected to fall below the tests scheduled. The degree to which the tests passed line falls below the planned test schedule is an indicator of the readiness of the system to have entered the test program. Wherever the test program reveals problems, these problem reports should be counted and indicated on the chart as a count of problems remaining open. As these problems are resolved, the number of problems remaining unresolved should decrease. The unresolved problem line reveals whether or not the contractor is solving more problems than identifying them. If the slope of the line is positive (increasing to the right), the test program is revealing problems faster than the contractor can solve them. If the slope of the line is negative, the contractor is

NUMBER OF TESTS/PROBLEMS

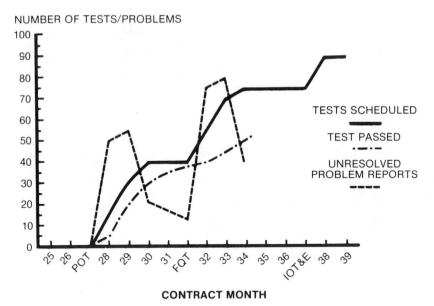

CONTRACT MONTH

Graph A-V.   Testing progress.

on a healthier path towards completing the tests. Note that an ambitious test plan may prevent the number of unresolved problems from decreasing. The testing progress indicators show a general view of testing progress. It is expected that the project office will establish a more detailed view for the project office's internal use by tracking the trouble reports. For example, the longevity of trouble reports can indicate how well the contractor is solving the difficult problems. The number of modules changed per trouble report can reveal how well functional partitioning has been preserved.

A plot of the cumulative count of planned PQT and FQT tests should be presented before PQT begins. The count of tests passed, problem reports filed, and unresolved problem reports will be updated at the end of each calendar month of the contract.

Rules of Thumb

1. The tests passed should converge to the tests scheduled as FQT approaches.
2. The problems unresolved should decrease toward zero as FQT approaches.

PERCENT (%)

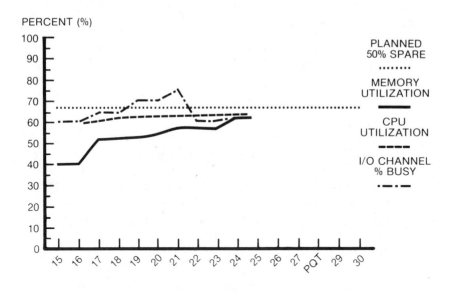

Graph A-VI. Computer resource utilization.

COMPUTER RESOURCE UTILIZATION

The computer resource utilization indicators are intended to show the degree to which the estimates of the target computer resources utilized are changing or approaching the limits of resource availability. The three major bottlenecks that can prevent a system from performing within the capacity of its hardware are computation power, memory, and input/output (I/O) channels. Regardless of whether the system architecture is distributed or centralized, these parameters should be carefully monitored to ensure the software design will fit within the resources planned.

It is typical for large software systems to specify that the completed system will have 50 percent spare capacity in memory, central processing unit (CPU), and peripheral device I/O. This is usually interpreted to mean that the software could require half again as much resources as it uses without exceeding the capacity of the hardware. Most development programs experience an upward creep in the amount of resources estimated to be used when the program is complete. If this upwards creep exceeds the 66 percent utilization limit, the program may elect to expand the capabilities of the hardware. Whenever a resource expansion is approved, the utilization curve, or curves, affixed will drop to a new (hopefully, below 66 percent) value.

The estimate for CPU, memory, and I/O resource utilization should be updated at the end of each calendar month of the contract. For projects where multiple computing resources are used (e.g., a distributed network) a separate plot should be developed for each resource.

Rules of Thumb

1. CPU utilization should allow a minimum of 50 percent spare.*
2. Planned memory utilization should allow a minimum of 50 percent spare.
3. Planned I/O utilization, channels and data rate, should allow a minimum of 50 percent spare.
4. Performance deteriorates when utilization exceeds 70 percent for real-time applications. (Worst-case peaks in load cause more frequent conflict among processes competing for processing resources.)
5. Resource utilization tends to increase with time. Plan for this expansion early in the software development cycle.
6. Schedule and cost can increase dramatically as the spare drops below 10 percent.
    *Note: Confusion exists surrounding the interpretation of "50% spare." Contractors often argue that the requirement means they must preserve room for 50 percent growth in their use of a resource; that is, 66 percent of the resource may be utilized, leaving 33 percent (50 percent of 66 percent) as spare. The government sometimes uses "50 percent spare" when they really intended to allow only 50 percent of the resource to be used. To be correct, the government should have requested 100 percent spare. "Margin" is the difference between what resource the contractor is allowed to use, and what is actually used.

PROGRAM VOLATILITY

The program volatility indicators are intended to show the degree to which changes in requirements, or changes in the contractor's understanding of the requirements, affect the development effort for a program. When a program is originated, the details of its operation and system design are rarely complete. Consequently, it is normal to experience changes in a system's specifications as requirements are better defined. At some point in the program's history, the requirements should be firm, as only design and implementation issues are usually caught at the preliminary design review (PDR) and critical design review (CDR). When the design reviews reveal inconsistencies, a discrepancy report is opened. The discrepancy may be closed (resolved) by modifying (or clarifying) the design or by modifying the requirements. When one of these requirements, design or implementation issues causes a change to the original scope of the project, an engineering change proposal (ECP) may be submitted.

The open (unresolved) review discrepancies are expected to spike upward at each review and then exhibit exponentially decreasing behavior.

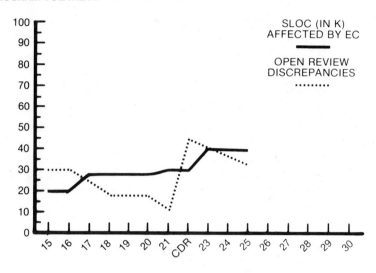

CONTRACT MONTH

Graph A-VII. Program volatility.

Programs that assure specifications which are clearly written will experience spikes that are low; programs that have good communications between the program office, system engineer, and contractor will have a high rate of decay to this curve. For each engineering change (EC), (i.e., an approved ECP) or closed discrepancy report, the portion of the software that will be affected should be reported. This indicator will track the degree to which ECs cause an increase in software development effort. Large numbers of ECs and affected SLOC indicate a program which has not established firm requirements before initiating a contract.

The number of discrepancies that are identified at each review must be recorded at the conclusion of the review. A discrepancy will be defined as any action item, clarification item, or requirements issue that must be resolved by either the contractor or the Government. The count of open discrepancy reports must be maintained by the program office and plotted at the end of each calendar month of the contract. The number of SLOC affected by ECPs will be derived by the contractor on each ECP submitted. The cumulative count will be changed only for ECPs that have been approved by the configuration control board. The cumulative count of SLOC affected by ECs will be updated at the end of each calendar month of the contract. The number of SLOC affected by each requirement, design, or implementation issue will be derived by the number of SLOC that is already developed and will remain as functional code after the EC. Total code is the new count of the total number of SLOC that will be in the system.

Rules of Thumb

1. Requirement uncertainty leads to changes (ECPs) which result in cost growth and delayed completion of system.
2. Firm requirements should be established before initiating a contract. Alternatively, a planned prototyping approach should be taken.
3. If program volatility has not settled down by CDR, the requirements should be frozen for an early delivery increment, and the program reopened for requirements review by the users before PDR of the second increment. Not that major requirements issues should have been settled by PDR; if the program volatility remains high to CDR the program is in serious trouble.

INCREMENTAL RELEASE CONTENT

The incremental release indicator is intended to reveal the contractor's ability to preserve schedule and system function. A common approach used to preserve schedule is to postpone program capabilities. This indicator is useful when the contractor's development plan calls for incremental software builds or "releases". Decrease in the plot of modules per release will indicate a program is off loading functions from early releases of the software to later releases. Increases in the plot of modules per release will indicate a program is having unanticipated growth in the complexity of the functions to be delivered.

Proper behavior would be for the number of modules to remain constant for each proposed release. Common behavior is for the number of modules in early releases to decrease as the release date approaches. The middle and later releases have decreasing numbers of modules; so, additional releases must be added to incorporate the delayed modules. In addition, increases in the program's size leads to additional modules added to the last releases. In a program where the PDR and CDR were adequate, the number of modules should not increase significantly after CDR. A program that is developing its capabilities on schedule will maintain the number of modules in each release constant.

The number of modules proposed by the contractor for each anticipated release should be updated at the end of each calendar month of the contract. The "actual" plot should show the number of modules reported for each release each month. The "planned" plot should show what the module counts are expected to be in future months. The plot of module count extends to the completion date for each release.

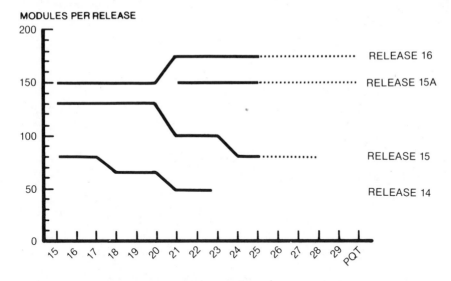

MODULES PER RELEASE

CONTRACT MONTH

Graph A-VIII.   Incremental release content.

Rules of Thumb

1. Number of modules should remain constant. However, it is common for the number of modules to increase as the program's design matures.

2. A significant increase in the number of modules per release might indicate the program is having unanticipated growth in the complexity of the functions to be delivered.

3. A decrease in the number of modules per release might indicate the program is off-loading functions from earlier releases to later releases.

4. To preserve the readability of code and improve maintainability, software should be divided into practical partitions of functions and subfunctions. It is commonly suggested that software units or modules should be sized at 50 lines of source code, and should not exceed 100 lines.

5. Testing should begin integrating pieces of the software as early as possible. Software builds should be encouraged to correspond to operationally useful capabilities as soon as is practical.

GLOSSARY

Abstraction.   A view of a problem that extracts the information relevant to a particular purpose and ignores the remainder of the information.

Acceptability Criteria.   The criteria used to judge the acceptability of a product.

Acceptance.   An official act by a customer to accept transfer of accountability, title, and delivery of an item on a contract.

Acceptance Testing.   Formal testing conducted in order to determine whether or not a system satisfies its acceptance criteria and to enable the customer to determine whether or not to accept the system. See also Qualification Testing; System Testing.

Accuracy.   (1) Freedom from error. (2) A quantitative measure of the magnitude of error. (3) A quantitative assessment of freedom from error. Contrast with Precision.

Actual Cost.   The costs actually incurred and recorded for the work performed and/or the materials purchased.

Adaptability.   The ease with which software satisfies differing system constraints and user needs.

Algorithm.   A finite set of rules for the solution of a problem in a finite number of steps; for example, a complete specification of a sequence of arithmetic operations for evaluating sin (x) to a given precision.

Alias.   An additional name, usually shortened, by which an item is known.

Allocated Baseline.   Basis for judging the acceptability of a configuration item. For a CSCI, an allocated baseline includes its functional requirements and associated interface information.

Analysis Phase.   See Requirements Phase.

Analytical Model. A representation of a process or phenomenon by a set of solvable equations. Contrast with Simulation.

Anomaly. (1) An observed deviation from specified or expected behavior. (2) An error.

Application-Oriented Language. (1) A computer language with facilities or notations applicable primarily to a single application area; for example, languages for statistical analysis or machine design. (2) A problem-oriented language that produces statements that contain or resemble the terminology of the occupation or profession of the user.

Application Software. Software specifically produced for the functional use of a computer system; for example, software for navigation, gun fire control, payroll, general ledger. Contrast with System Software.

Approval. Formal recognition of the validity and acceptability of an action or a product.

Approved Change. Any change to a controlled, data product that is approved and entered into a controlled, based project.

Architectural Design. (1) The process of defining a collection of hardware and software components, their functions, interfaces, and key characteristics to establish a framework for the development of a computer system. (2) The result of the architectural design process.

Architecture. See Program Architecture; System Architecture.

Assemble. To translate a program expressed in an assembly language into a machine language and perhaps into link subroutines. Assembling is usually accomplished by substituting machine language operation codes for assembly language operation codes and by substituting absolute addresses, immediate addresses, relocatable addresses, or virtual addresses for symbolic addresses. Contrast with Compile; Interpret.

Assembler. A computer program used to assemble. Contrast with Compiler; Interpreter.

Assembly Language. (1) A computer language giving instructions that correspond directly to computer instructions and that may provide such facilities as the use of macroinstructions. See also Assemble; Assembler. Contrast with Higher Order Language; Machine Language. (2) A machine-specific language giving instructions that correspond directly to computer instructions.

Assembly Program. See Assembler.

Audit. (1) An independent assessment of compliance with software requirements, specifications, baselines, standard procedures, instructions, codes, and contractual and licensing requirements. See also Code Audit. (2) An activity to determine the adequacy of and adherence to established procedures, instructions, specifications, codes and standards, or other applicable contractual and licensing requirements and the effectiveness of implementation.

Authorization.   Approval of or concurrence on a planned action. *Note:* An authorization does not necessarily imply that the results of the action are approved or concurred upon.

Automated Design Tool.   A software tool that aids in the synthesis, analysis, modeling, or documentation of a software design; for example, simulators, analytic aids, design representation, and documentation generators.

Automated Test Generator.   A software tool that accepts a computer program and test criteria as input, generates test input data that meet these criteria, and, sometimes, determines the expected results.

Automated Verification System.   A software tool that accepts a computer program and representation of its specification as input and produces, possibly with human help, a proof or disproof of the correctness of the program. See also Automated Verification Tools.

Automated Verification Tools.   A class of software tools used to evaluate products of the software development process. These tools aid in the verification of such characteristics as correctness, completeness, consistency, traceability, testability, and adherence to standards; for example, design analyzers, static analyzers, dynamic analyzers, and standard enforcers.

Baseline.   (1) A specification or product that has been reviewed and agreed on, and that thereafter serves as the basis for further development. A baseline can be changed only through change control procedures. (2) A configuration identification document or set of such documents formally designated and fixed at a specific time during the system life cycle. Baselines, including approved changes from those baselines, constitute the current configuration identification. For configuration management there are typically three baselines: (a) Functional baseline. The initial approved functional configuration. (b) Allocated baseline. The initial approved allocated functional configuration. (c) Product baseline. The initial approved or conditionally approved product configuration identification.

Baseline Configuration Management.   Procedures established to control changes to contractual baselines and documentation that have been approved by the customer.

BDR.   Build design review.

Block Diagram.   A diagram of a system, computer, or device in which the principal parts are represented by suitably annotated geometrical figures to show both the basic functions of the parts and their functional relationships.

Bottom-Up. Pertaining to an approach that starts with the lowest level software components of a hierarchy and proceeds through progressively higher levels to the top level component; for example, bottom-up design, bottom-up programming, bottom-up testing. Contrast with Top-Down.

Bottom-Up Design. The design of a system starting with the most basic or primitive components and proceeding to higher level components that use the lower level ones. Contrast with Top-Down Design.

Bridge Product. Engineering data product, including documentation that is independent of the software development methodology employed, and that relates to the management of development activities or the transition from one phase to another in the system life cycle.

Budget. The resources negotiated for a specific work task that serve as the measure against which variations are controlled.

Bug. See Fault.

Build. (1) An operational version of a software product incorporating a specified subset of the capabilities that the final product will include. (2) An operational configuration for a particular application; for example, launch-support build, or planetary encounter build.

Build Design Review (BDR). Meeting at which the design of a CSCI build is evaluated.

Build Testing. Aggregate of technical activities involved in verifying that as produced, a CSCI build satisfies the CSCI acceptability criteria allocated to the build.

Build Testing Configuration. A set of CSCI elements that represents the CSCI configuration to be used during build testing.

Build Test Plan. Document that identifies the tests planned to verify that a CSCI build satisfies the acceptability criteria allocated to the build. The procedure to be followed in conducting each identified test is appended to the build test plan.

Build Test Report. Documentation that summarizes the results of build tests identified in a build test plan.

CDR. Critical design review.

Certification. A process, which may be incremental, by which a contractor provides evidence to the contracting agency that a product meets contractual or specified requirements.

Change. A formally recognized revision to a specified and documented requirement.

Change Control. The process by which an engineering change is proposed, evaluated, approved or rejected, scheduled, and tracked.

Change Control Board (CCB). A management board that controls changes to formally established baselines.

Change Management. (1) The process of evaluating, approving or disapproving, and coordinating changes to controlled software after establishment of a baseline. (2) The systematic evaluation, coordination, approval or disapproval, and implementation of all approved changes in the configuration of a software product after establishment of baseline.

Change Management Authority. The individual responsible for approval of all proposed changes to baselines.

Change Review Board. The authority responsible for evaluating and recommending disposition of proposed engineering changes and ensuring implementation of the approved changes.

Class I Change. A change that affects specification documentation and associated designs and code, but does not affect an end item's form, fit, or function.

Class II Change. A change that affects specification documentation and associated designs and code, but does affect an end item's form, fit, or function.

Code Audit. An independent review of source code by a person, team, or tool to verify compliance with software design documentation and programming standards. Correctness and efficiency may also be evaluated. See also Audit; Inspection; Walk-Through.

Code Walk-Through. See Walk-Through.

Cohesion. The degree to which the tasks performed by a single program module are functionally related. Contrast with Coupling.

Compatibility. The ability of two or more systems to exchange information. Compare with Interoperability.

Compile. To translate a higher order language program into its relocatable or absolute machine code equivalent. Contrast with Assemble; Interpret.

Compiler. A computer program used to compile. Contrast with Assembler; Interpreter.

Complexity. The degree of complication of a system or system component, determined by such factors as the number and intricacy of interfaces, the number and intricacy of conditional branches, the degree of nesting, and the types of data structures.

Component. A basic part of a system or program.

Computer. (1) A functional unit that can perform substantial computation, including arithmetic and/or logic operations, without intervention by a human operator during a run. (2) A functional programmable unit that consists of one or more associated processing units, and peripheral equipment, that is controlled by internally stored programs, and that can perform substantial computation, including arithmetic and/or logic operations, without human intervention.

Computer Data. Data available for communication between or within computer equipment. Such data can be external (in computer-readable form) or resident within the computer equipment and can be in the form of analog or digital signals.

Computer Program. A sequence of instructions suitable for processing by a computer. Processing may include the use of an assembler, compiler, interpreter, or translator to prepare the program for execution as well as to execute it. See also Program. Contrast with Software.

Computer Software. A combination of associated computer instructions and data definitions required to enable the computer hardware to perform computational or control functions. See Software.

Computer Software Component (CSC). A functional or logically distinct part of a CSCI. Normally an individually loadable or functionally distinct software element.

Computer Software Configuration Item (CSCI). Software portion of a system that is managed, developed, documented, and demonstrated as a unit and that is formally designed for configuration management.

Computer Software Quality. The degree to which software is able to perform its specified and item use. See Software Quality.

Computer Software Top Level Design (CSTLD). Specification of the function, performance, data, and quality criteria to be used to evaluate the acceptability of a Computer Software Configuration Item (CSCI).

Concurrence. Agreement that a selected approach or a planned action is not contrary to contractual requirements. *Note:* Concurrence does not constitute either approval or acceptance.

Configuration. (1) The arrangement of a computer system or network as defined by the nature, number, and the chief characteristics of its software and/or hardware functional units. (2) The requirements, design, and implementation that define a particular version of a system or system component. (3) The functional and/or physical characteristics of hardware/software as set forth in technical documentation and achieved in a product.

Configuration Audit. The process of verifying that all required deliverable products have been produced and received in custody, that the current version agrees with specified requirements, that the technical documentation completely and accurately describes the baselined items, and that all change requests have been resolved.

Configuration Control. The disciplines associated with managing changes to controlled and managed data.

Configuration Control Board (CCB). A committee established to review and approve change requests, deviation requests, waiver requests, and change notices affecting products under configuration control.

Configuration Element.   Identifiable element of a CSCI.

Configuration Identification.   (1) The process of designating the controlled products in a system and recording their characteristics. (2) The approved documentation that defines a controlled configuration. (3) The currently approved or conditionally approved technical documentation for a controlled baseline as set forth in specifications, drawings and associated lists, and documents referenced therein.

Configuration Item.   A collection of hardware or software elements treated as a unit for the purpose of configuration management. (2) An aggregation of hardware and software or any of its discrete portions that satisfies an end-use function and is designated for configuration management. During development and initial production, configuration items are only those specification items that are referred to directly in a contract (or equivalent in-house agreement). During operation and maintenance period, configuration items are any reparable item designated for separate procurement.

Configuration Management.   (1) The process of identifying and defining the deliverable product set in a system, controlling the release and change of these items throughout the system life cycle, recording and reporting the status of product items and change requests, and verifying the completeness and correctness of the product items. See also Change Control; Change Management; Configuration Audit; Configuration Identification; Configuration Status Accounting. (2) A discipline applying technical and administrative direction and surveillance in order to: (a) identify and document the functional and physical characteristics of a product item, (b) control changes to those characteristics, and (c) record and report change processing and implementation status.

Configuration Status Accounting.   The recording and reporting of the information that is needed to manage a configuration effectively, including a listing of the approved configuration identification, the status of proposed changes to the configuration, and the implementation status of approved changes.

Contractual Baseline.   Configuration elements that represent contractually binding technical requirements.

Control.   The activities associated with measuring and assessing performance, and the identification and taking of actions to correct deficiencies.

Control Structure.   A programming language construct that determines the flow of control through a program.

Conversion.   Modification of existing software to enable it to operate with similar functional capability in a different environment; for example, converting a program from FORTRAN to Ada or converting a program that runs on one computer to run on another computer.

Correctness. (1) The extent to which software is free from design defects and from coding defects, that is, fault free. (2) The extent to which software meets its specified requirements. (3) The extent to which software meets user expectations.

Cost-Effective. The quality of having the best cumulative balance among cost, schedule, and technical requirements over the life cycle of an object.

Coupling. A measure of the interdependence among modules in a program. Contrast with Cohesion.

Critical Design Review (CDR). A review conducted for each configuration item when detail design is complete for the purpose of (a) determining that the detail design of the configuration item satisfies performance and engineering speciality requirements of the hardware development specifications, (b) establishing the detail design compatibility among the configuration item and other items of equipment, facilities, software, and personnel, (c) assessing configuration item risk areas on a technical, cost, and schedule basis, (d) assessing results of the procurability analyses conducted on system hardware, and (e) reviewing the preliminary hardware product specifications. For CSCIs, this review focuses on the determination of acceptability of the detailed design, performance, and test characteristics of the design solution and on adequacy of the operation and support documents.

Criticality. A classification of a software error, fault, or requirement based on evaluation of its degree of impact on the development or operation of a system (often used to determine whether or when a fault will be corrected, or when a requirement will be implemented).

Critical Path. The particular sequence of activities that consumes the longest time in reaching the end event or the activity completion.

Cross-Assembler. An assembler that executes on one computer to generate object code for a different computer.

Cross-Compiler. A compiler that executes on one computer to generate object code for a different computer.

CSC. Computer software component.

CSCI. Computer software configuration item.

Customer. A person or group for whom a product or service is being provided and who accepts delivery.

Data. A representation of information concepts, or instructions in a formalized manner suitable for communication, interpretation, or processing by human or automatic means.

Data Abstraction. The result of extracting and retaining only the essential properties of data by defining specific data types and their associated functional characteristics, thus separating and hiding the representation details. See also Information Hiding.

Database. (1) A set of data or part of a set of data consisting of at least one file that is sufficient for a given purpose or for a given data processing system. (2) A collection of data basic to a system. (3) A collection of data basic to an enterprise.

Database Configuration. Aggregate of the data elements in a CSCI database.

Data Control. The procedures applied in order to control the integrity and configuration of data products approved for use by the software.

Data Dictionary. (1) A collection of the names of all data items used in a software system, together with relevant properties of those items; for example, length and representation. (2) A set of definitions of the data flows, data elements, files, databases, and processes referred to in a data flow diagram.

Data Element. Imprecise designation for an element of a CSCI database; for example, for a data set, data record, and data item.

Data Flow Chart. See Data Flow Diagram.

Data Flow Diagram. A graphic representation of a system, showing data characteristics, relationships, and showing logical flow of data as links between the software functional elements.

Data Flow Graph. See Data Flow Diagram.

Data Item. An individual data element.

Data Set. A grouping of related data items.

Data Structure. A formalized representation of the order and accessibility relationships among data items without regard to their actual storage configuration.

Data Structure Analysis. An approach to software design that focuses on characterizing a problem in terms of the structure of its data and conforming the program structure to this structure.

Data Type. A class of data characterized by the members of the class and the operations that can be applied to them; for example, integer, real, and logical.

Debugging. The process of locating, analyzing, and correcting suspected faults. Compare with Testing.

Decision Path. Logic path to be executed as a result of a decision.

Definition Phase. Aggregate of technical activities involved in defining the acceptability criteria for a CSCI.

Delivery. (1) The point in the software development cycle at which a product is transferred to its intended users. (2) The point in the software development cycle at which a product is accepted by its intended user.

Demonstration Configuration. Set of CSCI elements that represents the CSCI configuration to be used during a demonstration of the CSCI to the contractor.

Demonstration Testing. Aggregate of technical activities involved in demonstrating that a CSCI meets its acceptability criteria.

Design. (1) The process of defining the software architecture, components, modules, interfaces, test approach, and data for a software system to satisfy specified requirements. (2) The result of the design process.

Design Analysis. (1) The evaluation of a design to determine correctness with respect to requirements, standards, system efficiency, and other criteria. (2) The evaluation of alternative design approaches. See also Preliminary Design.

Design Analyzer. An automated design tool that accepts information about a program's design and produces such outputs as module hierarchy diagrams, graphic representations of control and data structures, and lists of accessed data blocks.

Design Language. A language having special constructs and, sometimes, verification protocols, used to develop, analyze, and document a design.

Design Method. A systematic approach to creating a design through the ordered application of a specific collection of tools, techniques, and guidelines.

Design Phase. The period of time in the software life cycle during which the designs for architecture, software components, interfaces, and data are created, documented, and verified to satisfy requirements.

Design Requirements. Any requirement that affects or constrains the design of a software system or software system component; for example, functional requirements, physical requirements, performance requirements, software development standards, and software product assurance standards. See also Requirements Specification.

Design Review. (1) A meeting at which the preliminary or detailed design of a system is presented to a predesignated panel for inspection, comment, and approval. (2) The review of an existing or proposed design for the purpose of detection and remedy of design deficiencies that could affect fitness-for-use and environmental aspects, and identification of potential improvements in performance, safety, and economic aspects.

Design Specification. A document that records the design of a system or system component; typical contents include: system and/or component algorithms, control logic, data structures, data set use, input/output formats, and interface descriptions. See also Requirements Specification.

Design Verification. See Verification.

Design Walk-Through. See Walk-Through.

Desk Checking.   To detect faults through manual step-by-step examination of the source code for errors in logic or syntax.

Detailed Design.   (1) The process of refining and expanding the preliminary design to contain more detailed descriptions of the processing logic, data structures, and data definitions to the extent that the design is sufficiently complete to be implemented. (2) The result of the detailed design process.

Development Cycle.   See Software Development Cycle.

Development Life Cycle.   See Software Development Cycle.

Development Methodology.   A systematic approach to software creation that defines development phases and specifies the activities, products, verification procedures, and completion criteria for each phase.

Deviation.   Written authorization to develop a product that departs from established requirements.

Diagnostic.   (1) A program generated message indicating possible faults in another system component; for example, a syntax fault flagged by a compiler. (2) Pertaining to the detection and isolation of faults or failures.

Display.   To show, either on a terminal screen or hardcopy.

Document.   (1) A data medium and the data recorded on it that generally has permanence and can be read by human operator or machine. Often used to describe human readable items only; for example, technical documents, design documents, and requirements documents. (2) To create a document.

Documentation.   (1) A collection of documents on a given subject. (2) The management of documents, including the actions of identifying, acquiring, processing, storing, and disseminating. (3) Any written or pictorial information describing, defining, specifying, reporting or certifying activities, requirements, procedures, or results.

Documentation Configuration.   Aggregate of the documentation elements in a CSCI.

Driver.   A program that exercises a system or system component by simulating the activity of a higher level component.

Dump.   To write the contents of all or part of a storage, usually from an internal storage to an external medium.

Dynamic Allocation.   The allocation of addressable storage and other resources to a program while the program is executing.

Dynamic Analysis.   The process of evaluating a program based on its execution.

Dynamic Analyzer.   A software tool that aids in the evaluation of a computer program by monitoring execution of the program; for example, instrumentation tools, software monitors, and tracers.

Earned Value. A means of evaluating budgetary performance by relating actual expenditures to technical achievement as measured by a milestone accomplishment scheme.

Efficiency. The extent to which software performs its intended functions with a minimum consumption of computing resources.

Embedded Computer System. A computer system that is integral to a larger system whose primary purpose is not computational; for example, a computer system in an aircraft, or rapid transit system.

Embedded Software. Software for an embedded computer system.

Emulation. The imitation of all or part of one computer system by another, primarily by hardware, so that the imitating computer system accepts the same data, executes the same programs, and achieves the same results as the imitated system.

Emulator. Hardware, software, or firmware that performs emulation.

Encapsulation. The technique of isolating a system function within a module and providing a precise specification for the module. See Information Hiding.

End Item. An item of software or documentation that is deliverable to a user or customer.

Engineering Review Board (ERB). A development group that controls internal class changes and oversees technical analysis for Class I and Class II changes.

ERB. Engineering Review Board.

Error. (1) A discrepancy between a computed, observed, and measured value or condition and the true, specified, or theoretically correct value or condition. (2) Human action that results in software fault; for example, omission or misinterpretation of user requirements in a software specification, incorrect translation or omission of a requirement in the design specification. Not a preferred usage. See also Failure; Fault.

Error Analysis. (1) The process of investigating an observed software fault with the purpose of tracing the fault to its source, including cause of the fault, phase of the development process during which the fault was introduced, methods by which the fault could have been prevented or detected earlier, and method by which the fault was detected. (2) The process of investigating software errors, failures, and faults in order to determine quantitative rates and trends.

Error Category. One of a set of classes into which an error, fault, or failure might fall. Categories may be defined according to the cause, criticality, effect, life cycle phase when introduced or detected, or other characteristics.

Error Model. A mathematical model used to predict or estimate the number of remaining faults, reliability, required test time, or similar characteristics of a software system. See also Error Prediction.

Error Prediction. A quantitative statement about the expected number and/or nature of software problems, faults, or failures. See also Error Model.

Estimate. A projection of the resources necessary to accomplish a specific task made at different times and under varying degrees of uncertainty.

Exception. A deviation from a specified rule, practice, or plan.

Execution. The process by which a computer carries out an instruction or instructions.

Execution Time. (1) The amount of actual central processor time used in executing a program. (2) The period of time during which a program is executing. See also Run Time.

Executive Program. See Supervisory Program.

Exit. The point beyond which control is no longer exercised by a computer program, routine, subroutine, or instruction.

Failure. (1) The termination of the ability of a functional unit to perform its required function. (2) The inability of a system or system component to perform a required function within specified limits. A failure may be produced when a fault is encountered. (3) A departure of program operation from program requirements.

Failure Rate. (1) The ratio of the number of failures to a given unit of measure; for example, failures per unit of time, failures per number of transactions, failures per number of computer runs. (2) In reliability modeling, the ratio of the number of failures of a given category or severity to a given period of time; for example, failures per second of execution time and failures per month.

Failure Ratio. See Failure Rate.

Failure Recovery. The return of a system to a reliable operating state after failure.

Fault. (1) A condition that causes a functional unit to fail to perform its required function. (2) A manifestation of an error in software. A fault, if encountered, may cause a failure.

Fault Tolerance. The built-in capability of a system to provide continued correct execution in the presence of hardware or software faults.

FCA. Functional configuration audit.

Field. The space for one data item on a template or form; a field usually consists of a title and a data space.

Field Group. A set of fields to which specified processing rules apply. Members of the group are logically linked in some fashion; for example, a document and a version number.

Field Title. An identification for a field that appears on the template or form immediately preceding the field space occupied by data.

File. A set of related records treated as a unit. See also Logical File.

Final Build. Version of a CSCI that purportedly meets its acceptability criteria. The final build for a CSCI represents the last version of the CSCI to be subjected to demonstration testing.

Finite-State Machine. A model consisting of a finite number of states and transitions between these states.

Firmware. (1) A combination of a hardware unit and a computer program integrated to form a functional entity whose configuration cannot be altered during normal operation. The computer program is stored in the hardware unit as an integrated circuit with a fixed logic configuration that will satisfy a specific application or operational requirement. (2) Hardware that contains a computer program and data that cannot be changed in its user environment. (3) Program instructions stored in read-only storage.

Formal Language. A language whose rules are explicitly established prior to its use; for example, programming languages such as FORTRAN and Ada, and mathematical or logical languages such as predicate calculus and Boolian Algebra.

Formal Parameter. A name representing the possible set of data value or values to be transmitted between two software routines.

Formal Qualification Audit (FQA). The test, inspection, or analytical process by which a group of configuration items comprising a system is verified to have met specific contractual performance requirements.

Formal Qualification Test. The testing performed on an end item as a basis for its acceptance by a customer.

Formal Review. Formally scheduled meeting between buyer and builder of software during which CSCI development products are reviewed and approved; for example, preliminary design review.

Formal Specification. (1) A specification written and approved in accordance with established standards. (2) In proof of correctness, a description, in a formal language, of the externally visible behavior of a system or system component.

Formal Testing. The process of conducting testing activities and reporting results in accordance with an approved test plan.

FQA. Functional qualification audit.

Function. (1) A specific purpose of an entity and/or its characteristic action. (2) Mathematically, a single-valued mapping of an input domain onto an output range.

Functional Configuration Audit (FCA). A formal audit to validate that the development of a configuration item has been completed satisfactorily, has achieved the performance and functional characteristics specified in the functional or allocated configuration identification, and complies with the completed operation and support documents.

Functional Decomposition.   A method of designing a system by breaking it down into its components in such a way that the components correspond directly to system functions and subfunctions. See also Hierarchical Decomposition.

Functional Design.   The specification of the working relationships among the parts of a data processing system. See also Preliminary Design.

Functional Requirement.   A requirement that specifies a function that a system or system component must be capable of performing.

Functional Specification.   A specification that defines the functions that a system or system component must perform. See also Performance Specification.

Gantt Chart.   A chart illustrating a time-phased line of work activities.

Hardware.   Physical equipment used in data processing. Contrast with Software.

Hierarchical Decomposition.   A method of designing a system by breaking it down into its components through a series of top-down refinements. See also Functional Decomposition; Modular Decomposition; Stepwise Refinement.

Hierarchy.   A structure whose components are ranked into levels of subordination according to a specific set of rules.

Higher Order Language.   A programming language that usually includes such features as nested expressions, user-defined data types, and parameter passing not normally found in lower order languages and that can be used to write machine independent source programs. A single higher order language statement may represent multiple machine operations. Contrast with Assembly Language; Machine Language.

Host Machine.   (1) The computer on which a software system, program, or file is installed. (2) A computer used to develop software intended for another computer. (3) In a computer network, a computer that provides processing capabilities to users of the network.

HWCI.   Hardware configuration item.

Identifier.   (1) A symbol used to name, indicate, or locate. Associated with such things as data structures, data items, or program locations. (2) A character or group of characters used to identify or name an item of data and possibly to indicate certain properties of that data.

Implementation.   (1) A realization of an abstraction in terms of hardware, software, or both. (2) A machine executable form of a program that can be translated automatically to machine executable form. (3) The process of translating a design into code and debugging the code.

Implementation and Acceptance Test Phase. The period of time in the software life cycle during which a software product is created from design documentation, debugged, and incrementally acceptance tested.

Implementation Requirement. Requirement that affects or constrains the implementation of a software design; for example, design descriptions, software development standards, programming language requirements, software product assurance standards.

Independent Verification and Validation. Verification and validation of a software product by an organization other than the organization that created or implemented the original design. The degree of independence is generally a function of the importance of the software.

Informal Test. Any test that does not meet all the requirements of a formal test.

Information Hiding. The technique of encapsulating software designs in modules in such a way that the module's interfaces reveal as little as possible about the module's inner workings. Information hiding forbids the use of information about a module that is not in the module's interface specification.

Input Assertion. A logical expression specifying one or more conditions that program inputs must satisfy.

Inspection. An evaluation technique in which software requirements, design, or code is examined, observed, or measured to determine the conformity of materials, supplies, components, parts, appurtenances, systems, processes, or structures to predetermined quality requirements. See also Code Audit. Contrast with Walk-Through.

Instruction. (1) A program statement that causes a computer to perform a particular operation or set of operations. (2) In a programming language, a meaningful expression that specifies one operation and identifies its operands, if any.

Instruction Set. The set of instructions in a computer, in a programming language, or in the programming languages in a programming system.

Instrumentation. Software tools that monitor the internal characteristics of software as it is executed.

Integration. The process of combining software elements, hardware elements, or both into an overall system.

Integration and Test Phase. The period of time in the software life cycle during which a software product is integrated into its operational environment and tested in this environment to ensure that it performs as required.

Integration Testing. An orderly progression of testing in which software elements, hardware elements, or both are combined and tested until the entire system has been integrated. See also System Testing.

Integrity. The extent to which unauthorized access to or modification of software or data can be controlled in a computer system. See also Security.

Interactive. Pertaining to a system in which each user or operator entry causes a response from the system.

Interface. (1) A shared boundary; for example, a hardware component linking two devices or registers, or a portion of storage accessed and/or modified by two or more computer programs. (2) To interact or communicate with another system component.

Interface Requirement. A requirement that specifies a hardware, software, or database element with which a system or system component must interface, or that sets forth constraints caused by such an interface.

Interface Specification. A specification that sets forth the interface requirements for a system or system component; for example, the software interface specification document.

Interface Testing. Testing conducted to ensure that program or system components correctly pass data and/or control to one another.

Intermediate Build. Intermediate version of a CSCI that meets a subset of the CSCI's acceptability criteria, and that is not a formal, contractual, deliverable version.

Internal Review. A meeting scheduled and conducted for the purpose of reviewing one or more products of CSCI internal development; for example, module design review and module implementation review.

Interoperability. The ability of two or more systems to exchange and mutually use information. Compare with Compatibility.

Interpret. To translate and to execute each source language instruction before translating and executing the next instruction. Contrast with Assemble; Compile.

Interpreter. Software, hardware, or firmware used to interpret program instructions. Contrast with Assembler; Compiler.

Interrupt. Suspension of the execution of a computer program caused by an external event and performed in such a way that the process under execution can be resumed.

Interruption. See Interrupt.

Iteration. (1) Repeatedly executing a given sequence of programming language statements until a given condition is true. (2) A single execution of a loop.

Kernel. (1) A nucleus or core, as in the kernel of an operating system. (2) An encapsulation of an elementary function.

Language Processor. Software that performs processing functions such as translating or interpreting a specific programming language; for exam-

ple, a FORTRAN processor, a COBOL processor, a requirements specification language, a design language, or a programming language.

Level. A rank within a hierarchy. An item is of the lowest level if it has no
subordinates and the highest level if it has no superiors.

Level of Documentation. A description of required documentation indicating its scope, content, format, and quality based on intended usage.

Librarian. See Software Librarian.

Library. See Software Library; System Library.

Life Cycle. See Software Life Cycle; System Life Cycle.

Linkage Editor. A computer program used to create one load module
from one or more independently translated object modules or load modules by resolving cross references among the object modules and possibly by relocating elements. *Note:* Not all object modules require linking
prior to execution.

Listing. A human-readable, textual computer output.

Load Module. A program unit that is suitable for loading into main storage for execution; it is usually the output of a linkage editor.

Logical File. A file independent of its physical environment. Portions of
the same logical file may be located in different physical files, or several
logical files or parts of logical files may be located in one physical file.

Logical Record. A record independent of its physical environment. Portions of the same logical record may be located in different physical records, or several logical records or parts of logical records may be located
in one physical record.

Loop. A set of instructions that are executed repeatedly until a certain condition is met. See also Iteration.

Machine Language. A representation of instructions and data that is directly executable by a computer. Contrast with Assembly Language;
Higher Order Language.

Maintainability. (1) The ease with which maintenance of a functional unit
can be performed in accordance with prescribed requirements. (2) Ability
of an item under stated conditions of use to be restored, within a given
period of time, to a state in which it can perform its required functions
when maintenance is performed under stated conditions using prescribed procedures and resources.

Maintenance. See Software Maintenance.

Maintenance Phase. See Operation and Maintenance Phase.

Milestone. A scheduled event used to measure progress for which some
project member or manager is held accountable; for example, phase review, specification issuance, and product delivery.

Model.   An abstract or mathematical representation of a real world process, device, or concept. See also Analytical Model; Error Model; Simulation.

Modeling.   The evaluation of a software concept by developing a model of the software capability, then exercising it in a variety of configurations and simulated operational environments.

Modification.   (1) A change made to software. (2) The process of changing software.

Modular.   Pertaining to software that is organized into limited aggregates of data and contiguous code that performs identifiable functions.

Modular Decomposition.   A method of designing a system by breaking it down into modules. See also Hierarchical Decomposition; Modularity.

Modularity.   The extent to which software is composed of discrete components such that a change to one component has minimal impact on other components.

Modular Programming.   A technique for developing a system or program as a collection of modules. See also Modularity.

Module.   A discrete identifiable set of instructions usually handled as a single entity by an assembler, compiler, linkage editor, loading routine, or other type of routine or subroutine. It is frequently defined as the lowest stand-alone, testable set of executable code. Contrast with Unit.

Module Strength.   See Cohesion.

Multiprogramming.   A mode of operation that provides for interleaved execution of two or more computer programs by a single processor.

Network.   A pictorial display of the work activities that shows the interdependencies of activities and events among one another.

Object Module.   Version of a module that contains the internal instructions resulting from a translation of the symbolic instructions contained in a source module into instructions directly recognizable by a computer.

Object Program.   A fully compiled or assembled program that is ready to be loaded into the computer. Contrast with Source Program.

Operating System.   Software that controls the execution of programs, including such services as resource allocation and scheduling, input/output control, and data management. Although operating systems are predominately software, partial or complete hardware implementations are possible. See also System Software.

Operational.   Pertaining to the status given a software product once it has entered the operation and maintenance phase.

Operational Reliability.   The reliability of a system or software subsystem in its actual use environment, which may differ considerably from reliability in the specified or test environment.

Operational Test and Evaluation (OT&E). Testing performed on software in its normal operating environment by the end user.

Operation and Maintenance Phase. The period of time in the software life cycle during which a software product is used in its operational environment, monitored for satisfactory performance, and evaluated for change. Changes are made by re-entry into the development cycle.

Operator. (1) An individual who monitors or manipulates machines and input/output streams during the execution of a program or system. (2) In symbol manipulation, a symbol that represents the action to be performed in an operation; for example " $+$ ", " $-$ ", "$*$", and "$/$". (3) In the description of a process, that which indicates the action to be performed on operands. Contrast with User.

Operator Documentation. Documentation written to the operators of a program or system with instructions for interacting with that program or system during operations. Contrast with System Documentation e.g., Design Specification.

Overlay. (1) In a computer program, a segment that is not permanently maintained in internal storage. (2) The technique of repeatedly using the same areas of internal storage during different stages of a program. (3) In the execution of a computer program, to load a segment of the computer program in a storage area hitherto occupied by parts of the computer program that are not currently needed.

Parameter. (1) A variable that is given a constant value for a specified application and that may be named to denote the application. (2) A variable that is used to pass values between program routines.

Patch. (1) A modification to an object program made by replacing a portion of existing machine code with modified machine code. (2) To modify an object program without recompiling the source program.

PCA. Physical configuration audit.

PDL. Program design language.

Performance. (1) The ability of a computer system or subsystem to perform its functions. (2) A measure of the ability of a computer system or subsystem to perform its functions; for example, response time, throughput, number of transactions. See also Performance Requirement.

Performance Evaluation. The technical assessment of a system or system component to determine how effectively operating objectives have been achieved.

Performance Measurement. The process of generating quantitative information, based on plans and actual performance data, regarding the accomplishment of task activities.

Performance Requirement. A requirement that specifies a performance characteristic that a system or system component must possess; for example, speed, accuracy, and frequency.

Performance Specification. A specification that sets forth the performance requirements for a system or system component. See also Functional Specification.

Phase. An identifiable transitory state in a recurring cycle of changes. With respect to the system development cycle, a period of time characterized by a given activity; for example, the software design phase.

Physical Configuration Audit (PCA). A technical examination of a designated configuration item as built, conforming to the technical documentation definition.

Physical Requirement. A requirement that specifies a physical characteristic that a system or system component must possess; for example, material, shape, size, and weight.

Piloting. The early releases of a software system to a selected environment to evaluate a concept or system support.

Planning. The process of establishing in detail what will be accomplished, when, how, and by whom.

Portability. The ease with which software can be transferred from one computer system or environment to another.

Precision. (1) A measure of the ability to distinguish between nearly equal values; for example, four-place numerals are less precise than six-place numerals. (2) The degree of discrimination with which a quantity is stated; for example, a three-digit decimal numeral discriminates among 1000 possibilities. Contrast with Accuracy.

Preliminary Design. (1) The process of analyzing design alternatives and defining the software architecture, typically including definition and structuring of computer program components and data, definition of the interfaces, and preparation of timing and sizing estimates. (2) The result of the preliminary design process. See also Design Analysis; Functional Design.

Preliminary Design Review (PDR). Review conducted for each configuration item or aggregate of configuration items to: (a) evaluate the progress, consistency, technical adequacy, testability and risk resolution (on a technical, cost, and schedule basis) of the selected design approach; (b) determine its compatibility with performance and engineering speciality requirements of the Hardware Configuration Item (HWCI) development specification; (c)establish the existence and compatibility of the physical and functional interfaces among the configuration item and other items of equipment, facilities, computer software, and personnel; and (d) review the preliminary version of the operation and support document.

Preprocessor. A computer program that affects some preliminary computation or organization.

Procedure. (1) A portion of a computer program that is named and that performs a specific task. Compare with Function; Module; Subroutine. (2) The course of action taken for the solution of a problem. (3) The description of the course of action taken for the solution of a problem. (4) A set of manual steps to be followed to accomplish a task each time the task is to be done.

Process. (1) In a computer system, a unique, finite course of events defined by its purpose or by its effects, under given conditions. (2) To perform operations on data in process.

Product Assurance. A systematic plan of all actions necessary to provide confidence that the item or product conforms to established technical requirements.

Product Baseline. The data products that describe and document the as-built system.

Product Configuration Control. Project procedures established to control changes to CSC-prepared documentation that has been formally released for review.

Product Specification. See Design Specification.

Program. (1) A computer program. (2) A series of instructions or statements in a form acceptable to computer equipment, prepared to achieve a certain result and/or to perform a specified function within a system. (3) To design, write, and test computer programs. (4) A schedule or plan that specifies actions to be taken. (5) All the software that can interrelate, as an entity, to perform an activity.

Program Architecture. The structure and relationships among the components of a computer program, including the program's interface with its operational environment and specifications for high-level control, major data structures, module identification and coupling, clocking, protocols, and resource allocation strategies.

Program Block. In problem-oriented languages, a computer program subdivision that serves to group related statements, delimit routines, specify storage allocation, delineate the applicability of labels, or segment paths of the computer program for other purposes.

Program Correctness. See Correctness.

Program Design Language (PDL). See Design Language.

Program Development Notebook. A collection of material pertinent to the development of a given software segment, typically including the requirements, design, technical reports, code listings, test plans, test results, problem reports, schedules, and notes.

Program Instrumentation. (1) Probes, such as instructions or assertions, inserted into a computer program to facilitate execution monitoring, proof of correctness, resource monitoring, or other activities. (2) The process of preparing and inserting probes into a computer program.

Programming Language.   A formal language designed to generate or express programs.

Programming Support Environment.   The collection of available tools and facilities that provide programming support capabilities throughout the software life cycle, typically including tools for analyzing, designing, editing, compiling, loading, testing, configuration management and project management.

Program Set.   That part of the software component assigned to a task or subsystem.

Program Specification.   (1) Any specification for a computer program. See also Design Specification; Functional Specification; Performance Specification; Requirements Specification.

Program Support Library (PSL).   A controlled collection of software, documentation, and associated tools and procedures used to facilitate the orderly development and subsequent support of software. A software development library provides storage of and controlled access to software and documentation in both human-readable and machine-readable form. The library may also contain management data pertinent to the software development project.

Program Validation.   See Validation.

Project.   Any work effort, regardless of size, complexity, or type, of sufficient magnitude or importance that a dedicated organizational element is assigned overall responsibility for it.

Prototyping.   The rapid development of a functional representation of a system capability that serves to provide a test bench on which system and user interface concepts can be tested prior to development.

Pseudocode.   A combination of programming language and natural language used for computer program design. Compare with Design Language.

PSL.   Program Support Library.

Qualification Testing.   Formal testing to demonstrate that the software meets its specified requirements. See also Acceptance Testing; System Testing.

Quality.   The totality of features and characteristics of a product that bears on its ability to satisfy given needs. See also Software Quality.

Quality Assurance.   The project evaluation discipline that evaluates the form, structure, and/or compliance of software in relation to applied standards.

Quality Criteria.   Software attributes used as a basis for assessing the extent to which a CSCI reflects its quality requirements.

Quality Metric. A quantitative measure of the degree to which software processes a given attribute that affects its quality.

Real Time. (1) Pertaining to the processing of data by a computer in connection with another process outside the computer according to time requirements imposed by the outside process. (2) Pertaining to systems operating in conversational mode and processes that can be influenced by human intervention while they are in progress. (3) Pertaining to the actual time during which a physical process runs; for example, the performance of a computation during the actual time that the related physical process transpires.

Regression Testing. Selective retesting to detect faults introduced during modification of a system or system component.

Release. Formal delivery of a system or subsystem from one stage of the production process to another, or to a customer.

Reliability. The ability of an item to perform a required function under stated conditions for a stated period of time. See also Software Reliability.

Relocatable Machine. Machine language code that requires relative addresses to be translated into absolute addresses prior to execution.

Requirement. (1) A condition or capability needed to solve a problem or achieve an objective. (2) A condition or capability that must be met or possessed by a system or system component to satisfy a contract, standard, specification, or other formally imposed document. The set of all requirements forms the basis for development. See also Requirements Phase; Requirements Specification.

Requirements Phase. The period of time in the software life cycle during which the requirements for a software product, such as the functional and performance capabilities, are defined and documented.

Requirements Specification. A specification that sets forth the requirements for a system component; for example, a software product. Typically included are functional requirements, performance requirements, interface requirements, design requirements, and development standards.

Requirements Specification Language. A formal language with special constructs and verification protocols used to specify, verify, and document requirements.

Requirements Verification. See Verification.

Review. The evaluation of software products through presentation of form and technical content.

Revision Number. (1) The number automatically applied when the file is entered or updated in those control systems. (2) The number or letter assigned to a document each time the document is changed and/or updated.

Routine. A computer program unit that performs a specific task. See also Function; Procedure; Subroutine.

Run Time. (1) A measure of the time expended to execute a program. While run time ordinarily reflects the expended central processor time, peripheral accessing and processing may also be included. (2) The instant at which a program begins to execute. See also Execution Time.

Schedule. A graphic or tabular portrayal of activities and events in calendar time.

SCN. Specification Change Notice.

SDR. System Design Review.

Secretary/Librarian. The software librarian on a chief programmer team.

Security. The protection of computer hardware and software from accidental or malicious access, use, modification, destruction, or disclosure.

Segment. (1) A self-contained portion of a computer program that may be executed without the entire computer program necessarily being in internal storage at any one time. See also Component; Module. (2) The sequence of computer program statements between two consecutive branch points. (3) To divide a computer program into segments.

Simulation. The representation of selected characteristics of the behavior of one physical or abstract system by another system; for example, the representation of physical phenomena by means of operations performed by a computer system, and the representation of operations of a computer system by those of another computer system. Contrast with Analytical Model.

Simulator. A device, data processing system, or computer program that represents certain features of the behavior of a physical or abstract system.

Sizing. The process of estimating the amount of computer storage or the number of source lines that will be required for a system or system component.

Software. Computer programs, procedures, rules, and associated documentation and data pertaining to the operation of a computer system. See also Application Software; System Software. Contrast with Hardware.

Software Capability. Capability provided by a software element of a CSCI.

Software Component. (1) Used singly, a basic part of a software product. (2) Used collectively, the entire set of software within a system.

Software Configuration. Aggregate of the software elements in a CSCI or system.

Software Configuration Management. Configuration management applied to the software component of a system.

Software Database. A centralized file of data definitions and present values for data common to an operational software system.

Software Development Cycle. The period of time that begins with the approval to develop, improve, or maintain a software product and ends when the product is transferred to operational status; including requirements phase, design phase, implementation phase, system integration phase, acceptance test phase, and delivery phase. Contrast with Software Life Cycle.

Software Development Plan. Document that provides status information regarding contract requirements, to be updated monthly.

Software Development Process. The process by which user needs are translated into software requirements, software requirements transformed into design, the design implemented in code, and the code tested, documented, and approved for operational use.

Software Documentation. Technical data or information, including computer listings and printouts, in human-readable form, that specify or describe the functions, designs, or operations of a software component. See also Documentation; Operator Documentation; System Documentation; User Documentation.

Software Element. Imprecise designation for a part of a CSCI software.

Software Engineering. The systematic cost and schedule approach to the development, operation, maintenance, and retirement of software.

Software Integration. The process of combining specific software components into an operational software system configuration.

Software Librarian. The individual responsible for establishing, operating, and maintaining a software library.

Software Library. A collection of software and related items established to aid in software development, use, or operation. Types include software development support library, configuration management library, and operations support library. See also Program Support Library. Contrast with System Library.

Software Life Cycle. The period of time that starts when a software product is conceived and ends when the product is no longer available for use, including project planning (system/subsystem requirements analysis phase), task planning (system/subsystem functional design phase), software requirements analysis phase; implementation and acceptance test phase; system integration, test, and delivery phase, and the operation and maintenance phase. Contrast with Software Development Cycle; System Life Cycle.

Software Maintenance. Modification to a software product, after initial delivery, to correct faults, improve performance, or adapt the product to a changed environment.

Software Management Plan. A project plan for the development of the software component of a system or for the development of a software product.

Software Metrics. The specification of characteristics either in mathematical or statistical terms for the quantitative or qualitative evaluation of software quality.

Software Problem Report (SPR). A formal means to document and submit problems, questions, issues, or concerns that relate to controlled software or bridge products.

Software Product. A software entity designated for delivery to a user.

Software Product Assurance. See Product Assurance.

Software Quality. (1) The measure of acceptability of software products in relation to the application, environment, and role of the product in the context of the project. (2) The totality of features and characteristics of a software product that bear on its ability to satisfy given needs; for example, to conform to specifications. (3) The degree to which software possesses a desired combination of attributes. (4) The degree to which customers or users perceive that software meets their expectations. See also Computer Software Quality.

Software Reliability. (1) The probability that software, under specified conditions, will not cause the failure of a system for a specified time. (2) The ability of a program to perform a required function under stated conditions for a stated period of time.

Software Specification Document. See Program Specification.

Software Specification Review (SSR). A review of the finalized CSCI requirements and operational concept conducted when CSCI requirements have been sufficiently defined to evaluate the contractor's responsiveness to them.

Software Support. An organization that centralizes and consolidates all software data management and control functions.

Software Tool. A computer program used to help develop, test, analyze, or maintain another computer program or its documentation.

Source Language. (1) A language used to write programs. (2) A language from which statements are translated.

Source Module. Version of a module directly prepared by a programmer.

Source Program. (1) A computer program that must be compiled, assembled, or interpreted before being executed by a computer. (2) A computer program expressed in source language. Contrast with Object Program.

Specification. Documentation containing a precise, detailed, verifiable description of particulars with respect to the requirements, design, function, behavior, construction, or other characteristics of a system or system component.

Specification Language. A language, often a machine-processable combination of natural and formal languages, used to specify the requirements, design, behavior, or other characteristics of a system component. See also Design Language; Requirements Specification Language.

SPR. Software problem report.

SRR. System requirements review.

SSR. Software specification review.

Stepwise Refinement. A system development methodology in which data definitions and processing steps are defined broadly at first, and then with increasing detail. See also Bottom-Up; Functional Decomposition; Hierarchical Decomposition; Top-down.

Structured Design. A disciplined approach to software design that adheres to a specified set of rules based on the data flow and hierarchal decomposition.

Structured Program. A program constructed of a basic set of control structures, each one having one entry point and one exit. The set of control structures typically includes: sequence of two or more instructions, conditional selection of one of two or more instructions or sequences of instructions, and repetition of an instruction or sequence of instruction.

Structured Programming. (1) A well-defined software technique that incorporates top-down design and implementation and strict use of structured program control constructs. (2) Loosely, any technique for organizing and coding programs that reduces complexity, improves clarity, and facilitates debugging and modification.

Structured Programming Language. A programming language that provides the structured program constructs and facilitates the development of structured programs.

Stub. (1) A dummy program module used during the development and testing of a higher level module. (2) A program statement substituting for the body of a program unit and indicating that the unit is or will be defined elsewhere.

Subroutine. A program unit that may be invoked by one or more other program units.

Subsystem. A group of hardware assemblies and/or software components combined to perform a single function.

Supervisory Program. A computer program, usually part of an operating system, that controls the execution of other computer programs and regulates the flow of work in a data processing system.

System. A group of hardware and software subsystems united by some interactions or interdependence, performing many tasks, but functioning as a single unit to accomplish a set of specific functions.

System Architecture.   The structure and relationship among the components of a system including interface with its operational environment.

System Design.   (1) The process of defining the hardware and software architectures, components, modules, interfaces, and data for a system to satisfy specified system requirements. (2) The result of the system design process.

System Design Review (SDR).   Review conducted to evaluate the optimization, correlation, completeness, and risks associated with the allocated technical requirements. Includes a summary review of the system engineering process that produced the technical requirements, the engineering planning for the next phase of effort, basic manufacturing considerations, and planning for production engineering in subsequent activities. The SDR is conducted when the system definition effort has proceeded to the point at which system characteristics are defined and the configuration items are identified.

System Documentation.   Documentation of the requirements, design philosophy, design details, capabilities, limitations, and other characteristics of a system. Contrast with Operator Documentation; User Documentation.

System Library.   A controlled collection of system-resident software that can be accessed for use or incorporated into other programs by reference; for example, a group of routines that a linkage editor can incorporate into a program as required. Contrast with Software Library.

System Life Cycle.   The period of time that starts when a system is conceived and ends when the system is no longer available for use, including: system/subsystem requirements analysis phase, system/subsystem functional design phase, software development process, hardware development process, personnel procedures development process, system integration, test, and delivery phase, operation and maintenance phase, and, sometimes, a retirement phase. Contrast with Software Life Cycle.

System Reliability.   The probability that a system will perform required tasks for a specified time in a specified environment. See also Operational Reliability; Software Reliability.

System Requirements Review (SRR).   A review of the system (or software) requirements specification to determine that the functional requirements for an end item are complete, feasible, verifiable, and testable.

System Software.   Software for a specific computer system, or family of computer systems, that facilitates the operation and maintenance of the computer system and associated programs; for example, operating systems, compilers, utilities. Contrast with Application Software.

System Testing. The process of testing an integrated hardware and software system to verify that the system meets its specified requirements. See also Acceptance Testing; Qualification Testing.

System Validation. See Validation.

System Verification. See Verification.

Task. A work effort performed by a system and/or an organization.

Testability. The extent to which the establishment of test criteria, and the evaluation of the software with respect to those criteria, can be achieved.

Testbed. (1) A test environment containing the hardware, instrumentation tools, simulators, and support software necessary for testing a system or system component. (2) The repertoire of test cases necessary for testing a system or system component.

Test Case. A specified set of test data and associated procedures developed for a particular objective so as to exercise a particular program or to verify compliance with a specific requirement. See also Testing.

Test Data. Data developed to test a system or system component. See also Test Case.

Test Data Generator. See Automated Test Generator.

Testing. The process of exercising or evaluating a system or system component, by manual or automated methods, in order to verify that it satisfies specified requirements or identifies differences between expected and actual results. Compare with Debugging.

Testing Phase. Aggregate of technical activities involved in demonstrating that a CSCI, as designed and produced, meets its acceptability criteria.

Test Levels. The testing of software is organized in levels according to the structure of decomposition. Test levels typically range from 1 to 6, where level 1 is module testing and level 6 is a test of the software in its operational environment.

Test Log. A chronological record of all relevant details of a testing activity.

Test Phase. A period of time in the software life cycle during which various components of a software product are brought together and evaluated to determine whether or not requirements have been satisfied.

Test Plan. A document prescribing the approach for intended testing activities. The plan typically identifies the items to be tested, the testing to be performed, test schedules, personnel and equipment requirements, evaluation criteria, reporting requirements, and any risks requiring contingency planning.

Test Procedure. Detailed instructions for the setup, operation, and evaluation of results for a given test.

Test Readiness Review (TRR).   Review conducted for each CSCI to determine whether the software test procedures are complete, and to assure that the contractor is prepared for formal CSCI testing. Software test procedures are evaluated for compliance with software test plans and descriptions, and for adequacy in accomplishing test requirements. The contracting agency reviews the results of informal software testing and any updates to the operation and support documents.

Test Repeatability.   An attribute of a test indicating that the same results are produced each time the test is conducted.

Test Report.   A document describing the conduction and results of the testing carried out for a system or system component.

Test Specification.   Documentation that identifies which tests verify that a specific set of goals has been achieved.

Test Tools.   The software, hardware, systems, or other instruments that are used to measure and test an item.

Test Validity.   The degree to which a test accomplishes its specific goal.

Throughput.   A measure of the amount of work performed by a computer system over a period of time; for example, number of inputs per day.

Time-Sharing.   (1) An operating technique of a computer system that provides for the alternation of two or more processes. (2) Pertaining to an alternation on a computing system that enables two or more users to execute computer programs concurrently.

Tools.   A hardware device used to analyze software or its performance. See also Software Tool.

Top-Down.   Pertaining to an approach that starts with the highest level of a hierarchy and proceeds through progressively lower levels; for example, top-down design, top-down programming, and top-down testing. Contrast with Bottom-Up.

Top-Down Design.   The process of designing a system by identifying its major components, decomposing them into their lower level components, and iterating until the desired level of detail is achieved. Contrast with Bottom-Up Design.

Top-Down Testing.   The process of checking out hierarchically organized programs, progressively, from top to bottom, using simulation of lower level components.

Total Correctness.   In proof of correctness, a designation indicating that a program's output assertions follow logically from its input assertions and processing steps, and that the program terminates correctly under all specified input conditions.

Trace.   (1) A record of the sequences in which instructions were executed. (2) A record of all or certain classes of instructions or program events occurring during execution of a computer program. (3) To produce a trace.

Traceability.   The extent to which information exists in one software product that leads to its precedent or antecedent in another.

Translator.   A program that transforms a sequence of statements in one language into an equivalent sequence of statements in another language. See also Assembler; Compiler; Interpreter.

Tree.   An abstract hierarchical structure consisting of nodes connected by branches in which: (a) each branch connects one node to a directly subordinate node; (b) there is a unique node, called the root, that is not subordinate to any other node; and (c) every node except the root is directly subordinate to exactly one other node.

TRR.   Test Readiness Review.

Unit.   A part of a program segment, made up of one or more logically related modules, possessing the following characteristics: (a) it performs a specific, defined function that can readily be traced to the requirement; (b) it is developed by a single individual within an assigned schedule; (c) it is able to be thoroughly tested in a disciplined environment. Contrast with Module.

Unit Design Walk-through.   Internal meeting during which the software designs for a collection of units are evaluated for correctness and completeness before the corresponding code is generated. The planned module tests are also evaluated for completeness during a unit design walkthrough.

Unit Testing.   Aggregate of technical activities involved in demonstrating that a unit has been correctly coded, that the code and the design of a unit are consistent, and that the unit design is correct.

Unit Test Walk-through.   Internal meeting during which unit code is evaluated for correctness, consistency with the corresponding unit designs, and conformance to project programming standards; unit testing results are concurrently evaluated for completeness and practicality. Units are subjected to a unit test walkthrough after conducting computer unit tests.

User.   An individual or organization that normally supplies information for processing, or that receives, interprets, and utilizes the output or effect of such processing. Contrast with Operator.

User Documentation.   Documentation conveying to the end user of a system instructions for using the system to obtain desired results. Contrast with System Documentation; Operator Documentation.

User's Manual.   Reference information needed by CSCI users in order to effectively use the CSCI to perform its functions in an operational environment.

Utility Software.   Computer programs or routines designed to perform general support functions required by application software, the operating system, or system users.

Validation.   The process of evaluating the software development process to ensure compliance with software requirements. See also Verification.

VDD.   Version Description Document.

Verification.   (1) The process of determining whether or not the products of a given phase of the software development cycle fulfill the requirements established during the previous phase. See also Validation. (2) Formal proof of program correctness. (3) The act of reviewing, inspecting, testing, checking, auditing, or otherwise establishing and documenting whether or not items, processes, services, or documents conform to specified requirements.

Version.   The content of a product submitted to control. The revision number and/or the version number of the product is incremented.

Version Description Document (VDD).   A document prepared for each release and modification of an end item that describes the content of the end item and the changes incorporated in it since the preceding release.

Virtual Storage.   The storage space that may be regarded as addressable main storage by the user of a computer system in which virtual addresses are mapped into real addresses. The size of virtual storage is limited by the addressing scheme of the computer system and by the amount of auxiliary storage available, not by the actual number of main storage locations.

Waiver.   A formal authorization to deviate from stated specifications, practices, or plans.

Walk-Through.   A review process in which a designer or programmer leads one or more other members of the development team through a segment of design or code that he or she has written, while the other members ask questions and make comments about technique, style, possible errors, violation of development standards, and other problems. Contrast with Inspection.

WBS.   Work Breakdown Structure.

Work Breakdown Structure.   A tree diagram relating the hierarchical structure of the tasks in the project and the organizations developing them.

Work Item.   A detailed short-span job, or material item, identified for accomplishing work required to complete a task. It is the lowest level of the fully expanded WBS at which budgets are allocated and performance is measured. It is one WBS level below the work package.

Work Package.   The lowest WBS level at which costs are accumulated and measured against earned value. A work package is assigned to one responsible organizational function and has a separate budget, schedule, and task description.

BIBLIOGRAPHY

ARTHUR, L. J. *Measuring Programmer Productivity and Software Quality.* New York: Wiley, 1984.

BASILI, V. R. *Tutorial on Models and Metrics for Software Management and Engineering.* New York: Computer Societies Press, 1980.

BASILI, V. R. AND M. V. ZELKOWITZ, "The Software Engineering Laboratory: Objectives." *Proceedings of the Fifteenth Annual Conference on Computer Personnel Research.* New York: Computer Societies Press, 1978.

BECK, L. L. AND T. E. PERKINS. "A Survey of Software Engineering Practice: Tools, Methods, and Results," *IEEE Transactions on Software Engineering SE-9,* no. 5 (September 1983). 541–561.

BEIZER, B. *Software Testing Techniques.* New York: Van Nostrand Reinhold, 1983.

BOEHM, B. W. *Software Engineering Economics.* Englewood Cliffs, New Jersey: Prentice-Hall, Inc., 1981.

BOWEN, T. P., G. B. WIGLE AND J. T. TSAI, "Volume I, Specification of Software Quality Attributes, Volume II, Software Quality Specification Guidebook, and Volume III, Software Quality Evaluation Guidebook," *RADC Report,* TR-85-37 (February 1985).

BROOKS, F. P. *The Mythical Man Month: Essays on Software Engineering.* Reading, MA: Addison-Wesley, 1975.

BRUCE, P. AND S. M. PEDERSON. *The Software Development Project Planning and Management.* New York: Wiley 1982.

COOPER, J. D. AND M. J. FISHER. *Software Quality Management.* New York: Petrocelli, 1979

COUGAR, J. D. AND R. A. ZAWACKI. *Motivating and Managing Computer Personnel.* New York: Wiley, 1980.

DEAN, W. A., "Why Worry about Configuration Management?" *Defense Systems Management.* 2, no. 3 (Summer 1979).

DE MARCO, T. *Controlling Software Projects.* New York: Yourdon, 1983.

DE MARCO, T. *Structured Analysis and System Specification.* New York: Yourdon, 1978.

DEUTCH, MICHAEL S. *Software Verification and Validation: A Realistic Project Approach.* Englewood Cliffs, NJ: Prentice-Hall, 1982.

EVANS, M. *Productive Software Test Management.* New York: Wiley, 1984.

EVANS, M., P. PIAZZA, AND J. DOLKAS. *Principles of Productive Software Management.* New York: Wiley, 1983.

315

EVANS, M., P. SONNENBLICK, AND P. PIAZZA. "How to Salvage a Faltering Software Project." Paper presented at the National Science and Industrial Association Conference, Washington, DC, October 1981.

FAGAN, M. E., "Design and Code Inspections to Reduce Errors in Program Development," *IBM Systems Journal 15*, no. 3 (1976).

FREEDMAN, D. P. AND G. M. WEINBERG. *Handbook of Walkthroughs, Inspections and Technical Reviews: Evaluating Programs, Projects and Products.* 3rd ed. Boston: Little, Brown, 1982.

GLASS, L. AND A. NOISEUK. *Software Maintenance Guide Book.* Englewood Cliffs, NJ: Prentice-Hall, 1981.

GOEL, A., AND A. SUKERT, "A Guidebook for Software Quality Assessment," *In Proceedings of the 1980 Annual Reliability and Maintainability Symposium,* 186–190. IEEE Catalog no. 80CH1513R.

HANSEN, H. D. *Up and Running: A Case Study of Successful Systems Development.* New York: Yourdon, 1984.

HOWDEN, W. "Contemporary Software Development Environments," *Communications of the ACM, 25,* no. 5 (May 1982).

HUGHES, J. K. AND J. A. MICHTOM. *A Structured Approach to Programming.* Englewood Cliffs, NJ: Prentice-Hall, 1977.

IEEE Transactions of Software Engineering, SE-10, No. 1, (January 1984). Issue devoted to Software Engineering Project Management.

JENSEN, AND C. TONIES. *Software Engineering.* Englewood Cliffs, NJ: Prentice-Hall, 1982.

KENNINGHAN, B. W. AND R. PIKE. *The UNIX Programming Environment.* Englewood Cliffs, NJ: Prentice-Hall, 1984.

KIEDER, S. P., "Why Projects Fail," *Datamation,* (December 1974): 35–37.

MCCABE, T., "A Complexity Measure," *IEEE Transactions on Software Engineering, SE-2,* no. 4 (December 1976): 308–322.

MCCALL, J. A. AND M. T. MATSUMOTO, "Volume I, Software Quality Metrics Enhancements and Volume II, Software Quality Measurement Manual," *RADC Report,* TR 80–109 (April 1980).

MCCARTHY, R. "Applying the Technique of Configuration Management to Software," *Quality Progress,* (October 1975).

METZGER, P. W. *Managing a Programming Project,* rev. ed. Englewood Cliffs, NJ: Prentice-Hall, 1981.

METZGER, P. W. *Managing a Software Project.* Englewood Cliffs, NJ: Prentice-Hall, 1973.

MEYERS, G. J. *The Cost of Software Testing.* New York: Wiley, 1984.

MEYERS, G. J. *The Art of Software Testing.* New York: Wiley, 1979.

MEYERS, G. J. *Composite/Structured Design.* New York: Van Nostrand Reinhold, 1978.

MEYERS, G. J. *Software Reliability Principles and Practices.* New York: Wiley, 1976.

MEYERS, G. J. *Reliable Software Through Composite Design.* New York: Van Nostrand Reinhold 1975.

OSTERWEIL, L. J., "Software Environment Research: Directions for the Next Five Years," *Computer, 14,* no. 4 (April 1981).

PETERS, L. J. *Software Design: Methods and Techniques,* New York: Yourdon, 1981.

PRESSMAN, R. S. *Software Engineering: A Practioners Approach.* New York: McGraw-Hill, 1982.

REIFER, D. J. *Tutorial: Software Management,* 3rd ed. Silver Spring, MD: IEEE Computer Society Press, 1985.

REIFER, D. J. AND S. TRATTNER, A Glossary of Software Tools and Techniques. *In Tutorial: Automated Tools for Software Engineering.* Silver Spring, MD: IEEE Computer Society Press, 1979.

RIDDLE, W. E. AND J. C. WILEDEN, Eds. *Tutorial on Software System Design: Description and Analysis*. Silver Spring, MD: IEEE Computer Society Press, 1980.

SEMPREVIVO, P. *Teams in Information Systems Development*.New York: Yourdon, 1980.

SHOOMAN, M. *Software Engineering*. New York: McGraw-Hill, 1983.

TAUSWORTHE, R. C. *Standardized Development of Computer Software*. Vol. 1 *Methods*. Vol. 2 *Standards*. Englewood Cliffs, NJ: Prentice-Hall, 1979.

THAYER, T. A., *Software Reliability: A Study of a Large Project Reality*. New York: North Holland, 1978.

UNITED STATES AIR FORCE, "Software Management Effectiveness." (A paper in the public domain): Bedford, Massachusetts.

VICK, C. R. AND C. V. RAMAMOORTHY. *Handbook of Software Engineering*. New York: Van Nostrand Reinhold, 1984.

WEINBERG, G. *The Psychology of Computer Programming*. New York: Van Nostrand Reinhold, 1971.

Work Scheduling Handbook, Pamphlet no. 5–4–6, Department of the Army, (January 1974).

YOURDON, E. N. *Classics in Software Engineering*. New York: Yourdon, 1979.

YOURDON, E. N. *Structured Walkthroughs*. Englewood Cliffs, NJ: Prentice-Hall, 1979.

YOURDON, E. N. AND L. CONSTANTINE. *Structured Design*. Englewood Cliffs, NJ: Prentice-Hall, 1977.

ZELKOWITZ, M. *Principles of Software Engineering and Design*. Englewood Cliffs, NJ: Prentice-Hall, 1979.

INDEX